THE COMPLETE

TRAINING GUIDE FOR

ALL SPORTS

CROSS-TRAINING

GORDON BAKOULIS BLOCH

Foreword by Paula Newby-Fraser

A FIRESIDE BOOK • Published by Simon & Schuster
New York London Toronto Sydney Tokyo Singapore

FIRESIDE
Simon & Schuster Building
Rockefeller Center
1230 Avenue of the Americas
New York, New York, 10020

FIRESIDE and colophon are registered
trademarks of Simon & Schuster Inc.

DESIGNED BY BARBARA MARKS
Manufactured in the United States of America

10 9 8 7 6 5 4 3   Pbk.

Library of Congress Cataloging in Publication
Data

Bloch, Gordon Bakoulis.
  Cross-training : the complete handbook and
training guide for athletes of all sports and levels of experience / Gordon Bakoulis Bloch :
foreword by Paula Newby-Fraser.
      p. cm.
  Includes index.
  1. Physical education and training—Handbooks, manuals, etc. 2. Physical fitness—Handbooks, manuals, etc. 3. Exercise—Handbooks,
manuals, etc. I. Title.
GV711.5.B58 1992
613.7'11—dc20   91-35646
                                    CIP
ISBN: 0-671-74366-X Pbk.

To all who seek movement for better health

CONTENTS

ACKNOWLEDGMENTS

Many people helped make this book possible. First of all I want to thank all the researchers, scientists and others who shared their information in fields as diverse as medicine, exercise science, nutrition, coaching and sports marketing to fill the pages that follow here. I could not have continued without their time, patience and thoroughness. I also thank the dozens of individuals in public relations and media relations offices who answered my many questions and steered me toward sources of further information.

I thank my agent, Meredith Bernstein, for leading me to this project, and my editor, Kara Leverte, for her tremendous skill, enthusiasm and patience in overseeing it and bringing it to completion. I am grateful to photographer Cliff Grassmick of Boulder, Colorado, for his talents, humor and cooperation, and to fellow-writer Katy Williams, also of Boulder, for turning problems into challenges and unselfishly, enthusiastically helping me devise creative solutions.

I deeply appreciate the encouragement of my friends and family, and most of all, the unwavering support of my husband, Bradley.

FOREWORD

I'm a professional triathlete. While the term "cross-training" well describes the difficulty of training for the triathlon, which, for those of you who might not know, combines swimming, bicycling and running—something like an endurance decathlon—for me it speaks more of a lifestyle than a training regime.

When I was growing up in South Africa, I was very involved in sports—swimming and ballet dancing primarily. In those days, we did our sports one at a time. My friends growing up in different parts of the world shared the same experience. If you were a swimmer, well, then by God, you were a swimmer and you swam all day long. Other activities were strictly out, even serious weight-lifting, for fear of tightening those well-honed swimmer's muscles.

So the advent of a sport like the triathlon presented both psychological and physiological problems. How did one train for three different and apparently antagonistic activities? After all, runners can't carry around a swimmer's bulky upper body; cyclists need a massive set of quads that are superfluous in the other sports; and swimmers need flexibility from shoulders to toes that the other two activities don't afford. Besides, a top marathoner must train a minimum of seventy miles a week with a long run and two high-quality speed sessions; world-class cycling requires daily marathon rides including mountains and twice-weekly sprints; and long-distance swimmers must log several hours each day in the water, including high-intensity interval sessions.

Confused? So was I. The only thing I knew for sure was that if I tried to do all of this I'd be dead by the side of the road. The toughest thing about the triathlon in the early days, we thought, was settling for mediocrity in our approach to the three disciplines. The best we could do, we figured, was to just pick the highlights of the physical and training requirements of each sport.

But when we did this, interesting things began to happen. We triathletes found that despite lacking technique and base miles we hung pretty well on long, hard rides with national-class cyclists. In the longer road races we could keep the national-class runners in sight. Some of us even improved upon our personal-best swimming times despite doing only 15 percent of the swim training we had been doing when we were swimmers all day long.

So to us, the term "cross-training" came to mean something other than engaging in several activities on a regular basis. It took on the added meaning of using different activities to improve upon performance in a single sport by raising overall fitness level and lowering injury and burnout rate. This knowledge has spread to other sports. For example, world-class skaters now supplement their training with cycling. Cyclists spend time skating and running. Even swimmers now do some running.

Whether you're a world-class athlete, work out strictly for fun and fitness, or fall somewhere in between, you too can benefit from what we all now know about cross-training. Everyone has limits on the time they can devote to exercise, and cross-training simply gives you the best return on your investment—balanced fitness with minimum injury risk and maximum fun.

—Paula Newby-Fraser
August 1991

CROSS-TRAINING

ONE

INTRODUCTION TO

CROSS-TRAINING

As with almost everything else these days, we are presented in the sports and exercise realm with a mind-boggling array of choices. The potential fitness movement participant is faced with literally hundreds of ways to get the heart beating faster, trim excess weight, strengthen the muscles, improve flexibility, improve balance and coordination, hone physical skills, indulge the competitive urge and just plain have a good time through physical activity. Indeed, the array of choices can at times seem to overwhelm rather than inspire.

For this reason, it hardly seems fair to limit yourself to just one or two choices when picking a sport or fitness activity. I find this is true even for me, a competitive long-distance runner who has competed at the elite level in events ranging from the 5 kilometer (3.1 miles) to the marathon (26.2 miles), and who runs up to 100 miles a week during heavy marathon training periods. All year long, however—and *particularly* during those most intense training periods—I also bike, take brisk walks, do stretching and calisthenics and lift weights. And when opportunities present themselves I will also cross-country ski, rock climb, swim, play vigorous games of frisbee and even take an occasional aerobics class.

You, too, probably have a sport or two about which you're passionate— either as a participant or as an observer. You would go to great lengths to engage in or observe this sport—as I do with my long-distance running—and you would probably feel a tremendous sense of loss if it ever ceased to be part of your life. But if you've picked up this book, and if you are like most active, fit people, or people who would like to be fit, you probably also like a bit of variety in the sports and physical activities you pursue—or those you would like to try.

Origins of Cross-Training

Indeed, when you think about it, seeking variety in physical activity is a natural thing for human beings to do. After all, we evolved as creatures who depended on a number of different physical attributes and adaptations for our very survival. For example, primitive humans needed to travel long distances on foot to find food and shelter. They also had to move quickly—running, climbing or crossing streams, rivers and other bodies of water—to escape from predators and track down prey. Whether they were hunting, raising crops, building shelter, storing food or transporting goods, they relied on their endurance, speed, strength, flexibility, coordination and balance for their livelihood. To this day, while human beings are not the fastest species on earth, they are said to have the greatest endurance—at least in terms of covering ground on dry land.

Beyond being a means of survival, physical competence in a variety of areas became an athletic and a cultural ideal as ancient societies made sports a major part of their community life. More than twenty-five hundred years ago, the ancient Greeks adulated well-rounded athletes whose training made them fast, strong, flexible, skilled and beautiful. Indeed, all these traits together in one athlete became celebrated as the Olympic ideal.

Development of Cross-Training in the Modern Age

In our own era, the past several centuries have seen the ever-increasing urbanization of most "developed" societies. This trend has led to a gradual turning from a naturally active lifestyle—farming, for the most part—toward more sedentary living, as more and more people spend their days in offices, on factory assembly lines or running their homes with the help of an array of modern conveniences. As a result, more and more people have been forced to seek exercise in the context of their leisure-time activity, rather than as a life-sustaining necessity.

While the *ways* in which we seek physical activity have changed drastically through the centuries, and vary today among different cultures, our physical ideals have remained remarkably constant. Well-rounded athleticism—what we now call cross-training—has continued to set an athletic standard. From the worldwide embrace of the modern Olympic movement, which celebrates excellence in sports of almost every conceivable variety, to advertisements for children's sneakers that help one "run faster, jump higher and stop quicker," we have shown an unbroken passion for multisport activity and the ideal of well-rounded fitness. Although no one knows when and how the term "cross-training" was first used, it's clear that the concept is nothing new.

The immediate background of the modern cross-training movement, however, made it appear nothing short of revolutionary. The most recent Western fitness boom—which began in the mid-1970s—started, at least in the United States, with the worship of what for most people was an awe-inspiring but unrealistic, unbalanced ideal, the super-long-distance (marathon) runner. Frank Shorter's gold-medal performance at the 1972 Olympics triggered "marathon mania" in this country. The number of people entering the New York City Marathon—a 26.2-mile race—increased from just over one hundred in 1970, the race's first year, to more than two thousand in 1976. It has continued to grow over the next fifteen years, reaching twenty-five thousand in 1991. In addition, other marathons and even longer running races (100 miles and more) have sprung up and flourished around the country and the world.

Participation in marathons has leveled off over the past few years, as millions of people have sought a more balanced, moderate means of staying in shape. Many have turned to cross-training: Instead of just running, they have added various types of exercises that contribute to flexibility and strength, adding these effects to the excellent cardiovascular benefits that long-distance running affords. (See Chapter Three for a full description of all the benefits of a variety of fitness activities.)

As you can see, the current fitness ideal thus hearkens back to the one that has been with us in Western culture virtually throughout history: to be well-balanced, sensibly trained and accomplished in a variety of areas.

What Is Cross-Training?

Cross-training is defined today by exercise physiologists, fitness instructors and people who engage in it as any fitness program that incorporates a variety of activities in a systematic way to promote balanced fitness. In other words, instead of just running or swimming or playing tennis or taking an aerobic dance class, or participating in any one of a myriad of sports or activities, someone who cross-trains will do a little of a number of different types of exercise—from two to half a dozen or more.

One of the beauties of cross-training is that it is limited only by the interests, imagination, energy and time of the person who is putting together the exercise program. One of the goals of cross-training (I will go into this goal and others in much greater detail in later sections of this book) is to give *variety* to physical activity. The reasons for doing this are briefly outlined below.

1. *Cultivating total-body fitness* (you'll soon find out exactly what that means). The components of fitness are outlined by the American College of Sports Medicine as cardiovascular fitness (achieved by raising the heart rate to a certain critical level for a prescribed period of time on a regular basis); muscular endurance (gained by working the various major muscle groups in a repetitive, rhythmic manner); muscular strength, which comes from stressing a muscle at a level approaching its maximal capacity; flexibility (maintained or improved by stretching or gentle movement exercises or both); and body composition (muscle-to-fat ratio), which can be set and controlled by regular calorie-burning exercise combined with reasonable eating.

Of course, sports and fitness activities can stress and improve other areas of sports and physical performance as well, such as speed, coordination, balance, concentration, and various sports techniques and skills, but the basic fitness components mentioned above should never be totally neglected.

2. *Avoiding injury.* Think for a minute about various sports injuries. With the exception of those that result from accident or miscalculation—a race car driver smashing into a wall, a football player getting caught in a crushing tackle, a cyclist taking a bruising spill—the vast majority of problems are what is called *repetitive motion* injuries. What happens is that a muscle, an area of connective tissue or some of the protective material around a joint starts to hurt or feel strained or inflamed simply because an athlete has used the body part too often or vigorously without taking adequate rest.

Long-distance running has a notoriously high rate of repetitive motion injuries: shin splints, "runner's knee," heel spurs and plantar faciitis (a painful inflammation of the connective tissue of the foot), to name a few. Common problems in other sports come quickly to mind as well: tennis elbow, pitcher's arm, swimmer's shoulder and so forth. The solution (and whether the hurting athlete decides to accept it or not is, by the way, often another story, as you'll discover when I discuss injuries in Chapter Eight) almost always includes a period of rest or decreased activity until the injury begins to heal itself.

One of the great benefits of cross-training is that repetitive motion injuries are far less likely to occur than in a single-sport exercise program, because each activity, ideally, is engaged in at most once every other day, allowing for longer rest periods between bouts of exercise affecting a certain area. For example, a cross-trainer who jogs on Mondays and Thursdays, swims on Tuesdays and Fridays, lifts weights on Wednesdays and Saturdays and uses Sundays as a day of rest from exercise, is much less likely to develop a repetitive motion injury—runner's knee or swimmer's shoulder, for example—than someone who runs every day. Avoiding and dealing with injuries is discussed in much greater detail in Chapter Eight.

3. *Banishing boredom.* How many times have you started a new sport or exercise program only to find yourself starting to skip workouts a few weeks or perhaps months later? You find you simply can't get motivated to work out every day or even every other day, and when you finally sit down and ask yourself why you are having so much trouble, you admit that the activity is starting to bore you to tears.

Sure, we all have workouts that are tough, when our mind travels elsewhere, when we're really just going through the motions. But most people find that these sessions are much easier with a little variety, when no session is quite the same as the one the day before.

As another way of keeping boredom at bay, cross-training programs can be designed to be flexible: You can set up a workout schedule that allows you to swim, cycle, run, jazz dance or lift weights, for example, on any given day of the week, depending on how you feel. (For variety, and to reduce the risk of injury, you might want to stipulate that you will not repeat the activity you did during your last workout.) To cite myself as an example: In addition to my running, I try to get in two or three weight-lifting sessions and ninety minutes of stationary bicycle riding every week. But I rarely plan the exact days and times I'll do these workouts; I let my schedule, my moods and my energy levels be the determining factors. I find such an approach keeps me fresh, eager and more likely to be looking forward to my next workout, no matter what it may be.

Of course, as this book will explain in later chapters, cross-training doesn't mean you can just engage in any sport you feel like on any given day with no thought to your overall plan—not if you want to achieve balanced, total-body fitness and avoid injury, potential boredom and burnout down the line. Every sport has its own physical requirements, and dabblers—who tend to jump into a session of a new activity without the proper instruction, training or warmup, and who may well overextend themselves in their enthusiasm—are at high risk for injury. As you'll see, the overall pattern of a quality cross-training program needs to be planned, and stuck to, in order to avoid injury, boredom and burnout, and to accrue maximum fitness benefits from the work you put into it.

4. *Steering clear of burnout.* Burnout—which can be physical, mental, emotional or all three—can occur any time that an overabundance of energy or intensity is put into a single pursuit over an extended period. Just about everyone has felt burnout at one time or another—when working on a school assignment, pushing to finish a project at work, even trying to resolve a challenging issue in a personal or family relationship.

Athletes who become burned out on their sport can suffer from sudden, drastic decreases in their performance level; fatigue; lethargy; loss of interest in their sport (which can sometimes even be permanent); and other symptoms. In serious cases of burnout, an athlete may quit a sport altogether, as I have seen a number of competitive road runners do. As with repetitive motion injuries, the less drastic solution to burnout is usually a period of backing off or avoiding the activity for some time. This successfully "cures" many cases.

Again, cross-trainers are much less likely to get burned out on sports or exercise, because they devote their energies to a variety of activities rather than just one. This is true at the highest levels of sports and on down through the ranks. Professional triathletes, for example, whose sport combines swimming, cycling and running (see Chapter Nine for more on triathlons and triathletes), tend to have long careers of performing at or near the top level of their sport, probably in large part because they don't get burned out on any one of the three activities. For example, Dave Scott, two-time Ironman Triathlon champion and among the top-ranked triathletes in the world, has been competing at the elite level since 1975 with very few injuries.

Athletes in other sports often perform better in a new sport if they come from a background in another activity: Their approach is likely to be fresher, and their injury rate may be lower over the long haul. For example, runner Ingrid Kristiansen, the world record holder in the marathon (26.2 miles), has a background as a competitive cross-country skier, and still cross-trains with the activity during the Norwegian winters. And former Olympic marathon gold medalist Frank Shorter, now in his forties, has extended his career by competing in duathlons, which combine running and cycling (see Chapter Nine for more on this sport as well).

Of course, in any physical activity, periodic rest is needed to provide a physical, emotional and mental break. In fact, the higher the level of training and competition, the more essential these planned periods away from the activity become.

Who Cross-Trains?

That's a good question, since it isn't easy keeping track of the vast numbers of people who engage regularly in two or more sport or fitness activities. But some statistics may help.

The National Sporting Goods Association (NSGA) in Mount Prospect, Illinois, one of the largest sporting-goods trade-industry groups in the world, keeps track of Americans' participation in forty-six different sports and fitness activities. Although NSGA does not keep track of the number of people who cross-train, their figures for individual sports indicate that the numbers must be high. For example, 71.4 million Americans aged seven and over walked for fitness in 1990, and 67.5 million pursued swimming in some fashion. With only about 250 million people in the country altogether, there is bound to be some overlap in those two groups alone. The list of sports tracked by NSGA, and the number of participants for each (in millions), is shown in the table on page 22. Again, notice that the numbers total well over the 250 million population of the United States (not all of whom, of course, engage in *any* physical activity at all), suggesting that there must be a sizable contingent of cross-trainers out there.

Keep in mind, however, that NSGA counts even one-time engagement in the activity in question as "participating." Thus, according to the definition, someone who took a single snorkeling lesson while vacationing in the Caribbean last winter is as much a snorkeling participant as the competitive cyclist logging five hundred miles a week is a participant in cycling. Even so, it's clear that among active people, engaging in more than one sports or fitness activity is not unusual.

Another organization, American Sports Data, Inc., in Hartsdale, New York, tracks sports participation figures for corporate and business leaders. According to ASD president Harvey Lauer, it's impossible to estimate the total number of cross-trainers in the country. "The number is way up there, but any estimate would be a grossly meaningless figure," he says. What ASD is able to estimate are numbers of people who engage in various combinations of activities, either consistently (at least one hundred days in a year) or merely once in a twelve-month period (these numbers, of course, are larger). Data from ASD from 1990, the most recent year for which figures are available, are reprinted in the table on pages 23–25.

1990 Sports Participation

(Participated more than once [in millions], seven years of age and older)

1. Exercise Walking	71.4		24. Target Shooting	12.8
2. Swimming	67.5		25. Table Tennis	11.8
3. Bicycle Riding	55.3		26. Skiing (Alpine)	11.4
4. Fishing	46.9		27. Soccer	10.9
5. Camping	46.2		28. Backpacking	10.8
6. Bowling	40.1		29. Water Skiing	10.5
7. Exercising with Equipment	35.3		30. Badminton	9.3
8. Boating (Motor)	28.6		31. Canoeing	8.9
9. Billiards/Pool	28.1		32. Croquet	8.2
10. Basketball	26.3		33. Racquetball	8.1
11. Running/Jogging	23.8		34. Skateboarding	7.5
12. Aerobic Exercising	23.3		35. Ice/Figure Skating	6.5
13. Volleyball	23.2		36. Archery	5.6
14. Golf	23.0		37. Skiing (Cross-Country)	5.1
15. Hiking	22.0		38. Sailing	4.9
16. Softball	20.1		39. Mtn/Rock Climbing	4.7
17. Hunting with Firearms	18.5		40. Roller Skating/In-Line	3.6
18. Tennis	18.4		41. Bocce	2.6
19. Roller Skating/2x2	18.0		42. Ice Hockey	1.9
20. Dart Throwing	16.4		43. Snowboarding	1.5
21. Baseball	15.6		44. Surfboarding	1.5
22. Football	14.5		45. Boardsailing	0.9
23. Calisthenics	13.2		46. Squash	0.4

Note: 20.3 million people indicated they "worked out at club" in 1990, versus 16.6 million in 1989.
Source: National Sporting Goods Association, Mount Prospect, Illinois.

Information from the Triathlon Federation/USA on the increase in participation in triathlons and other multisport events (see Chapter Nine) is also an indication that nationwide interest and participation in competitions based on cross-training principles has grown and continues to increase.

Can Anyone Be a Cross-Trainer?

Another of the beauties of cross-training is that virtually anyone can do it, in many different ways. Individuals who call themselves cross-trainers comprise

Frequent Cross-Participation—1990
(100 or more days both activities)

Running, Jogging

Weight Training	1,827,000
Resistance Machines	883,000
Stationary Cycling	807,000
Swimming (Laps/Fitness)	796,000
Fitness Cycling	765,000

Fitness Cycling

Fitness Walking	895,000
Stationary Cycling	690,000
Weight Training	569,000
Swimming (Laps/Fitness)	547,000

Fitness Walking

Stationary Cycling	1,865,000
Swimming (Laps/Fitness)	1,064,000
Running/Jogging	1,033,000
Weight Training	820,000

Aerobics (Regular) 1990 Cross-Participation
(At least once in both activities)

	Cross-Participants	%	Index
Aerobics (Low-Impact)	5,295,000	42.8	596
Stationary Cycling	5,122,000	41.4	212
Running/Jogging	4,520,000	36.6	257
Fitness Walking	3,878,000	31.4	218
Weight Training	3,864,000	31.3	239
Fitness Cycling	3,584,000	29.0	228
Swimming (Laps/Fitness)	3,076,000	24.9	226
Resistance Machines	3,046,000	24.6	326
Stair-Climbing Machine Exercise	2,781,000	22.5	407
Treadmill Exercise	1,737,000	14.1	271

Cross-Participation Gains 1987–1990

Stair-Climbing Machine Exercise	2,237,000
Fitness Walking	1,483,000
Treadmill Exercise	1,003,000
Aerobics (Low-Impact)	671,000
Weight Training	493,000
Stationary Cycling	94,000
Resistance Machines	(181,000)
Swimming (Laps/Fitness)	(249,000)
Running/Jogging	(700,000)
Fitness Cycling	(785,000)

Fitness Walking 1990 Cross-Participation
(At least once in both activities)

	Cross-Participants	%	Index
Stationary Cycling	11,326,000	35.4	182
Fitness Cycling	6,737,000	21.1	166
Running/Jogging	6,517,000	20.4	143
Swimming (Laps/Fitness)	6,062,000	19.0	173
Aerobics (Low-Impact)	5,251,000	16.4	229
Weight Training	5,081,000	15.9	121
Aerobics (Regular)	3,878,000	12.1	218
Resistance Machines	3,554,000	11.1	147
Treadmill Exercise	3,175,000	9.9	192
Stair-Climbing Machine Exercise	3,049,000	9.5	173

Cross-Participation Gains 1987–1990

Stationary Cycling	3,826,000
Stair-Climbing Machine Exercise	2,584,000
Aerobics (Low-Impact)	2,512,000
Treadmill Exercise	1,966,000
Swimming (Laps/Fitness)	1,655,000
Weight Training	1,630,000
Running/Jogging	1,627,000
Aerobics (Regular)	1,483,000
Fitness Cycling	1,277,000
Resistance Machines	1,025,000

Weight Training
1990 Cross-Participation
(At least once in both activities)

	Cross-Participants	%	Index
Stationary Cycling	12,221,000	42.1	216
Running/Jogging	11,618,000	40.0	281
Resistance Machines	9,786,000	33.7	445
Fitness Cycling	7,942,000	27.3	215
Swimming (Laps/Fitness)	6,831,000	23.5	214
Stair-Climbing Machine Exercise	6,164,000	21.2	383
Fitness Walking	5,081,000	17.5	121
Aerobics (Low-Impact)	4,062,000	14.0	194
Treadmill Exercise	3,972,000	13.7	264
Aerobics (Regular)	3,864,000	13.3	239

Cross-Participation Gains 1987–1990

Stair-Climbing Machine Exercise	5,220,000
Stationary Cycling	2,939,000
Treadmill Exercise	2,378,000
Fitness Walking	1,630,000
Resistance Machines	1,579,000
Aerobics (Low-Impact)	1,336,000
Swimming (Laps/Fitness)	1,028,000
Running/Jogging	775,000
Fitness Cycling	677,000
Aerobics (Regular)	493,000

Source: American Sports Data, Inc., Hartsdale, New York.

a wide range of ages, fitness pursuits, abilities and commitment levels. Some are serious professional or semiprofessional athletes, training dozens of hours a week. Others are weekend fitness buffs, whose exercise commitment is important but limited by other lifestyle constraints. And there are literally millions of people in between. Remember that anyone who combines two or more sports or fitness activities is a cross-trainer, no matter what their age, sex, ability or fitness level. Chapter Five looks at some of the many different types of people for whom cross-training can be beneficial, and at how they can adapt it to their bodies, lifestyles, interests and personalities.

Although it's hard to gauge any increase in the level of interest and participation in the vast area of cross-training when data are so hard to come by, a strong case can be made that the sport has grown over the years since the latest boom of cross-training popularity began in the late 1970s and early 1980s. As one gauge of the growth, the number of people competing in triathlons (swim-bike-run races) in the United States increased from 10,000 in 1982 to an estimated 250,000 to 300,000 in 1991. The growth has been equally impressive in the duathlon, the triathlon's run-bike-run offshoot (see Chapter Nine), which began in this country only in the mid-1980s. Only 6,000 people participated in the Coors Lite Biathlon Series (duathlons were known as biathlons until 1990), a nationwide group of races, in 1988, the first year it was held. By 1990, however, the number of participants had risen to 20,000 and was continuing to grow.

Many signs indicate that it is also quite likely that cross-training's popularity will continue, and is even likely to increase. The main reason for this is that as the large group of people in our population known as "baby boomers"—who now range in age from the mid-to-late twenties to the mid-to-late forties—grow older, they will be more and more attracted to the benefits of multisport activity, for all of the many reasons mentioned above.

Indeed, I think it is quite likely that the type and number of cross-training programs will increase greatly. People have found that single-sport fitness can be unbalanced, dull, injury-producing and unadventurous. Cross-training, on the other hand, can give them balance, variety, excitement and flexibility.

It should be noted that it can take decades for the wear and tear of overuse of a muscle or joint or connective tissue to catch up with someone who engages in just one sport, year after year. And for those who take up regular physical activity later in life, older body parts are less forgiving than young ones. For example, a seventeen-year-old high school athlete can happily thrive playing four hours of basketball a day, week after week, month after month, with no noticeable bodily protests. But for the average forty-year-old, the same regimen would be quite another story. A regular, moderate cross-training program can prevent a midlife fitness program from being a major reclamation project.

Why Should You Cross-Train?

One of the many reasons I decided to write this book was to try and answer this question for as many people as possible, and in quite a bit of detail. At this point, suffice it to say that you should consider making cross-training the foundation of your fitness plan primarily because it is likely to keep you active, healthy and interested in whatever physical activities you do for longer than any single-sport or activity plan that you could dream up.

In particular, if you've ever been in any of the following situations, or are in one of them now, you are a prime candidate for a cross-training program:

- You want to try a new activity for the first time
- You feel bored with or unmotivated by your current routine
- You suffer from sports or exercise-related fatigue
- You have, or have had, a sports- or fitness-related injury
- You feel you need a fitness plan that's more flexible than the one you now have
- You want to get your whole body more fit
- You want to start exercising for the first time, or after a significant fitness layoff

How This Book Can Help

Cross-training should never be a random pursuit. As flexible, versatile and subject to change as a cross-training program can be, it doesn't make sense to undertake it in a haphazard fashion. Rather, there are certain basic sports and fitness principles that any active person must follow in order to get maximum benefit from whatever activity she or he decides to engage in. (These principles are discussed in detail in Chapter Two.) And when activities are combined to try to get the most, performance-wise, from an exercise program without injury, boredom or burnout, following these principles becomes all the more important.

I've written this book as a complete guide to cross-training. First, in Chapter Two you will learn some basic principles of exercise science (which I promise aren't as tough or intimidating as they may sound) that are necessary for understanding how fitness benefits are achieved. You'll also learn the importance of using cross-training to make your mind fit along with your body—a principle that more and more exercise scientists, psychologists, physical educators and fitness participants are discovering and recommending.

Chapter Three is a comprehensive guide to getting started in cross-training. It outlines how to choose the best activities for you, allowing you to pick among many possibilities you may not even have thought of—things like boardsailing, rock climbing, bowling and more. It outlines the benefits of many popular sports and fitness activities, as well as quite a few esoteric ones. You will also learn the principles of combining activities in ways that create a long-lasting program that builds maximum fitness.

Chapter Four then shows you how to set up a workable cross-training schedule—no matter what your interests and the constraints on your time may be. You'll learn how to set goals, establish and maintain a program that is both regulated and flexible and fully integrate cross-training with the rest of your busy, active life.

Chapter Five discusses how cross-training can work successfully for many different kinds of people—men, women, children, teenagers, senior citizens and those with physical and emotional disabilities. Chapter Six covers nutrition—an area that is neglected and misunderstood by many active people. The chapter includes sports nutrition basics; losing, maintaining and gaining weight; and special diets. Chapter Seven addresses body weight, taking advantage of the latest information on what "healthy" weight and body fat levels really are and showing how exercise of all kinds can help attain and maintain them. Injuries—yes, they can and do happen to anyone—are addressed in Chapter Eight, including first aid, long-term care, and how to exercise right in all your cross-training activities, so that you avoid both acute and chronic (overuse) injuries in the first place. Chapter Nine covers multisport events—not only the familiar triathlons and duathlons, but those combining horse racing, mountain climbing, kayaking, basketball, dogsledding and more. You will also learn how cross-training can enhance the abilities of many athletes to compete in their one sport or event of choice.

Finally, Chapter Ten is a guide to equipment, because no matter what your sport, you need to know how to buy the best, maintain it and not get taken for a ride by a salesperson who is overeager, ignorant, misinformed or all three. And in the back of the book you'll find references and resources for much more information on sports and exercise science, nutrition, injury prevention, competitions, coaching, equipment and more.

Throughout this book, you will find charts, lists, schedules and plans to help you start and follow through on the cross-training program you design. Just remember: All that any book can do is give you tools to work with. It's up to *you* to adapt them to your situation—and then go out and use them!

I am eager to share all of this information with you. I've been fortunate enough to have been a fit, active person all my life. As I mentioned earlier, long-distance running is my main sport: I started running on a regular, semistructured basis in the summer of 1978, and I have been a national-class competitive distance runner since 1985.

Looking back, I know that I have also been a cross-trainer since before I got out of diapers—although at times I didn't even realize it. For example, as a child I took part in every vigorous outdoor game the kids in my neighborhood went in for—from baseball, football, basketball and soccer, to Capture the Flag, Home Free, hide-and-seek, various versions of tag, Red Rover, Mother May I, follow the leader, and many more. No matter what the season, I was constantly running, jumping, throwing, catching, kicking, swimming, lifting, balancing—and all with no thought that what I was doing would someday be given a name and become an enormously popular national pastime.

Later, in my teens, I joined a gymnastics team, did a bit of competitive springboard diving and went out for my junior high and high school field hockey, lacrosse, basketball and track teams. During my summers I stayed just as active, going on bicycle trips, to summer camps and on camping and beach trips with my family, where I was constantly involved in a variety of sports and fitness pursuits.

Today, as an elite competitive athlete, I run up to one hundred miles each week and enhance my training program with biking, swimming, walking and weight lifting. I do this not necessarily to become a better runner (there are raging debates over whether cross-training can improve sports performance in a particular activity, as you will learn in Chapter Nine), although I believe my nonrunning activities help keep me injury-free and will probably increase the number of years I remain competitive. Rather, I cross-train mainly because I enjoy a variety of activities and feel better—both physically and mentally—when I add them to my fitness regimen. Frankly, I couldn't imagine limiting my physical repertoire to just one activity and excluding all others, nor would I ever feel comfortable telling any fit (or would-be fit) individual that he or she ought to do so.

Obviously, if you're reading this book, you are a physically active person, too—or you are at least thinking about becoming one and wondering how to go about it. You will find that the chapters that follow are written with your situation in mind. They encourage you to get out and *do* the activities suggested, and as you're learning, making choices and trying out different sports and combinations, to make decisions about what sort of program to set up.

Doubtless you've read or heard about the many benefits of regular physical activity. The largest studies, which were conducted by Ralph Paffenbarger, M.D., at Stanford University in California and by Steven Blair, Ph.D., at the Institute for Aerobics Research in Dallas, show that moderately active men and women of all ages live longer, on average, than those who exercise minimally or not at all. Fit people are less likely to have heart attacks, high blood pressure or diabetes, or to develop some types of cancer, than are those who are unfit. They also have lower rates of osteoporosis, which can cause crippling and even death in old age, especially among women.

The message is clear: For most people, *any* activity at all is better than none. This book is about opening up your possibilities to as many forms of movement as possible, so that sports and exercise can become a part of life for more and more people.

Without further ado, let's get started!

TWO

Some basic (and painless)

exercise science

What does it mean to be "physically fit"? It sounds like a straightforward question, yet the answers vary enormously, depending on whom you ask. Exercise and sports scientists—professionals whose work involves defining, quantifying, qualifying and analyzing physical activity—have devoted a considerable amount of energy and time to putting together a definition of physical fitness.

The main group responsible for defining fitness in this country is the American College of Sports Medicine (ACSM), which is the largest national organization of sports and fitness professionals in the United States (see Appendix for information on contacting the ACSM and other organizations). The ACSM is made up of several thousand doctors, nurses and people with undergraduate and advanced degrees in exercise and sports science, exercise physiology, kinesiology, biomechanics and related fields.

And how does this august group define fitness? According to the latest guidelines issued by the ACSM, last updated in April 1990, there are five basic physical fitness components:

- Cardiovascular-respiratory endurance
- Muscular strength

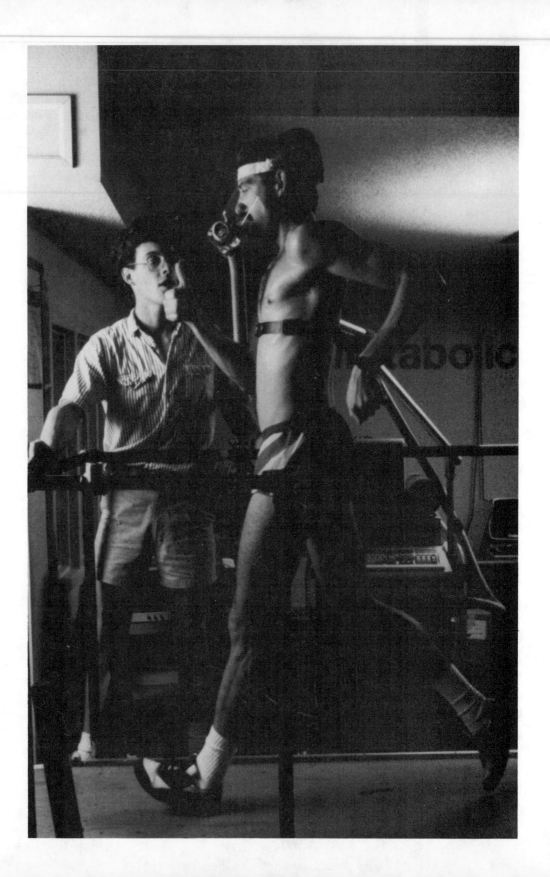

- Muscular endurance
- Body composition
- Flexibility

Until the spring of 1990, the ACSM had proscribed guidelines for attaining basic fitness in only the cardiovascular-respiratory (also known as aerobic) category. All five areas were previously considered important by exercise scientists—and indeed, they are essential for total, balanced fitness—but the organization saw fit to tell the general public how to go about meeting basic fitness requirements only for aerobic fitness for several reasons, the main one being that this is the area thought to be most directly connected to overall health maintenance and disease prevention. It has been shown in epidemiological (population) studies that simply by being aerobically fit one can significantly reduce the risk of premature death or disease in a number of areas, primarily heart disease and heart attack. (You'll read more later on just how this protection can take place.)

However, in the spring of 1990, the ACSM broadened its recommendations on suggested levels and types of activity to the area of muscular strength. Why was this done? According to the ACSM: "The addition of resistance/strength training to the position statement results from the need for a well-rounded program that exercises all the major muscle groups of the body."

The main reason for the extension of the definition is further explained by Michael Pollock, M.D., a professor of exercise science at Florida State University in Tallahassee, who was chairman of the ACSM committee that drew up the new recommendations. "Strength is an essential component of fitness," he says. "It doesn't necessarily entail having big, bulky muscles, but rather muscles that are put through a regular program of exercise designed to preserve their function. This is especially important for the upper-body muscles, which in most people do not perform the types of tasks in daily living designed to stress the major muscles. Muscle-strengthening exercises can help preserve function, maintain bone-mineral density, and avoid lower back problems, which afflict so many people of all ages."

Further statements made by the ACSM have yet to address the other three basic components of fitness—muscular endurance, body composition and flexibility—although they may do so in the future. The organization—like most people working in the area of sports and exercise science—feels that for now, since aerobic and muscle strengthening conditioning are the most important aspects of fitness as they relate to health, they should be stressed to the public above the others. The other components, however, are still considered vitally important for fitness, and again, should be part of any well-rounded program. Stay tuned for future pronouncements on them.

Fitness Step by Step

Here we will take a more detailed look at the five basic components of fitness (cardiovascular endurance, muscle strength, muscle endurance, body composition, and flexibility), what each one involves, how specific types of physical activity can help people achieve each of them, and why a person who strives for balanced physical fitness must embrace them all. It will become even clearer in later chapters of this book why it is important to keep all five aspects in mind when planning any cross-training program concerned with total fitness.

1. Cardiovascular (or Cardio-Respiratory or Aerobic) Endurance This is, quite simply, the ability of the cardiovascular system (heart, lungs and the circulatory apparatus—arteries, veins and blood) to work harder than it does at its resting rate to supply working muscles with oxygen, their main fuel. The ACSM first laid out its guidelines for attaining cardiovascular fitness in 1978, and those standards still apply: The organization recommends performing an activity that raises the heart rate to between 60 percent and 90 percent of its maximum attainable level, for at least twenty to sixty minutes at a time, and doing this three times a week. This will keep the average healthy person cardiovascularly, or *aerobically*, fit.

One of the beauties of this simple guideline is that (depending on a person's preferences and level of fitness) raising the heart rate to the 60 percent to 90 percent of maximum level (often referred to as the *training range* or *training zone*) can be accomplished in an enormous variety of ways. This is good news for the cross-trainer. Walking, jogging, rowing, cross-country skiing, cycling, racquet sports, in-line skating and aerobic dance are but a few of the more popular ways.

Another beauty of this guideline is that you can start working out aerobically right away; you don't need to "work up" to doing it. For example, someone who is completely out of shape could start by walking at a two- to three-mile-per-hour pace in order to raise his or her heart rate into the range that produces a training effect. However, as that person becomes more fit, this will no longer work; a walk at the two- to three-mile-per-hour intensity will no longer be an aerobic activity. It would not be hard, however, to continue to get a training effect; the person must simply increase the exercise's intensity by walking more briskly, or perhaps eventually even jogging at, say, a six-mile-per-hour rate, to continue getting an aerobic workout.

To give an opposite example, a well-trained swimmer might have to churn through the water at a speed that would leave most other people gasping for breath after half a lap in order to get the heart beating significantly above its resting pace—and then move up to an even higher level as training progresses through a competitive season.

To achieve an aerobic fitness benefit, the experts say, you must get the heart beating in its *training zone.* There's a crude, simple, and not always reliable way to calculate the training zone: In beats per minute, it is 60 to 90 percent of 220 minus your age.

For example, a forty-year-old woman (the formula is the same for both sexes, by the way) wants to know how fast her heart should be beating to get a training benefit from her jogging program. She would work the formula as follows:

$$220 - 40 = 180$$
$$180 \times 0.6 \ (60\%) = 108$$
$$180 \times 0.9 \ (90\%) = 162$$

The woman concludes that her heart should be beating between 108 and 162 times every minute of the twenty to thirty minutes of her thrice-a-week jog in order to maintain fitness at her current level. (Note: She should remember to gradually warm up to that level with five to ten minutes of easy movement, and to cool down for the same amount of time afterward.) Keep in mind that the guidelines are rough: They assume that maximum attainable heart rate declines at a steady rate with age, which is not true across the board. Heart rate seems to be somewhat genetically based, and to vary with current fitness level as well.

There is some question whether exercise bouts that are shorter than twenty minutes or less intense than the 60 percent to 90 percent of maximum can have any effect on fitness. Until recently the consensus was no, but such exercise bouts were still thought to be beneficial to health. This was good news: With the population aging, and with people of all ages feeling that they have less and less time to exercise, the idea that shorter, less intense sessions could keep one healthy had great appeal. (The exact health benefits of aerobic activity will be explained later.)

Several recent studies have looked at the health and fitness benefits of shorter periods of aerobic and subaerobic activity—that is, periods both at and below the training range (for example, walking up flights of stairs, or raking leaves for just five or ten minutes at a time). The results have been illuminating: It has been found that people who sprinkle such activities throughout their day—even if they're otherwise inactive—have lower rates of heart disease than people who do absolutely no physical exercise at all.

Most exercise experts agree that if you're sedentary, starting with *any* activity is better than continuing to do nothing. And doing just about anything other than sitting around will raise your heart rate—not necessarily into the training range (which improves or maintains fitness), but at least to a point that seems to improve health.

It should be noted that there are other, slightly different, definitions of training range, established by other health and fitness-related organizations. For example, the American Heart Association's definition suggests that for basic fitness, an activity should raise the heart rate only to the 60 percent to 75 percent of maximum range. And the Institute for Aerobics Research, a Dallas-based organization founded by Kenneth H. Cooper, M.D., M.P.H., which has conducted extensive exercise science research (see Appendix), advises working out at between 65 and 80 percent of your maximum.

Whatever organization's advice you take, it is generally recommended that beginning exercisers stay on the low end of the range, while workouts for intermediate and advanced fitness buffs can approach the high end.

How Can You Measure Your Heart Rate?

The best way to measure your heart rate is by taking your pulse. You can do this by placing your index and middle fingers lightly on a place on your body where blood flows through a vein or artery close to the skin. The inside of the wrist and the point on the neck just below and in front of the ear are two of the most popular pulse-taking places.

Find your pulse, then count the number of beats in ten seconds. Multiply by six to get your pulse rate in beats per minute. (If you are stopping in the middle of an exercise session to take your pulse, don't time it for a full minute; this will give you an inaccurate reading because your heart rate will start to fall significantly during that time.)

There is also a wide range of pulse-taking equipment that can do the job for you; check sporting-goods stores or ads in the back of reputable health and fitness magazines. See also Chapter Ten, on equipment, for general advice on buying the best exercise-related gear. In addition, you can find a variety of heart-rate monitors, which measure the beating of the heart directly.

. . .

What Is Aerobic Exercise?

Now that you know *how* to exercise aerobically, you might wonder what exactly goes on inside the body when you do so. First of all, it is important to distinguish between aerobic activity and what's known as *anaerobic* activity. *Aero* is a Latin word meaning "air," so *aerobic* can be loosely translated as "with air" or "with oxygen." In aerobic activities, oxygen is inhaled by the lungs, passed along to the bloodstream through the blood-gas exchange process in the lungs' tiny air sacs (called alveoli) and carried to the working muscles, all at a rate that is sufficient to keep up with the muscles' demands for fuel.

This is all in contrast to *anaerobic* activities, in which the muscles work, in part, "without air" (or oxygen). In other words, anaerobic activity is that which is performed at a level that is more intense than the body's aerobic (oxygen-delivering) system can keep up with.

Aerobic activity is also defined as any physical work that raises heart rate to within the training zone. The idea is that this work can be maintained at that pace steadily and, in theory at least, indefinitely—although of course the body at some point, depending on other fitness factors, must slow down. Examples of aerobic activity are brisk walking, jogging, swimming, rowing, cycling and cross-country skiing, performed at a pace within the training range.

Anaerobic activities, on the other hand, generally are either all-out or nearly all-out efforts, such as a hundred-yard dash, a twenty-five-yard swimming sprint, a fast break to the basket, stealing a base, an intense weight-lifting effort or a lightning-quick pass or run into the end zone in football. These activities range in length from about five seconds to two minutes. An activity that starts out anaerobically must either stop or convert to an aerobic activity within a couple of minutes. An example would be the start of a cross-country running race, in which the competitors must sprint for position, then settle into a pace they can maintain over several miles.

During anaerobic activities, the working muscles call upon two fueling systems: ATP-CP (adenosine triphosphate–creatine phosphate) and ATP-lactic acid. To explain this process in simple terms: ATP is a chemical stored in the muscles that allows them to contract. The ATP-CP system is used for the first quick burst of energy (five to thirty seconds). It fuels the activity of fast-twitch muscle fibers—those that propel the body in short, quick bursts. ATP then combines with another chemical, ADP (adenosine diphosphate), to resynthesize ATP. Thus the system is self-sustaining. However, the resynthesization process doesn't happen instantaneously, and so after thirty seconds or so of all-out effort, when CP starts to run out, a backup source of energy is needed.

The body then calls upon *glycogen* stored in the muscles, which is produced when food is converted to sugar in the bloodstream. It can make enough energy immediately available for use to fuel about two minutes of intense activity. At that point, lactic acid (the by-product of the breakdown of glycogen) builds up in the muscles to the point where their activity becomes inhibited.

At that point (which can be extended somewhat through training), the muscles need oxygen to continue their work. This means that the aerobic system must be activated for muscle activity to carry on. Oxygen is the chief resynthesizing agent in the process of replenishing the muscles with ATP, although the system uses primarily glycogen for the actual fuel. Theoretically, the aerobic system can continue indefinitely—or at least until muscle fatigue or other factors cause the exerciser to finally take a break.

There is almost always some overlap between the aerobic and anaerobic systems; which one is used is not an either/or question. However, the aerobic system gradually takes over a greater share of the work as the anaerobic system is no longer able to sustain the load. As you can see, the great majority of time in most exercise activities is spent using the aerobic energy-delivery system.

How Can Aerobic Activity Improve Your Health?

As mentioned above, aerobic activity has many health and fitness benefits. By stressing the heart, it makes that organ stronger, so it has to work less hard to sustain the body's functions at rest. This greater efficiency is thought to preserve heart function, reducing the risk of heart disease and heart attack. Aerobic activity is also thought, over time, to increase the number of blood vessels surrounding and feeding the heart. In addition, it increases the capacity of the lungs and the efficiency of the arteries, veins and tiny capillaries that carry blood to all parts of the body.

Any cross-training program should include at least one regular aerobic activity (for example, walking, jogging, swimming, cycling, rowing or aerobic dancing). And fortunately, it isn't hard for most people to find one that they enjoy.

2. Muscle Strength Strength is a muscle's capacity to exert maximal effort or to resist maximal opposing force. It is often measured in terms of pounds lifted or force exerted against a fixed weight.

Muscles work by contracting. Every muscle is made up of many bundles of *muscle fibers*, each of which is only a few millionths of an inch in diameter. The muscle contraction process works like this: An electrical impulse from the brain travels down the spinal cord along a *motor neuron* to the muscle. This causes many thousands of fibers to shorten (contract) for just a small fraction of a second. This mass of tiny, short contractions adds up to one big, discernible muscular effort. As a result, you are able to lift a weight, step forward to begin a jogging workout, or simply pick up a pen to write a shopping list. The muscle *spindles* then immediately send a message back to the brain that the muscle has received the message and is ready for more information.

During vigorous physical activity, the brain and various muscles are in constant communication, receiving and sending back signals to fire, contract and respond. That is part of the reason why in order to improve performance in a particular activity, you must perform that activity over and over, training yourself *neuromuscularly*. It also helps you understand yet another reason why cross-training can allow you to become more fit overall than working out in any single sport: When one set of muscles becomes neuromuscularly fatigued, you can give them a rest and turn to exercising another set.

Muscle strength is important for carrying out daily tasks. Think about it: Everything from picking up a bag of groceries to opening a heavy door requires a degree of muscle strength. Some people naturally have greater strength than others because of their greater muscular bulk; they simply have more muscle fibers. I'm an example of the opposite case: I'm naturally thin, with small muscles (fewer muscle fibers), particularly in the upper body. Everyone, however, can improve muscle strength with a program of resistance training; I'll outline basic strength-training programs in the following paragraphs.

Strong muscles serve many functions. For example, they safeguard vulnerable parts of the body (for example, a strong abdomen protects the lower back). As you will see later, muscle strength is vitally important for people of all ages and both sexes.

The American College of Sports Medicine (ACSM), recognizing the importance of muscle strength, recommends at least two weekly sessions of resistance (weight) training. Within each session, one should perform a set of eight to twelve repetitions of eight to ten different exercises that work the various muscle groups.

As you will see later, muscle strengthening work is highly specific, meaning that the particular muscles that you are trying to make stronger must be the ones doing the work. This differs from cardiovascular conditioning, in which one exercise, such as running or swimming, trains the entire system, and gains through one activity can be transferred to another. Like cardiovascular training, however, strength training must be continuous to be effective—you cannot build up your muscles and then "store" the strength for later use.

A muscle that goes without training is said to *atrophy*, or lose strength. It becomes smaller and weaker. The number of fibers actually decreases, and the individual fibers get smaller and weaker as well. Gaining muscle strength is referred to as the process of *hypertrophy*.

3. Muscle Endurance Endurance in a muscle is not defined by how much work it can do in a single bout (that is strength), but rather by how long it can keep performing the same contraction over and over. Muscle endurance is primarily developed through repetitive activity; it's the reason your legs get stronger from regular walking or jogging, or your arms from swimming. As a result of endurance training, the trained muscles can carry you farther over land or through the water (or use more power in the same place if you're using a stationary exercise machine).

A fit body, one conditioned through cross-training, has muscles possessing both strength and endurance. Lifting weights can primarily either develop endurance, if one follows a program using low resistance and a high number of repetitions, or promote strength, with a program of high weights and low repetitions. Muscles developed through endurance tend to be long, lean and toned, whereas those developed through strength tend to become shorter and bulkier. As you will see later, both muscle strength and muscle endurance are important for total fitness, and a good cross-training program will develop both of them.

4. Body Composition In fitness terms, this generally refers to the ratio of fat tissue to muscle tissue. Whether a body contains a greater or lesser percentage of fat depends on many factors, including genetic background (if people in your family, particularly your parents, naturally tend to carry a lot of extra body fat, you will too, all things being equal), diet and activity level. In addition, sports and exercises that burn a lot of calories—for example, jogging, aerobic dancing, cross-country skiing and "action" sports, such as soccer and singles tennis— tend to produce physiques with a low body-fat content.

The average American adult male carries about 15 to 20 percent of his weight as fat, while women, who are thought to need more weight to meet the energy needs of menstruation, pregnancy and breastfeeding babies, tend to carry slightly more, in the 25 percent range, on the average. It is important to note, however, that wide variations exist; body-fat percentages of greater than 50 percent are not uncommon among obese individuals, and it's possible for these people to still be fit and healthy. Male world-class marathon runners, on the other hand, have body-fat levels in the 5 percent range, with some measuring as low as 2 to 3 percent.

Many types of exercise are effective at lowering or maintaining body fat, which has been recognized in recent years as a more important indicator of health than total body weight. A six-foot tall, two-hundred-pound man, for example, if he is sedentary, is likely to be carrying too much body fat; however, the same two hundred pounds on a very fit man would probably be perfectly healthy, as a far greater proportion of the weight would be muscle. High body fat is associated with increased risk of heart disease, hypertension, diabetes, gallbladder disease and some forms of cancer.

The chart on page 42 gives the recommended healthy body weights from the 1990 Dietary Guidelines for Americans, published by the federal government's Department of Health and Human Services. Higher rates of premature mortality and some diseases exist in groups of people both above *and below* these standards.

This book cannot offer a complete discussion of the health risks of being overweight, although there is a more detailed treatment of the topic in Chapter Seven. If you are concerned about your weight and its impact on your health, you should consult a health or medical professional.

Cross-training programs are effective in promoting overall fitness because they strengthen the major muscles in all parts of the body. It is extremely important to note, however, that the loss of body *fat* through exercise is body-wide. In other words, there is no such thing as "spot-reducing," which refers to trimming fat off a particular body area—the thighs, for example—by exercising the muscles beneath the fat.

Another widespread myth is that stopping exercise can "turn muscle into fat." This is incorrect. However, exercise can strengthen and tone muscle in specific areas, while encouraging body-wide fat loss if calories burned are greater than calories consumed. ("Spot-reducing," "turning muscle into fat" and other body-weight and exercise myths are discussed and refuted in Chapter Six.)

The quest to carry as little body fat as possible can sometimes be taken to extremes that are both physically and emotionally unhealthy. Despite the premium placed on low body fat in sports such as running, cycling, gymnastics and body-building—as well as the perception among the general public that "you

Recommended Healthy Body Weights

Height*	Weight in Lb†	
	19 to 34 years	35 years and over
5'0"	97–128	108–138
5'1"	101–132	111–143
5'2"	104–137	115–148
5'3"	107–141	119–152
5'4"	111–146	122–157
5'5"	114–150	126–162
5'6"	118–155	130–167
5'7"	121–160	134–172
5'8"	125–164	138–178
5'9"	129–169	142–183
5'10"	132–174	146–188
5'11"	136–179	151–194
6'0"	140–184	155–190
6'1"	144–189	159–205
6'2"	148–195	164–210

*Without shoes.
†Without clothes.
Source: U.S. Departments of Agriculture and Health and Human Services.

can never be too rich or too thin''—it is not desirable, either from a health or a fitness standpoint, to carry too little body fat. Fat is needed to perform such basic body functions as maintaining the balance of hormones, processing food and insulating and protecting organs.

Keep in mind that even the world's best athletes, whose livelihoods depend on their low body-fat levels, are as concerned with keeping their body fat *up* to a certain level as they are with keeping it down. In addition, too-low body fat is associated with higher rates of some types of disease. Finally, preoccupation with body-fat levels can lead to unhealthy attitudes about food and exercise, in extreme cases developing into eating disorders such as anorexia and bulimia. (See Chapter Seven for more on these problems.)

5. Flexibility This is the ability of muscles, joints and the material that links muscles and bones—known as connective tissue—to move through a full range of motion, to extend without causing stiffness or pain. While some people are naturally more flexible than others, it is nonetheless possible to enhance flexibility by working muscles and joints through their full range of motion.

Stretching is the most common, readily accepted way to improve or maintain flexibility. Unfortunately, however, stretching incorrectly can do more harm than good to flexibility. But the good news is that it has also been shown that any activity that works large muscles, causing them to contract rhythmically in a regular, repetitive manner, can enhance flexibility. (By the same token, muscles that are not used in regular physical activity tend to lose their flexibility.)

While it is perfectly possible to be fit without being flexible, suppleness of muscles, joints and connective tissues can immensely improve the enjoyment of exercise, and indeed that of physical activity of all types. Stiffness is uncomfortable, and it limits performance in sports and activities that call upon a wide range of motion, such as dance, tennis and figure skating. In addition, flexibility may reduce the risk of injury.

Unfortunately, current research is notoriously inconclusive on the question of whether stretching really does *prevent* injury in various activities. There are several reasons for the lack of certainty: One, human beings are extremely varied in their flexibility; two, flexibility changes with the weather, time of day and other factors; and three, consistent, reliable flexibility measurements simply do not exist.

Many active people do stretch in some way as part of their fitness program, usually to prepare for vigorous activity or to keep muscles and joints from becoming stiff after the exercise session. (There is a more thorough discussion of stretching and its benefits, risks, and right and wrong techniques in Chapter Eight.)

Personally, I find stretching an invaluable part of my long-distance-running training program. It feels good, it's relaxing and I believe it helps keep me injury-free. Often, when I feel unusually fatigued during or after a training run for no apparent reason, I'll look in my training log to see when was the last time I had a nice, long, thorough stretch. I'll almost invariably discover that it has been a while.

Like most active people, I don't always do what I know is best for me when it comes to promoting optimum health and fitness. I find that, despite my best intentions, the "I don't have time" excuse is regrettably easy to call up. But I always tell people (myself included) to *make* time for stretching. It is an investment you will win back many times over.

The chart on page 45 summarizes the five basic components of fitness, briefly explaining what each one is and listing sports and exercise activities that

Fitness Components: What They Are and What Activities Enhance Them

Component	What It Is	Activities that Enhance It
1. Cardiovascular endurance.	The ability of the heart, lungs and circulatory system to supply the working muscles with oxygen.	Any activity that raises heart rate into the *training zone* for at least twenty consecutive minutes, ideally three or more times a week: brisk walking, jogging, stair climbing, swimming, cycling, rowing, rope-jumping, cross-country skiing, in-line skating, aerobic dance, water aerobics, walking or jogging in water, vigorous tennis, squash, racquetball, soccer and so forth.
2. Muscle strength.	The muscle's capacity to exert maximal effort or apply maximal opposing force.	Weight-lifting (free weights and machines) and calisthenics (pushups, pullups, and so forth) are considered most effective, although *any* activity that uses a muscle will strengthen it to some degree.
3. Muscle endurance.	The ability of a muscle to repeatedly sustain a contraction.	Activities that involve repeated use of large muscle groups, such as walking, jogging, swimming, rowing, cycling and other aerobic activities.
4. Body composition.	The ratio of body fat to lean tissue.	Activities that burn a lot of calories through sustained, repetitive use of large muscle groups: swimming, cross-country skiing, water aerobics, water running or walking, jogging, walking, aerobic dance, jazz dance, stair-climbing, in-line skating, rope-jumping, high-level racquet sports, soccer and so forth.
5. Flexibility.	The ability of muscles, joints and connective tissue to move through a full range of motion.	Activities that rely on gentle, nonstressful movements, such as stretching, yoga, tai chi and some martial arts. Warming up before vigorous activity and cooling down afterward may also help prevent stiffness.

encourage each. As you can see, some sports foster fitness gains in more than one area. It's important to notice, however, that no single activity helps develop fitness in all five areas. If you wish to do that, as has already been noted, you must cross-train under a program designed to promote total fitness.

Other Fitness Components

There are a couple of other attributes that, while not considered by the ACSM to be essential to fitness, are thought to be important in enhancing full enjoyment of sport and exercise and in improving quality of life.

1. *Coordination.* Sports scientists will tell you that in large part, coordination is something you are born with (or, in many cases, without). However, coordination in a particular activity—serving a tennis ball, passing a football, skiing a slalom course—can be learned and improved through practice. While many cross-training programs do without a coordination component, and coordination is not essential to fitness, adding activities that enhance coordination can enhance the quality of a program. Most sports, whether team or individual, can help develop coordination. Tennis, racquetball, squash, baseball, aerobic dance, softball, basketball, hockey, lacrosse, water polo, diving, yoga and crew are but a few sports that can do the trick.

2. *Concentration.* Another element of sport and physical activity that is not essential to fitness, concentration nonetheless can result from both engaging in fitness activities and developing sports skills. Concentration is part mental, part physical, and in most sports both are needed for optimal performance.

Believe it or not, some of the sports in which the skill needed to perform the activity is one of the least important components actually require the greatest levels of concentration. Marathon running is an example. In countless postrace interviews top runners will assert that the moment in which they either made a move in a competition or lost their momentum occurred not because of a physical breakthrough or inadequacy, but rather at the instant that they either bore down mentally, establishing an edge, or let their attention wander just long enough to let the race slip from their grasp. "I lost it." "I just spaced out." "I zoned." These are all ways of saying the same thing, and add up to a situation athletes try to avoid at all costs. In some sports, such as race car driving, mountaineering, rock climbing, and boxing, a loss of concentration—even for an instant—can literally be a matter of life and death.

Mind-Fitness

Do you ever wonder what sports and fitness activities do for the gray matter between your ears? You probably have read in some magazine or newspaper article, book or advertisement, something about the concept of mind-fitness (sometimes also called the mind-body connection). What is this phenomenon, and what does it have to do with cross-training?

The first ten or so years of the contemporary fitness boom emphasized complete—some would say excessive—development of the body, the physical self. It seemed that just about everybody who was "into" being fit was running marathons, spending hours in aerobics classes, going for "century" (hundred-mile) bicycle rides and the like. Now, with the evidence from the sports science labs telling us that more exercise isn't always better—and that in fact it may often be detrimental to overall health—a new emphasis has developed on conditioning the *mind* along with the body, to bring about total mental and physical health.

Of course, this concept of body-mind fitness is hardly brand new; in fact, it has been around for thousands of years, at least since the ancient Greeks noted that a sound mind cannot exist within an unsound body. The contemporary body-mind movement also claims its roots in Eastern physical disciplines such as yoga and tai chi, which have a strong mental component, as well as in various forms of both Eastern and Western meditation.

Important input into the mind-fitness movement also comes from recent discoveries in the field of sport psychology showing that repetitive, rhythmic movements—the type one performs when doing aerobic activities such as brisk walking, jogging, swimming, dancing, and cross-country skiing—can encourage activity on the right side of the brain, which is the creative, intuitive half. (The left side of the brain, on the other hand, is more concerned with linear, analytical thought.) It is also well known that these types of exercises can induce a sense of calm, happiness and well-being—the fabled "exercise (or runner's) high."

Any cross-training program is enhanced by activities specifically designed to encourage mind-fitness, as well as, of course, aerobic activities that seem to encourage calm and relaxation naturally by themselves. In fact, leaving the mind-fitness component out of a cross-training program—or any exercise program, for that matter—seriously undermines the routine's potential benefits. It's like exercising without eating a well-balanced, nutritious diet, without getting enough sleep or without keeping stress levels under control.

When I'm tired, anxious, hassled and under stress—and who isn't from time to time?—I'll deliberately use a training run as a form of meditation rather than concentrating on the activity's physical benefits. I'll turn my watch off, put in as much or as little mileage as I want (within reason) and concentrate on staying relaxed. That means breathing easily, keeping my arms, shoulders and back loose and not being concerned with pace. I may notice my body's effort, but I'll try not to feel the least bit of anxiety about it. Rather than letting my mind wander (which in my case usually leads to thinking about problems or anxieties), I'll focus on feeling my breathing, listening to the slap of my running shoes against the pavement and noticing the environment as I pass through it.

After a few miles, inevitably, more pleasant, relaxed thoughts come naturally to mind. I become calm. If I am lucky, this feeling lasts until the end of the run and beyond. Of course, I've also garnered the physical fitness benefits of a run, but compared to what it has done for my head, those are almost beside the point at the time.

This feeling of well-being during and after aerobic activity has been the subject of much research, as psychologists and sport scientists attempt to understand exactly what brings it about. The idea is that if they can pinpoint the cause, perhaps they can move on to the next step, bringing the phenomenon about at will, controlling it, perhaps even reproducing it somehow *without* exercise. In the meantime, however, activity that raises the heart rate will have to continue to be part of the formula.

It is thought that *endorphins*, which are hormonelike substances released in greater quantities into the bloodstream during heart-rate-raising activity, lead to the sense of calm and equilibrium many people feel after exercise. Other factors that may play a role are neurotransmitters, increased blood flow to the brain and the "high" that the sense of accomplishment from completing a workout can bring on. Research will continue to focus on this important area over the next few years.

It should be abundantly clear from these first two chapters why cross-training is beneficial, and how the kind of balanced, varied exercise program a cross-training regimen offers can help you achieve full physical and mental fitness. Now, with no further delay, it's time to get started on planning the best cross-training program for you.

THREE

Getting Started

Now that you've learned what cross-training is and why building a fitness program around it can be so beneficial, both physically and mentally, you should be ready to pick your activities and start moving.

Of course, it's important to keep in mind that the sports you choose and the schedule you set up are never set in stone. Occasionally picking your day's activity or activities on a whim can allow for spontaneity, providing a welcome break in a schedule that has become too predictable or overly regimented. That's fine, every now and then. In the end, however, you'll appreciate being grounded in a program that you've mapped out in advance, giving thought to maximizing its potential for fitness (including mind-fitness), variety, injury prevention and fun. This chapter will help you give some advance thought to how you're going to combine your exercise modes. This planning will help you to get the most from your cross-training plan.

Finding the Right Activities

With all the sport and exercise choices available to most people in this country today, it seems inconceivable that an active person could get stuck in a fitness rut, to the point where he or she even gives up exercise altogether because the particular sport he or she has decided to pursue is boring or lacks variety. It also seems hard to believe that a sedentary individual would refuse to take up exercise because he or she feels that there's no single activity that holds particular appeal over the long haul.

Hasn't it occurred to such people to try cross-training? After all, the sheer number and variety of sports available is astounding: The National Sporting Goods Association (NSGA), a trade-industry group for sporting-goods manufacturers and retailers based in Mount Prospect, Illinois, tracks sales and participation figures for forty-six sports, recreational activities and fitness pursuits. (See page 22 for a complete list of the activities, with numbers of participants in each for 1990, the most recent year for which figures are available.)

Perhaps you already have a main activity or group of activities that you regularly engage in. If so, one of the reasons you are reading this book may be that you want to build a more comprehensive program around them or take a more systematic approach to engaging in them. Or perhaps you are bored with, burned out on or injured from pursuing your current sport (or sports) and want to try something completely new. It's also possible that you're new to physical activity altogether, or are returning after a layoff, and for various reasons you don't want to limit yourself to one sport.

These are all good reasons for beginning a cross-training program. Whatever your current situation, here are some general suggestions for designing a cross-training regimen that will work for you.

1. *Pick activities that you enjoy.* Make a list, consulting the list of sports on page 22 if you're at a loss or just looking for some inspiration. Don't worry about how long the list is or whether the activities seem intimidating or impractical. For now, think of it as a "wish list"; you can choose from among what you've come up with later.

2. *Don't be hobbled by your past experiences.* One of the greatest benefits of cross-training is that it allows many people to start up anew with activities that they have previously had to give up because of injury, burnout or other factors. They may have given up the pastime because they pursued it in the past with overly single-minded devotion. One of the advantages of making the activity part of a cross-training program is that it reduces the chance of someone making that mistake again.

For example, someone who repeatedly tried and abandoned running because her knees kept giving out may well be able to work running into a cross-training schedule. Under the new plan she may do the activity only one or two days a week, instead of her customary five or six. Even people who have been advised by a doctor *never* again to engage in a particular sport may find they can do so as part of a carefully planned and executed cross-training program. (It's a good idea, though, to seek a second medical opinion if you fall into this category.)

3. *Consider an activity's psychological benefits.* Look back to the section on "mind-fitness" in the previous chapter for advice on how to increase an activity's mental benefits. Too often people approach a sport armed with a vision solely of the positively transforming effect it will have on their body. For example, an aspiring walker or jogger may want thin thighs, while a would-be weight-lifter or body-builder might yearn for impressive biceps.

Overlooking a sport's mental component, however, can easily short-circuit a fitness plan. For example, a driven type of person wanting relief from life's pressures might inadvertantly choose an intensely competitive activity, but then quickly abandon exercise if all it means is engaging in "killer" activities such as bicycle racing, squash or tennis. By the same token, a gregarious soul probably wouldn't be happy doing nothing but swimming laps in a pool or running solitary miles—whereas trying an aerobics class at an exercise studio might be just the thing to keep her moving.

While it is of course possible to try and then reject activities because of mental unsuitability, there are probably also quite a few that, with some thought, can easily be eliminated in advance.

4. *Consider whether the activities you are drawn to fit comfortably into your lifestyle.* Here, now, is where practicality enters the picture—but again, don't let either past experiences or current realities stifle you. For example, if you used to cycle but gave it up when you moved to a congested urban area, you don't necessarily have to leave cycling off your activity "wish list." Rather than working out outdoors, investing in an inexpensive indoor exercise bike, or a device with rollers to which you can attach your outdoor model, can easily allow indoor pedaling to continue to be a part of your fitness plan. In fact, just about any sport can be accommodated to various lifestyle options: For example, someone who enjoys aerobic dance but doesn't want to take classes at a health club or exercise studio can work out in front of the VCR at home to a choice of literally hundreds of exercise videos. And a running or walking enthusiast who lives in the desert can move his training program to an indoor treadmill or walk or run in a swimming pool during the hottest few months of each year.

Even living in New York, with its cold, sloppy winters, I never miss a day of working out in some fashion. Among the reasons for my consistency are that I keep indoor options open, have a flexible training program, and know I can get some kind of aerobic workout by engaging in activities other than running. Keeping an open mind can go a long way toward making sure you remain engaged in a variety of activities.

Major Muscles Used in Activities Front View

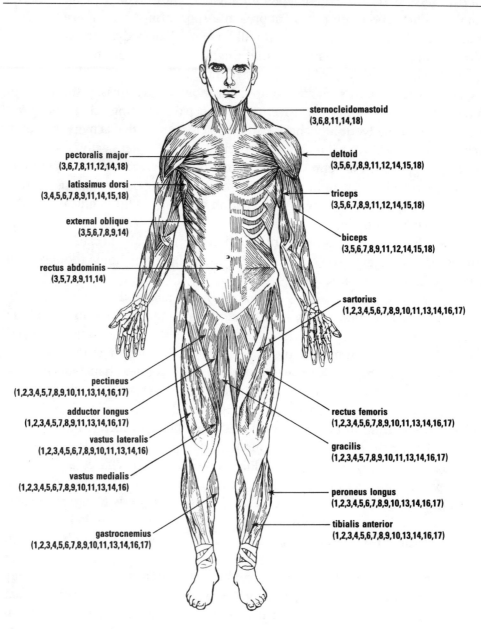

sternocleidomastoid
(3,6,8,11,14,18)

pectoralis major
(3,6,7,8,11,12,14,18)

latissimus dorsi
(3,4,5,6,7,8,9,11,14,15,18)

external oblique
(3,5,6,7,8,9,14)

rectus abdominis
(3,5,7,8,9,11,14)

deltoid
(3,5,6,7,8,9,11,12,14,15,18)

triceps
(3,5,6,7,8,9,11,12,14,15,18)

biceps
(3,5,6,7,8,9,11,12,14,15,18)

sartorius
(1,2,3,4,5,6,7,8,9,10,11,13,14,16,17)

pectineus
(1,2,3,4,5,7,8,9,10,11,13,14,16,17)

adductor longus
(1,2,3,4,5,7,8,9,11,13,14,16,17)

vastus lateralis
(1,2,3,4,5,6,7,8,9,10,11,13,14,16)

vastus medialis
(1,2,3,4,5,6,7,8,9,10,11,13,14,16)

gastrocnemius
(1,2,3,4,5,6,7,8,9,10,11,13,14,16,17)

rectus femoris
(1,2,3,4,5,6,7,8,9,10,11,13,14,16,17)

gracilis
(1,2,3,4,5,7,8,9,10,11,13,14,16,17)

peroneus longus
(1,2,3,4,5,6,7,8,9,10,13,14,16,17)

tibialis anterior
(1,2,3,4,5,6,7,8,9,10,13,14,16,17)

Find your cross-training activities on the list opposite, then check the corresponding numbers on the illustrations above to find out which muscles can get a workout.

Rear View

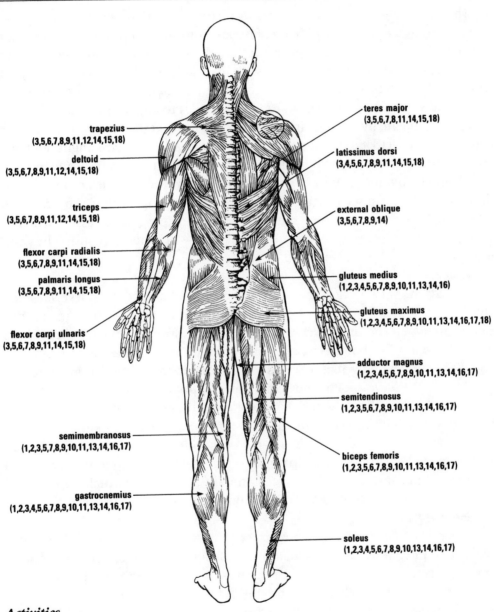

trapezius
(3,5,6,7,8,9,11,12,14,15,18)

deltoid
(3,5,6,7,8,9,11,12,14,15,18)

triceps
(3,5,6,7,8,9,11,12,14,15,18)

flexor carpi radialis
(3,5,6,7,8,9,11,14,15,18)

palmaris longus
(3,5,6,7,8,9,11,14,15,18)

flexor carpi ulnaris
(3,5,6,7,8,9,11,14,15,18)

semimembranosus
(1,2,3,5,7,8,9,10,11,13,14,16,17)

gastrocnemius
(1,2,3,4,5,6,7,8,9,10,11,13,14,16,17)

teres major
(3,5,6,7,8,11,14,15,18)

latissimus dorsi
(3,4,5,6,7,8,9,11,14,15,18)

external oblique
(3,5,6,7,8,9,14)

gluteus medius
(1,2,3,4,5,6,7,8,9,10,11,13,14,16)

gluteus maximus
(1,2,3,4,5,6,7,8,9,10,11,13,14,16,17,18)

adductor magnus
(1,2,3,4,5,6,7,8,9,10,11,13,14,16,17)

semitendinosus
(1,2,3,5,6,7,8,9,10,11,13,14,16,17)

biceps femoris
(1,2,3,5,6,7,8,9,10,11,13,14,16,17)

soleus
(1,2,3,4,5,6,7,8,9,10,13,14,16,17)

Activities

1. walking
2. running/jogging
3. swimming
4. cycling
5. rowing
6. racquet sports
7. aerobic dance
8. weight-lifting
9. cross-country skiing
10. downhill skiing
11. water skiing
12. golf
13. roller/ice skating
14. martial arts
15. softball/baseball
16. soccer
17. ice/field hockey
18. boxing

The Benefits of Popular Sports

The primary goal of cross-training is to combine activities that you enjoy—and those that mesh easily with your lifestyle—into an exercise program designed to build all-around fitness. The program should also keep you motivated, healthy and injury-free. In order to come up with the right combination, you first need to know the benefits—physical, psychological and lifestyle—of various sports.

How do you decide which sports and activities to engage in? The following pages examine the most popular sports in terms of what they have to offer. Look carefully at the activities that interest you—as well as others you might not have considered—to assess whether they might give you the physical and mental fitness and enjoyment paybacks you are looking for. Refer to the accompanying drawings so you can see exactly which muscles are being worked. You can also refer to these pages at any time during your training program to assess whether your current sports are best meeting your needs—or whether you might want to experiment with others instead.

Walking

Physical benefits: Can help maintain healthy weight and body-fat levels; associated with increased longevity, even at moderate levels; brisk walking can improve cardiovascular health; improves muscle endurance, strength and tone in the legs; muscles in buttocks, abdominals, arms and upper body can benefit from race walking; some studies show that it seems to help maintain adequate bone density.

Psychological benefits: Provides companionship when done with others and opportunities for solitude when done alone; rhythmic, repetitive nature can be calming and soothing, may stimulate right-brain (creative) thinking.

Lifestyle benefits: Accessible to people of a wide range of fitness levels and ages from toddlers to great-grandparents; can be used for transportation; minimal equipment and instructional needs; culturally acceptable virtually anywhere; can be performed both indoors and outdoors.

Jogging-Running

Physical benefits: Can help maintain or lose excess weight and body fat; improves and maintains cardiovascular fitness; associated with lower rates of heart disease, hypertension and so forth; improves muscle strength and endurance in the lower body; may help maintain bone density in the lower body.

Psychological benefits: Like walking, can provide either companionship or solitude; regular jogging-running has been associated with lower rates of anxiety and depression; racing can provide a competitive outlet.

Lifestyle benefits: Accessible to many different types of people, with minimal equipment and instructional needs; can be performed both indoors (on a tread-mill) and outside; time investment need not be extensive; for many people, can be a lifelong activity.

Swimming/Water Exercise

Physical benefits: Improves and maintains cardiovascular fitness; can help with weight and body-fat control (although it seems to be less effective at calorie burning than out-of-water aerobic activities); works virtually every major muscle group, providing overall muscle endurance, strengthening and toning; non-stressful to joints; may have some bone-strengthening effect.

Psychological benefits: Can induce a calm, relaxed state, which may help with stress control; rhythmic, repetitive nature has been associated with increase in right-brain (creative) activity; its solitary nature can be soothing.

Lifestyle benefits: Accessible to many different types of people, with minimal equipment needs; can be performed indoors and out; nonstressful nature makes it suitable to many among the elderly and disabled; body's buoyancy in water is ideal for the obese and for pregnant women; an important safety skill for those who spend time on or near the water.

Cycling

Physical benefits: Improves/maintains cardiovascular fitness; strengthens and tones muscles in legs, buttocks and (to a lesser degree) arms and shoulders; doesn't tend to cause joint injury through pounding; can help with weight and body-fat maintenance or loss.

Psychological benefits: Rhythmic, repetitive nature can calm, relax; may be helpful for stress relief; can provide both individual and team competitive outlet, but is also soothing if performed alone.

Lifestyle benefits: Can do "double duty" by serving as transportation; workouts can be done alone or with others; equipment need not be overly expensive; minimal instruction and supervision needed; easily accessible indoors (with sta-tionary cycling machines) or out.

Rowing

Physical benefits: Can improve and maintain cardiovascular fitness; a good over-all muscle strengthener and toner; works all major muscle groups without pound-ing joints; can help contribute to weight and body-fat loss and maintenance.

Psychological benefits: Is rhythmic and repetitive (see other aerobic activities); can be engaged in individually or as part of a team, competitively or not, pro-viding either solitude or companionship.

Lifestyle benefits: Can be performed both indoors (on rowing machines) and outside on water; outdoor version allows for interaction with natural setting;

allows opportunities for both individual and team competition; rowing machines widely accessible in gyms and health clubs; can be a lifelong activity.

Racquet Sports

Physical benefits: Strengthens and tones muscles in arms, shoulders, back, legs and, to a lesser degree, buttocks, abdomen; can provide some aerobic benefit if pursued at high levels; may contribute to weight and body-fat control and to strengthening bone mineral, reducing the risk of osteoporosis.

Psychological benefits: Many people find these sports helpful for stress relief and channeling competitive urges.

Lifestyle benefits: Easily accessible to people in most areas of the country; can be pursued indoors and out; sports tend to be social; instruction is widely available.

Aerobic Dance

Physical benefits: Provides good cardiovascular benefits; workouts can strengthen and tone all major muscle groups; may be helpful in weight and body-fat loss and maintenance; can improve and maintain range of motion and flexibility; may strengthen bones.

Psychological benefits: Rhythmic and repetitive (see other aerobic activities); generally noncompetitive, but sessions can be lively and fun.

Lifestyle benefits: Great popularity; classes and videotapes for all levels widely available; minimal equipment and instructional needs; can be a social outlet.

Weight-Lifting

Physical benefits: Strengthens, improves endurance and tones muscles; can target particular areas not worked in other sports or by daily living; may be helpful in injury prevention by strengthening the muscle and connective tissue that protects the joints; recommended by the American College of Sports Medicine as part of total fitness program (see Chapter Two).

Psychological benefits: Many report increased feelings of self-confidence; the activity itself can be calming; can build capabilities in other sports and in life.

Lifestyle benefits: Equipment widely available for home or gym and health club use; instruction and guidance available in most gyms and clubs; can be made accessible to the elderly, pregnant and disabled.

Cross-Country Skiing

Physical benefits: Considered the ideal "total-body" exercise because it strengthens and tones all major muscle groups and provides an excellent cardiovascular workout; nonstressful to joints; can be helpful in maintaining flexibility; excellent for weight and body-fat maintenance and control; low injury rate because nonpounding.

Psychological benefits: Is rhythmic and repetitive (see other aerobic activities);

solitude can be soothing; can be pursued competitively although tends to be noncompetitive for most people.

Lifestyle benefits: Indoor machines available for home or gym and health club use; not difficult to master; can be pursued by people of all ages; equipment relatively inexpensive; allows for the exploration of and communion with natural settings.

Downhill Skiing

Physical benefits: Excellent for strengthening and toning muscles in the legs, buttocks and, to a lesser degree, arms and shoulders; improves balance, coordination and agility.

Psychological benefits: Can fulfill competitive and risk-taking urges; many find the excitement and challenge very stimulating.

Lifestyle benefits: Often forms the basis of daylong trips, weekends, and longer vacations; can be pursued alone or in groups; social outlet for many; equipment costs can be high but rentals are available.

Water Skiing

Physical benefits: Strengthens and tones muscles all over—in arms, shoulders, legs, buttocks, back and abdomen.

Psychological benefits: The thrill and fun can be very satisfying for many; skill mastery builds confidence for other sports and pursuits.

Lifestyle benefits: Allows enjoyment of natural setting; not limited to certain age levels; can be social outlet; equipment needs must be considered, but rentals widely available; can be used as off-season sport for downhill skiers.

Golf

Physical benefits: If players walk briskly and carry clubs, offers benefits of walking (see above); can contribute somewhat to muscle toning in arms and shoulders; may improve balance and coordination.

Psychological benefits: Develops concentration; many people find playing relaxing; can also be a competitive outlet.

Lifestyle benefits: Generally a very social experience, although it can be practiced or played solo; usually pursued in pleasant outdoor surroundings; easily accessible in most parts of the country.

Roller/Ice Skating (Including In-Line Skating)

Physical benefits: Strengthens and tones muscles in the legs, ankles, buttocks and, to a lesser degree, arms and shoulders (if they are swung as in speed skating); at high intensities can improve and maintain cardiovascular fitness; can contribute to weight control; helps develop balance and coordination.

Psychological benefits: Same as for other rhythmic, repetitive aerobic activities; speed skating can satisfy the competitive urge, but is also relaxing if performed alone.

Lifestyle benefits: One activity or the other can be performed year-round in most locales; equipment needs are not excessive and rentals are often available; suitable for transportation in some areas; suitable for solo or group workouts.

Martial Arts

Physical benefits: Some types of martial arts provide a cardiovascular workout; they can help develop muscle tone and strength, flexibility, balance and concentration; considered an effective "total-body" workout; may help with weight and body-fat control and maintaining healthy bone density.

Psychological benefits: Some types are considered calming and relaxing, others more stimulating; can be pursued combatively and competitively; focus is often on helping the body and spirit feel "centered" and connected to each other.

Lifestyle benefits: Can be done alone or with others; group instruction is widely available; accessible to people of widely ranging ages and fitness levels; equipment needs are minimal and equipment is inexpensive.

Softball/Baseball

Physical benefits: If practiced regularly, there is some development of shoulder and arm muscles from swinging bat and throwing (especially for pitchers); activity during practice and games usually not sufficient to improve or maintain cardiovascular fitness, although vigorous batting practice may have some effect.

Psychological benefits: Can help develop concentration; competitive aspect enjoyable to many, but more often engaged in recreationally; team orientation pleasing to many.

Lifestyle benefits: Can be social, building a spirit of camaraderie; opportunities to learn and play on amateur teams exist in most communities; can be pursued by people of a wide range of ages, abilities and fitness levels.

Soccer

Physical benefits: Helps strengthen and tone the lower-body muscles; practice sessions may promote cardiovascular conditioning, and at high levels players at some positions may develop aerobic fitness; can help improve and maintain speed and agility; may help maintain bone-mineral density.

Psychological benefits: Competitive and team aspects are emotionally enjoyable to many.

Lifestyle benefits: Instruction and opportunities to play and compete are widely available to people of all ages; equipment needs are minimal; can be played indoors and out; a very popular sport worldwide.

Ice Hockey/Field Hockey

Physical benefits: Can help strengthen and tone muscles in the legs and, at advanced levels, the arms and shoulders; can help improve and maintain speed, agility and coordination; at high levels some players develop aerobic fitness.

Psychological benefits: Competitive and team aspects are enjoyable to many; can help develop concentration.

Lifestyle benefits: One version or the other of the sport can be played year-round in most places; equipment needs aren't excessive; team nature makes for social enjoyment.

Boxing

Physical benefits: Training provides excellent cardiovascular workout, especially when jumping rope is included; workouts strengthen, tone and improve endurance in muscles all over the body, particularly arms and shoulders; promotes speed, coordination, grace and dexterity; flexibility exercises are encouraged in training.

Psychological benefits: Helps promote feelings of power and strength; can be a confidence-builder, particularly for women, who are relatively new to the activity.

Lifestyle benefits: Skills can be used in self-defense if needed; convenient as an "all-in-one" workout; inexpensive and widely accessible in gyms and training centers; equipment is inexpensive and easy to rent or purchase.

Combining Activities in a Cross-Training Program

Once you have picked a set of sports and fitness activities that you find appealing, and that you think will suit your schedule and lifestyle, the next step in creating a cross-training program is to work on shaping your choices into a well-rounded fitness regimen. There are a few simple rules you should follow in doing this, which are outlined below. Beyond those, however, your interests (which may change—so remember not to become a slave to habit) and imagination are your best guides. Let the following guidelines help you shape a cross-training program designed to bring you maximum fitness and enjoyment for your investment, with minimum risk of burnout, overuse, illness or injury.

Keep in mind that these rules are meant to promote total-body fitness, so you may wish to modify them if your goal is to develop your muscular strength and endurance in only one particular part of the body (the legs, for example). Remember, however, that if you strengthen muscles selectively, you risk injury—or at least imbalance—resulting from overworking some areas and underworking others.

Rule 1: Combine upper-body and lower-body activities. Ideally, you want the stress on your arms, shoulders and upper back to be roughly equal that on the legs, buttocks and lower back. You might also want to include separate exercises to work the abdominal muscles. If your program emphasizes one particular sport (running, for example) and uses others secondarily for variety and injury prevention, those other activities should work parts of the body that the primary sport does not (a runner should consider sports such as swimming and tennis, for example).

There are many sports that naturally work the lower body more than the upper body—think of walking, jogging, cycling and most team and individual sports in which participants spend most of their time on their feet. Consequently, to attain balanced fitness, most people have to make a special effort to exercise the upper body. In fact, recent exercise-science studies show that people of average fitness who add upper-body training exercises to their regimen (in this case sessions on an upper-body ergometer) develop their cardiovascular fitness more efficiently than those who follow just a lower-body training program.

As a runner, I generally find that I feel stronger, more balanced and less prone to injury when I faithfully stick to my weight-training program, which concentrates on my upper body. Activities that develop muscle strength and endurance in the upper body include weight-lifting, calisthenics, racquet sports (tennis, squash, racquetball and so forth), swimming, rowing, canoeing and to some extent cross-country skiing.

Rule 2: Make your program a combination of aerobic and strengthening workouts. Fitness, as defined by the American College of Sports Medicine (ACSM), has cardiovascular, muscle strength, muscle endurance, flexibility and body-composition maintenance components. The ACSM rates the first two as most important for people of all ages and fitness levels (see Chapter Two). Therefore, if one of your goals is to develop optimum fitness, you should try to include in your cross-training program exercises that stress the cardiovascular system and strengthen major muscle groups. Secondarily, your program should include some flexibility work, which will enhance your enjoyment of all physical activity.

Rule 3: Choose both activities that stress movement and activities that stress skill. As you can see from the list of sports on the previous pages, there are a number of sports and activities that can be performed by most people throughout life without a great deal of instruction, supervision or equipment. These include walking, jogging/running, swimming, cycling, rowing and other activities often referred to as "life sports," both because they are life promoting and because they can be enjoyed throughout life. These sports are terrific for body-fat management, cardiovascular fitness, and building muscle endurance.

Other activities, on the other hand, including softball/baseball, football, water skiing, downhill skiing and golf, rely quite a bit more on skill. These sports may demand a high sports *talent* level without doing much to develop cardiovascular fitness or muscle strength in and of themselves. For example, a star baseball player will rely on strength to throw and to hit the ball hard and on speed to run the bases quickly. But the limited amount of time and intensity that he devotes to doing these things in a game of baseball isn't enough to develop them to any great extent. So this baseball player finds that he must lift weights and adopt a running program that includes both aerobic jogging and anaerobic sprints in order to be optimally trained. He must also possess a modicum of raw skill—talent that he is born with and builds upon through practice.

Rule 4: Combine activities that are more stressful to the joints with those that are less stressful. How many people do you know who have had to give up running, soccer, aerobic dance or another activity that involves a lot of pounding to the knees, or swimming, tennis or another sport that's tough on the arms, back and shoulders, because of one or a series of injuries? Many of these people could have continued to engage in their sport safely and comfortably if they had combined it with another activity or activities that skipped the upper-body pounding (swimming, rowing, walking and cycling would all be good choices) or lower-body stroking (any lower-body activity would do the trick).

One famous example of a former one-sport athlete who now engages in multisport activity is Olympic marathon champion Frank Shorter, now in his forties and still almost as physically active as he was twenty years ago. Shorter finds that years of running and dozens of injuries have taken such a toll on his body that he can no longer train at the level it takes to be one of the top in the sport, even as a masters (over forty) competitor. Instead, he has turned to duathlons (competitions that involve cycling and running; see Chapter Nine for a complete discussion of this sport).

Shorter claims that he can recover from workouts and races far more quickly now than in his running-only days. He places highly in competitions and plans to remain active in the sport for the foreseeable future.

The following are a few suggestions for combining sports. Keep in mind that the combinations are endless, and that it is possible to experiment to your heart's content. As discussed in Chapter Four, it is probably best to have your core training program consist of no more than four activities, although with proper preparation, care and recovery, you can from time to time add another activity as the mood, the occasion and the availability of the activity strike you.

Sample Two-Activity Combinations

1. *Jogging/running and biking:* This classic combination actually takes the form of a popular sport, the run-bike-run duathlon (see Chapter Nine). Although both activities work the lower body, the muscles used to engage in each are different.

Biking uses mainly the quadriceps muscles in the front of the thigh, especially when toeclips are used on the feet, while running relies more on the back-of-thigh hamstrings and the calf muscles.

Those who wish to pursue running and biking with equal intensity may want to adopt an every-other-workout schedule. Alternatively, it's possible to concentrate on one activity, adding one or two workouts a week of the other for injury and burnout prevention. Upper-body strength and endurance must be developed separately, along with flexibility, perhaps through a stretching and calisthenics program twice a week.

2. *Rowing and weight-lifting:* People who row on the crew team in college discover that these two sports can complement each other very well. Rowing provides an aerobic workout when performed in the training zone for at least twenty minutes at a time (this is especially easy to monitor when rowing on an indoor machine), while weight-lifting can strengthen and improve endurance of the muscles, guarding against injury and providing a break from the regular grind of the cardiovascular rowing activity. Rounding out the two activities with regular stretching can keep the muscles used limber and better able to withstand the stress placed upon them.

3. *Racquet sport (tennis, squash or racquetball) and swimming:* Unless they are pursued at a very high competitive level, racquet sports are not aerobic. If done every day, however, they will involve a great deal of running in spurts (anaerobically), burn a large number of calories and cause pounding to the lower body (ankles, knees and hips) and strain to the arms and shoulders from repeated swinging at the ball.

A swimming program can be an excellent complement to racquet sports because of its aerobic nature and because it involves no pounding to the joints. A swimmer must be careful, however, not to overdo the activity to avoid straining the shoulder, as this joint is involved in both activities and can easily be overstressed. Building up the intensity in both activities and taking a day or two off (no workout at all) each week should minimize these problems.

Sample Three-Activity Combinations

1. *Tennis, aerobic dance and swimming:* This is a good program for someone looking for a strong cardiovascular program with upper-body (tennis) and lower-body (aerobic dance) muscle endurance and strength building. The swimming component helps improve overall muscle tone and cardiovascular fitness without excessive stress to the joints. Aerobic dance routines can be varied to emphasize upper-body or lower-body development. Depending on the season, the routines can be performed indoors or outside.

2. *Boxing, cross-country skiing and soccer:* As mentioned above, the training involved in boxing (calisthenics, jumping rope, punching a bag, sparring) develops cardiovascular fitness, muscular strength and endurance and flexibility. Cross-country skiing (either in snow or with a ski machine) is a good complement because it is gentler on the joints, can sustain aerobic activity for longer periods and still works all the major muscle groups. Soccer is a team sport that allows one to partake of the fitness benefits gained in the other two sports while providing a light workout of its own. Along with these attributes, it also provides fun, camaraderie and competition.

Sample Four-Activity Combinations

1. *Golf, weight-lifting, rowing and downhill skiing:* Here, one gets a good cardiovascular workout from the rowing; this can help sustain aerobic fitness during lengthy downhill skiing stints. Golf also affords a mild aerobic benefit if the clubs are carried and a golf cart isn't used to get from hole to hole; the activity also develops concentration and offers a competitive outlet. A weight-lifting program can help strengthen muscles, particularly those in the legs, buttocks and lower back that are used in downhill skiing. Rowing can also improve the endurance of those muscles, as well as strengthen those in the abdominals and back. Many people also use the activity to control weight by burning calories. Downhill skiing improves agility and can add a social aspect and excitement to the total cross-training program.

2. *Walking, softball, water aerobics and racquetball:* The purposes of walking are to establish an aerobic base, useful in the other activities, as well as to provide greater endurance for the tasks of daily life. Walking also burns calories, is relaxing and can be used for transportation. Softball can be social and fun, build concentration and sports skills (catching, throwing and so forth) and contribute mildly to upper-body strength and endurance. Water aerobics (also called aqua- or hydro-aerobics) can be a great cardiovascular workout and fat-burner. It is suitable for pregnant women, the elderly, or anyone with injury-prone joints. Racquetball, besides being competitive (if desired) and fun, also burns calories, enhances skills, contributes to upper-body strength and builds endurance, and at high levels can provide an aerobic workout.

These are just a few of literally thousands of combinations of activities. Be adventuresome and flexible, and you will come up with many of your own; really, there is no limit to the mixes that you can create. Now, read on for suggestions about the best ways to put a program together into a schedule that works for you, keeping you fit, excited and injury-free.

FOUR

MAKING THE

MINUTES COUNT

All the pages devoted in the last chapter to discussing which activities to combine with which, and what they will do for the body, are very well and good. I hope that after reading them and giving them some thought, you have a fairly clear, coherent idea of which sports and activities most interest you and how to combine them with other exercises that complement them in order to build a well-balanced total fitness program.

Now, however, we must turn to some of the more practical questions that are posed by many of those who would like to cross-train. The most pressing of these—almost invariably, I have found—is, "How will I find the time for all these activities? How can I fit them into my life?"

Lack of time is the most common reason (or perhaps "excuse" is sometimes a better word) people give for not exercising regularly. From world-class athletes to weekend warriors, we all use the excuse. More often than not, the best of intentions are there: Witness the number of people who begin every January by carrying out their New Year's resolutions to get in shape and lose weight, or those who hit the jogging trails, bike paths or aerobic studios with the onset of spring, after reaching a milestone birthday, or when the scale starts to register an ungodly number.

But then what happens? The days and weeks pass, and these well-intentioned souls find that putting in the requisite twenty to thirty minutes per day becomes a challenge. Then soon it is a burden. They spend a few late nights at the office, some friends come in from out of town, they are forced to deal with a child's illness (or their own), and the commitment is broken—regretfully, but lost none-theless, until the urge to reform strikes yet again.

Estimates vary, but the consensus is that well under half the people who start a regular exercise program are still pursuing it six months down the road. And since fitness gains must be maintained to do any good, either health or fitness-wise (in other words, the gains cannot be "stored" for periods of time), stopping the activity unfortunately can cause the benefits of those hours, days and weeks invested to go up in smoke.

What Gets People Exercising?

It should be fairly obvious by now—even if you are not yet a regular ex-erciser—that consistent physical activity, like most endeavors, is not just a matter of one's ability, but of careful planning and commitment as well. Cross-training can either ease and simplify the problem or make it more challenging and complicated. The result depends both on the activities involved and on the approach one takes to pursuing them.

So how does one continue exercising once a program is under way? I've found, through my own experience, talking to others and doing a great deal of reading, that the best exercise programs, no matter at what level they are pursued, combine the following elements:

- Commitment
- Goal setting
- Flexibility
- A clear, honest assessment of how the program fits into the overall pattern of your life

Breaking down and understanding those elements can give someone plan-ning a cross-training program the tools to make that program work—not just for the first few exhilarating weeks, but for the months and years that the program lasts.

The plan outlined below can help guide you through the four steps to ex-ercising regularly that I've listed above. I know it has helped me many times to get motivated, start a training program and keep going.

1. Make a Commitment. Everything follows from this point, whether you are an absolute beginner or a potential world champion. When PattiSue Plumer, one of the premier middle-distance track runners in the world, was asked how she fits in her running every day (she is also a wife and a full-time attorney, living in Palo Alto, California), she replied, "I don't have to think about it, I just do it. It's like brushing my teeth. The decision has already been made."

That's commitment. Years ago, Plumer sat down and decided she was going to devote the requisite energy and time to becoming the best athlete she possibly could, while at the same time living a normal (if crammed-full) life. As she laces up her running shoes each day, she doesn't have to ask herself if she wouldn't really rather be doing something else, such as going to sit in the backyard to sunbathe, or whipping up a five-course dinner for herself and her husband. She doesn't have to wonder whether it is too cold, too hot, too windy, or raining too hard to go for a run. *The decision has already been made.*

It's easy to look at someone like Plumer and think, "Well of course she's going to go out and train every day. Looks what's at stake. She has talent. She is an Olympian who holds national records. If I had that kind of talent I'd go out and train every day, too!"

Okay, maybe you would. Keep in mind, however, that running (or any sport) is no different from any of life's endeavors in one respect: For every athlete who enjoys a career as successful as Plumer's, there are hundreds of others with equal or near-equal talent and potential who fall by the wayside. What gave Muhammad Ali, years after he lost the world heavyweight title, the will and the ability to come back and reclaim it from George Foreman in 1974? In large part it was Ali's commitment, to himself and to the sport of boxing, a promise to himself that he was going to do it, or at least to give it his best effort.

That same attitude can motivate people who exercise simply for enjoyment and fitness. After I ran the New York City Marathon in 1984, finishing in a respectable but strictly recreational time of about three hours and forty minutes (I barely placed in the top three thousand of a field of fifteen thousand), I felt sick and tired of running. For the next three months I hardly ran at all while I gave my mind and body a rest.

Come spring, however, I felt a longing to get back out on the roads. I realized, however, that I didn't just want to run long and regularly, but also run *fast*. So I made a commitment to doing some quicker training, with the goal of running a fast time in the L'eggs (now Advil) Mini Marathon, a ten-kilometer race held every spring in Central Park.

Once I'd made the commitment to run L'eggs, my training fell into place.

No, the running wasn't easy; in fact it was physically more challenging than anything I had done before, because I had decided to test the limits of my capabilities at the time. I found, however, that everything just seemed to flow from that decision. I ran L'eggs in 38:52—a respectable time for someone who was not on a formal training program—and was subsequently asked to join Atalanta, an elite women's running team that I continued to train with for six years.

You will discover that it's not necessarily those people with the best cardiovascular systems, the strongest muscles, the most favorable body-fat percentages or the greatest flexibility who stick with their chosen activity or activities. Rather, those who stick with it tend to be the ones who have made a commitment, who have said, "This is something that is important to me, that I enjoy, and for which it is worth making some sacrifices and shifts in my priorities."

For most people, of course, a commitment to cross-training (or any regular exercise program) must be adjusted to fit in around numerous other commitments and responsibilities—to work, family, friends, community affairs and so forth. Most people don't—and shouldn't—work out every day. In addition, most people tend to go through several periods a year when their commitment to exercise is at a low ebb. Their workouts may go completely by the boards for a few days, a week or longer.

Exercise scientists call this practice "periodization" and recommend it to athletes at all levels. (Obviously a cross-training program must also be modified for illness, injury—see Chapter Eight for more detail on avoiding and overcoming injuries—and other interferences.) Taking periodic, planned breaks, the experts find, helps maintain commitment over the long haul. These regularly scheduled times of less-intense activity should be built into everyone's yearly schedule (this is also discussed in Chapter Eight).

The inclusion of rest periods doesn't mean a slacking off of the overall commitment to sports and physical fitness; in fact, it can strengthen that promise. For example, world cross-country champion Lynn Jennings announced in 1990 that she planned to run in the Olympic marathon in the 1996 Games in Atlanta. This was making a commitment to an event six years away. But after defending her national cross-country title that year, Jennings said she was "on vacation" from running for the next month. This is a clear example of a planned rest break built into an overall training program for the express purpose of lengthening and strengthening an overall commitment to a sport. Professional team players, too, while they tend to stay in at least adequate shape year-round, aren't always going full steam. Why else do you think pro baseball teams have spring training every year?

2. Assess Your Goals As an intelligent person wanting to make a commitment to cross-training, one key question should leap instantly into your mind: "Why am I doing this? What do I hope to gain from these activities?"

The answer (or answers) that you come up with to that question should set the stage for virtually every other decision you make about how, when, where, with whom and how often you cross-train. The key point—one often forgotten by exercisers from the beginner to the elite competitive level, as well as many coaches and trainers—is that the goals of your exercise program are *yours* and *yours alone*. As such, they will be different from the cross-training goals held by anyone else.

Clearly, the reasons for cross-training regularly are many and varied. For many people—but not everyone—maintaining or improving fitness ranks high among those first mentioned. Other goals often cited are maintaining or improving appearance, controlling weight and body fat, meeting people and socializing and warding off the effects of advancing age.

The American public has become increasingly well-educated about the short-term and long-term health benefits of being in good physical condition. Other reasons commonly given for exercising are:

- To feel better
- To give myself a challenge
- To relieve stress
- To set a good example to others (such as children)

These are all valid goals. It is important to realize, however, that they are very diverse goals, and that therefore the means to achieving will also be different for each person. Given that, entering into a cross-training program without goals will likely consign you to a random, poorly conceived pattern of activity.

Most people who cross-train have more than one exercise goal; indeed, having multiple objectives is often one of the reasons why they choose a multiactivity exercise program in the first place. That's fine. Problems can arise, however, when cross-training goals are in conflict—either your own contradictory goals, or those you have that may clash with someone else's.

An example of the first case would be a woman who has set two goals for her cross-training program: She wants to lose some weight and to relieve anxiety and stress. As the pounds start to drop, however, she sets a more concrete goal: She wants to lose twenty pounds by the day of her daughter's wedding. As the date draws near, she sees that the weight-loss goal is going to be difficult to attain unless drastic steps are taken. Under the current cross-training program, however, she has felt relaxed. Her activities fit comfortably into her schedule, increase her energy level rather than draining it and make her as fit as she wants and needs to be. In short, she feels no particular desire to exercise more—except that it would probably help her lose the extra weight that she is carrying.

Thus, the woman feels torn between her two goals. Exercising more, while helping her accomplish one goal (weight loss by a certain date) will detract from another (stress reduction) by making her feel anxious, tired and pressed for time. What she needs to do is sit down and decide which of the two goals is most important. This does not necessarily mean she has to completely abandon one goal or the other. She may decide, for example, that she can be satisfied with a slower-than-planned rate of weight loss, as long as she has the trade-off of feeling less stress. She will then set up a program appropriate to meeting her newly thought-out goals.

From this example, you can see the importance of setting goals that are not only realistic, but also not in conflict with one another. You will find that anticipating and planning to avoid these potential conflicts can save a lot of trouble in the long run.

3. Be Flexible In cross-training, as in almost any aspect of life, you may notice that things don't always go as planned. Ideally, involving yourself in several different types of exercise should make it *more*, not less, likely that you will be able to be active in *some* way during any given period of time. For example, if you are a cross-country skiing enthusiast who previously followed no formal exercise program during the warmer months, setting up a cross-training program that includes brisk walking or jogging in the spring, summer and autumn can keep you active year-round. (Making arrangements to work out indoors on a cross-country ski machine or treadmill during inclement weather can further guarantee that you'll never have to experience a time of forced inactivity.)

In order to keep yourself moving, however, you must develop an attitude that I call "planned flexibility." For example, suppose that you set up a program that is designed to accommodate several different aerobic activities, such as walking, cycling and rowing, and a couple of strengthening and flexibility exercises, such as calisthenics and weight-lifting. Having a flexible attitude about what you do, and when you do it, will mean that the activity that you choose on any given day will depend on a number of factors, including your mood, the activity's accessibility, the weather and what you have been doing over the past several days.

On the other hand, if your plan is set up according to a rigidly prescribed schedule that must be followed to the letter (racquetball on Monday, wind-surfing on Tuesday, walking on Wednesday and so forth), sticking to the plan will be very tough, especially if the activities depend on having partners, fancy equipment or favorable weather.

The best plan, therefore, is one that is prescribed, yet flexible, that aims for a certain amount, type and variety of activity to achieve certain goals each week but is not overly rigid in dictating how those goals are attained. For example, here is how Jeff Hildebrandt, a twenty-seven-year-old manager at a career consulting firm in Boulder, Colorado, who bikes, runs, swims, walks his dog and competes in triathlons and mountain running races, describes his cross-training schedule: "I have an idea of how I'm going to fit my workouts in each week, but I never know exactly how, when or where I'm going to do it. How can I know? I have a full-time job, relationships, the weather to contend with. Fortunately, I never have a problem with motivation, so I know the workouts will get done. It's just that with my busy lifestyle, and the number of different sports I do, I'm more comfortable just keeping things loose and flexible."

Another active person I know, a doctor, kept himself in decent physical shape during a grueling residency in internal medicine at a New York City hospital. He would go out for runs in Central Park whenever he could fit them in—time of day or number of hours recently slept notwithstanding. He also kept an exercise bike in his apartment to catch shorter workouts during his rare hours at home. On a program that included ten-mile runs at 6:00 A.M. following thirty-six-hour stretches without sleep, he was able to complete the 26.2-mile New York City Marathon.

"My time in the race wasn't great," he reported, "but that didn't matter. The goal at the time was to just stay in one piece, mentally and physically, during a stressful period in my life. Running and biking whenever I could helped me to do that. I realized that I couldn't be compulsive. I didn't have the luxury of knowing when and for how long I'd be able to exercise. Once I accepted that, the program worked great for me."

Flexibility doesn't mean that you're constantly picking your activities on a whim, or giving no thought to how they combine with other exercises and fit into your total cross-training program. As you learned in Chapter Three, combining activities in the right ways is one of the secrets of a cross-training program's success. But being flexible does open your cross-training to a healthy measure of whimsy, which can take a lot of the stress out of exercise for most people. More important, by opening up more possibilities to you, it increases the chances that you will exercise regularly.

4. Fit Cross-Training into the Rest of Your Life As you probably know or can surmise, most people find it pretty challenging to do this. Like most serious exercisers, I am a veteran of workouts done before dawn, late at night, during lunchtime—any time I can manage to fit them in around work, family, social, community and other commitments and responsibilities. I've worked out at airports, from bus and train stations, during magazine photography shooting sessions, and on breaks while attending professional conventions. I've shown up to meet friends at movies, dinner dates and at parties fresh from working out, still breathless from rushing to be on time.

I know from my own experience and that of many others the lengths that a dedicated exerciser will go to in order to schedule workouts. At times I have felt frustrated that it seems there's never quite enough time to fit exercise into a life that's rich, busy and productive in other ways as well.

There's some comfort in knowing that other active people, at all levels, also find it hard to squeeze in workouts from time to time. For example, Joan Benoit Samuelson, the 1984 Olympic marathon gold medalist, is now a mother of two who claims to devote "only" a maximum of three hours a day to training. She still managed on this schedule to run one of the top marathon times in the country for 1991. When Samuelson's time gets really crunched, she reported to *Runner's World,* and she has an appointment away from home, one workout strategy she has adopted is to start out on a run as hard as she can in the direction she has to go. Her husband then at some point comes along in the car and picks her up and drives her the rest of the way to wherever she's headed—whether to the airport to catch a flight to go run in a race or give a speech, or to the market to buy groceries. And I thought running laps around an airport parking lot was crazy! Still, the program works for Samuelson: Although she is not running at quite the level that produced her Olympic gold medal performance and national record marathon time, she is still highly competitive, yet manages to be a full-time mother as well.

In some ways, the flexibility built into a good cross-training program actually can make fitting in exercise *less* hassle. For example, if you're short on time and can't make it to the health club for an aerobics class, taking a run around the neighborhood or pedaling a stationary bike at home (or even in the office if you're able) can be an acceptable substitute. On the other hand, as mentioned earlier, an overly regimented program can take a toll in the long run. For example, if your schedule says you simply *must* play two hours of tennis on Saturday, and a hurricane is raging, you'll likely get zero exercise that day unless you have an alternative plan. However, if you're content to pop an exercise video into the VCR and work out at home instead, you've at least gotten some sort of activity in, even if it wasn't precisely what you had planned.

Just a word on setting limits on your sports and fitness activities: There is a danger that cross-training can reinforce many people's tendency to be compulsive about exercise, to do too much, too soon, without setting reasonable limits. After all, haven't you ever felt the tendency, which can be especially strong when one first successfully establishes a regular fitness regimen, to think that if some activity is good, then more activity must be even better?

If you aren't careful, cross-training, with its multiplicity of activities, can reinforce this compulsive urge to do more, and more, and more. When you start, it may seem for a while that you have no limits, that the more you work out, the better you feel. This feeling can persist for weeks, even months, as you increase your level of activity to unsustainable, unnecessary and even dangerous levels. You may ignore friends, family, work assignments, community responsibilities and worse—at least for your continued participation in an active life—signs of ill health and impending burnout and injury, brought on by excess activity.

Recognizing and avoiding burnout and overuse injuries are discussed in detail in Chapter Eight. For now suffice it to say that if you don't put limits—physical and emotional—on the time and energy you put into cross-training, eventually those limits will be put in place for you. When this happens, you probably won't like the way it comes to pass. Your alternative is to be reasonable and realistic about the role of exercise and to understand the effects of overdoing it on both the body and mind. It is not your whole life. Even world-class athletes back off when they're tired, sick or starting to feel stale, or when they have important family, work or other situations to attend to. You will learn to back off, too, if not now, then eventually. Whether you do so by choice or are forced to is up to you.

Surprising Ways to Make Cross-Training Part of Your Life

At the other end of the spectrum from compulsive overexercisers are those people who exercise only sporadically or not at all because they say they "don't have time" to fit it in. They may start and stop, wondering why they can't stick with a program. What they may not realize is that they could probably fit a lot more "exercise" into their lives if they were more creative and open-minded in their view of what constitutes exercise.

The American College of Sports Medicine (ACSM), as you will recall from Chapter Two, says that for an activity to have an aerobic benefit it must be performed at a level that gets the heart beating at 60 percent to 90 percent of its maximum rate for between twenty and sixty consecutive minutes, at least three times a week. In addition, to adequately strengthen the muscles, says the ACSM, one should do a set of eight to twelve repetitions of eight to ten different exercises that work the major muscle groups, at least twice a week. Do the above, as well as maintaining adequate flexibility and acceptable body composition, and you are generally considered fit.

However, several studies on very large groups of people have found that for *health* benefits—living longer and reducing the risk of heart disease and other killing conditions—less intense and shorter bouts of regular activity may be effective. In what's probably the best-known study, Ralph Paffenbarger, M.D., of Stanford University, found that of more than sixteen thousand men of all ages, those who expended at least two thousand calories a week were less likely to die prematurely than those who expended fewer calories per week in exercising less. He found that the magic two thousands calories' worth of activity could be accomplished by performing ordinary tasks such as climbing stairs, raking leaves and performing household chores. Another large study of several thousand female subjects conducted at the Institute for Aerobics Research in Dallas found that regular, moderate activity had a life-enhancing effect for women as well. It is notable that neither study looked at whether the activity was performed in the aerobic training range.

Recent research has also called into question the dictum that aerobic activity must continue for at least twenty consecutive minutes. This may be needed for *fitness* reasons, says the argument, but is it really also essential for enhancing and maintaining *health* (rather than fitness)?

Studies by William Haskell, Ph.D., also of Stanford University, found that health benefits (reduced risk of heart attack and so forth) did not suffer when aerobic activity was broken up into three ten-minute segments, rather than performed as one thirty-minute session. The segments in this study included such activities as brisk walking, climbing stairs at a good clip and light calisthenics, although again, heart rate wasn't measured.

This is very good news for anyone who wants to be more active, but has a hard time fitting "exercise" time into the day. It means that with a little creativity, you needn't beat your head against the wall to stay reasonably healthy. For example, if the hours or the nature of your job or your duties at home keep you working right through lunchtime, it's probably impossible for you to schedule a half-hour aerobics session at the health club (which, while also entailing getting to the club, changing, warming up, and then showering, changing and getting back to home or work afterward, would likely stretch the entire operation to an hour or longer). But how about sneaking out for ten minutes of brisk walking sometime in the midmorning or midafternoon? Or, if the weather is lousy, trotting up and down the stairs in your building for a quick ten minutes? (Just make sure you wear supportive shoes, raise your heart rate gradually, and cool down with a couple of minutes of low-level activity afterward.) Combine your midday break with a walk in the morning—taking your dog out, accompanying your child to school or to the bus stop, hoofing it part or all of the way to the office—and perhaps ten minutes of stretching and calisthenics in the evening before bed, and you've got your thirty minutes of exercise made for that day. *And* you are following a cross-training program, for balanced fitness.

The following list of activities, and the sample schedules for employed and at-home people, show you the many, varied ways in which you can fit a variety of regular, moderate exercises and activities into your life, often in ways that you may not have expected. Whether you work in an office or at home, are married or single, with children or without, these strategies can give you ideas for designing a cross-training program that fits your life.

Remember, no one is "too busy" to exercise. When you keep in mind all the benefits you will get back—not just better health and fitness, but improved efficiency in performing daily tasks, better concentration, enhanced ability to relax, better sleep, improved overall feelings of well-being and more—you will see that your investment in exercise has become one of the wisest decisions you will ever make.

Twenty Excuse-Proof Ways to Fit More Exercise into Your Day

Here are a score of ways to make sure you don't catch yourself saying "I don't have time to cross-train."

1. Walk to work. If this isn't practical or feasible, get off the bus, train or subway and walk the last half-mile to your workplace, or park half a mile away instead of right outside the front door or in the company parking lot. Jogging

or running to or from work, or both, may even be feasible for some people who have showering and changing facilities at either end. One advantage: It can sure cut down on commuting time and costs.

2. If you work at home, walk your children to school or to the bus stop daily.

3. Take a baby for a walk in a stroller or baby carriage.

4. If you don't have kids, walk to get the morning paper or to do some errands.

5. If none of these options works for you, then just take ten minutes to walk for the pure health of it.

6. Whenever you can, walk to social engagements—parties, the movies, restaurants, to visit friends and so forth. This is particularly healthful and safe if you plan to drink, because walking saves the worry of who is going to be the "designated driver" for the trip home.

7. Take the stairs any time it is feasible. If you live in an apartment building, get in the habit of walking a few floors (or all of them) instead of taking the elevator.

8. Walk between floors at work or school, if the building security allows it. Walk to upper-floor appointments in other buildings, too—when seeing clients, at the library, at your health club (*especially* there) and so forth.

9. Do it by hand in the kitchen. Dicing, slicing, chopping, stirring, mixing, kneading—they all can work up a minor sweat, burn calories, and make your arm and hand muscles stronger.

10. Roughhouse with your kids—or your spouse, sibling, roommate, whoever is around and in the mood.

11. Get some chores done around the yard: Mow the lawn with a nonpower mower, rake leaves, prune hedges or shrubbery, plant bulbs, seeds, grown plants or grass seed, lay down sod, pull up weeds, water and so forth. You name it, and it probably burns calories, works major muscle groups and may even be aerobic if performed at a sufficient intensity. Just remember to ease into strenuous activities (such as brush clearing or leaf raking) gradually, do some gentle stretching, and wear gloves to protect your hands against blisters.

12. If you don't have a yard, or despise yardwork, or it's the wrong time of year, get busy indoors: Dust, vacuum, scrub (*really* scrub) a floor, sweep, mop, clean walls and woodwork or do whatever needs doing. Or you can really get ambitious and tackle a big job you have been putting off for months: painting a wall, floor or ceiling; putting up wallpaper; hanging pictures; stenciling on

decorations or refinishing a piece of furniture. Just don't concentrate so hard on making the activity aerobic that you do a sloppy job.

13. Play with your pet dog, cat, rabbit, mouse, gerbil, hamster, bird or raccoon. I haven't yet figured out a way to frolic with goldfish, but I'm working on it.

14. Play with your kids. They'll probably demand it anyway, so why not enjoy yourself? And if they *don't* want to play active games, then you can take the initiative. Take a walk, jog or bike ride together; play any one of an infinite variety of games of tag; kick, throw and catch a ball; shoot baskets; punch a child-size punching bag; rent, borrow or buy a canoe or rowboat and go paddling—the list is endless. (See Chapter Five for a more complete look at children's cross-training activities.)

15. Don't write off playing with your teenage children, either—toss a Frisbee or football, go for a walk, run or bike ride, whatever. Exercising together not only improves teens' fitness, it can also get adolescents to let down their guard and be more communicative—and that is no mean feat.

16. Run in place for five minutes. Close your office door at work or stand up from whatever you're doing at home, and as the commercials say, just do it. Alternatively, you can jump rope—but work up gradually to doing even five minutes if you're a beginner.

17. Keep a set of small (one-half to three-pound) weights in your home or office to do light weight-lifting exercises. Do not strain yourself.

18. Take an after-dinner stroll instead of watching a TV program you don't really care about.

19. Do some stretching, aerobics or calisthenics while watching TV in the evening.

20. Make friends with someone who lives within walking distance from you and make a pledge to each other to walk whenever feasible when you get together.

Cross-Training for "Too-Busy" Office and At-Home Workers

With your excuses gone, you are ready to set up a cross-training schedule that you will stick with. Here are suggested programs, whether you work at home or in an office.

Office Worker

Monday: Walk fifteen minutes to (or part way to) work and home or part way home (thirty minutes total).

Tuesday: Do light stretching and calisthenics for fifteen minutes in the office at lunchtime (or whenever you have some free time); walk to (or part way to) a dinner appointment in the evening, or part way home.

Wednesday: Arrange to visit a health club with a coworker to swim, bike, take an aerobics class or do some sort of aerobic activity. If something comes up, promise each other you'll get the workout in tomorrow.

Thursday: Walk to and from work, as on Monday. If that's not possible, walk or climb stairs at a moderate pace for half an hour at lunchtime.

Friday: Rest day. If you can fit some extra activity in, fine; if not, that's fine, too.

Saturday: Do some light stretching and calisthenics for fifteen minutes in the morning. Take a thirty-minute walk, jog, bike ride or swim in the afternoon.

Sunday: Spend an hour or so in the afternoon gardening or doing yardwork or chores around the house.

Home Worker

Monday: Take a walk—to school or the bus stop with your child, pushing a baby in a carriage or stroller, or by yourself to do an errand. Try to keep moving at a brisk pace for twenty to thirty minutes. Take fifteen minutes to do some calisthenics and stretch in the evening if you have time.

Tuesday: Put a half-hour exercise video of your choice in the VCR for a daytime workout, at whatever time you get the chance. Try to stick to the time you set aside for the activity, though. Many videos are suitable for both children and adults, so you can have your kids work out with you.

Wednesday: Walk in the morning as on Monday. Then, later in the day, do some strengthening calisthenics or light weight-lifting exercises for about twenty minutes. If you have a baby or small child, this is best done while the young one is napping; older children can join in with calisthenics and *light* weights as long as you supervise them carefully. (See Chapter Five for more on kids' fitness.)

Thursday: Arrange to get out of the house to exercise, leaving children with a sitter or trusted neighbor. The activity is up to you—just remember to warm up and cool down properly before and after the activity.

Friday: Cycle or walk for transportation on an errand, keeping your heart rate in your training zone for at least twenty consecutive minutes.

Saturday: Do an hour or so of vigorous yardwork or housework, with other members of your family if you wish. Many chores will raise your heart rate into the lower end of your training zone and improve strength and endurance in the major muscle groups. It's a good idea to do some light stretching and gradually ease into the activity.

Sunday: You've worked hard all week—so relax. If you get exercise, make sure it's something you thoroughly enjoy, and that you don't overtax yourself.

That's it, so there go all your excuses. You won't become an Olympian on this activity schedule, but you won't grow moss lounging in the recliner, either. Now, read on for more specifics on how various types of people can adapt cross-training programs to their lives.

FIVE

SPECIAL NEEDS FOR

SPECIAL PEOPLE

When it comes to physical activity, as you have certainly heard, no two of us are quite the same. To begin with, we are endowed with widely differing physiques, from a seven-foot seven-inch basketball player, to a 215-pound world-champion boxer, to a petite four-foot eight-inch, 75-pound gymnast. These variations naturally suit us to a wide variety of sports and activities.

If we have the interests and are fortunate enough to have access to the activities of our choice, then we will very likely gravitate toward those that best suit our talents, shape and size. For example, a big-boned, fearless young boy might turn to football, and a girl with broad shoulders and great cardiovascular endurance might decide to go out for her school's swim team.

We are also blessed—again to an extraordinarily varying degree—with sports-related talents, such as the coordination, concentration, and sense of timing it takes to connect a baseball bat with a ball hurtling toward us at ninety miles per hour, or to dodge a phalanx of opponents and leap high into the air to score in basketball. Of course these skills must be honed to bring out the best in them (and in us). It is well known, however, that most people could practice tennis twenty hours a day and never begin to hold their own in a match with Steffi Graf or Boris Becker, because of the coordination, concentration and sense of timing that these and other extraordinary athletes possess.

Credit: Karen Schulenberg.

Our physical adaptations to exercise are in large part genetically determined—there is a limited amount we can do to change them. Long-distance runners such as Grete Waitz and Bill Rodgers may train one hundred miles a week or even more to get the fastest times possible out of their bodies on race day. But, like the baseball player who bats .320 or the jockey who survives a streak of scores of races without a loss, these athletes are set apart to begin with by their inborn gifts—in the case of the runners, most crucially by strong cardiovascular systems, naturally lean body types and efficient running styles. They had a head start over the rest of us before we even got started.

Variations in how we adapt to various forms of physical activity extend down from the elite athletes into the general population. You may jog with your friend every day, doing the same course at the same speed, both of you also doing some supplemental biking and weight-lifting on the side. You may find, however, that she effortlessly beats you when you both enter a local fun run.

To draw on a personal example, I shocked my teammates, my coach and most of all myself when I was timed for the first time running a mile after going out for track in high school. I beat all the other girls by at least thirty seconds. "How did that happen?" I wondered. "We've been doing all our training together—same mileage, same pace, same workouts in the weight room." Obviously, I was blessed with a combination of a stronger and more efficient cardiovascular system, a lean body type and a more efficient running style, and these qualities, combined with my conditioning, allowed me to outperform against my teammates when going all-out against the clock.

I talked about custom-designing a fitness program to meet your physical capabilities, interests and lifestyle back in Chapter Three. Here, we look at some of the differences in how cross-training affects a variety of broad groups of people, including men and women, children and teens, the elderly and the disabled. Ignoring these broad differences among groups, as you will soon see, can strike a death knell for a cross-training program. On the other hand, paying attention to them can help ensure that the program best meets your needs, whether you work out alone or with others. The process, when properly handled, will become liberating instead of limiting.

Cross-Training for Men/Cross-Training for Women

With the passage of Title IX of the Civil Rights Act or 1972, women and girls gained equal access to sports programs in schools that receive federal funding.

That watershed event ushered in the past two decades of phenomenal growth and progress in women's and girls' sports and fitness activities. Female participation in high school sports programs increased from 294,000 in 1972 to 1,858,659 in 1990 (the most recent year for which figures are available), according to the Women's Sports Foundation, a nonprofit foundation based in New York City that supports female equality in sports.

In addition, we have seen the money awarded to top women athletes in sports across the board rise to a level commensurate with (and sometimes even greater than) that given to men. For example, tennis player Martina Navratilova was the highest-paid athlete (male or female) in the world in 1988. Women have won the right to participate in a greater number of world-class events, such as the Olympic Marathon—beginning in 1984 with Joan Benoit's brilliant gold-medal performance in Los Angeles—and Olympic race-walking events, which will be open to females for the first time in Barcelona in 1992. (Male race walkers, by the way, have competed in the Olympics since 1908.)

Running parallel to this progress at the elite level has been a huge mushrooming of women's participation in exercise and fitness activities. One of the most dramatic examples is aerobic dance, a sport that was practically unheard of fifteen years ago and experienced phenomenal growth during the 1980s. An estimated 90 percent of aerobic-dance participants are women, according to IDEA: The Association for Fitness Professionals, in San Diego. Perhaps a more telling figure, showing the extent to which women have led the fitness movement of the past two decades, is this one from American Sports Data, in Hartsdale, New York: Women consistently make up 50 to 60 percent of all *new* participants in exercise activities each year.

Without question, women have been a massive, vital part of the "fitness boom" that has been going on in this country since the mid-1970s. They walk, jog, swim, cycle, lift weights and more, plus play every team sport imaginable, either alongside men or on their own.

Partly in response to this vast growth in women's sports and fitness at all levels has been an accompanying growth in research on active women. At the annual meeting of the American College of Sports Medicine (ACSM) it is now estimated that roughly 20 percent of the research findings reported are on topics relating solely to females. These include studies on topics such as pregnancy, menstruation, breastfeeding, amenorrhea, eating disorders, menopause and osteoporosis, all of which pertain solely or primarily to women and have little or no relevance to men. This is a far cry from the situation twenty or thirty years ago, when to have even *one* study reported on, say, osteoporosis (a bone-thinning condition that primarily affects postmenopausal women and is thought to be related in various ways to exercise) at a sports-medicine gathering would have been considered an astounding breakthrough in the area of research on females.

Of course, despite years of lags in the research realm, scientists and laypeople have long been fairly certain that when it comes to physical activity, men and women are significantly different. Men are generally larger, and have a greater percentage of muscle mass, while women tend to carry a higher proportion of fat. Whether fitness-trained or not, men tend to have a higher average maximum oxygen uptake (VO_2 max), considered an index of cardiorespiratory fitness. Compared with the average, equally trained woman, the average man is stronger, faster and should have superior muscular and cardiovascular endurance. However, there are two areas in which females seem to be superior, in general. One, for reasons that aren't clear, women tend to be more flexible than men; and two, at ultra-long-distance endurance events there may be a female advantage, possibly because of women's superior ability to store and use fat to fuel muscle activity.

The problem, until the past thirty or so years, was that this was about as far as the knowledge of male-female fitness differences went. Unfortunately, this situation worked very much to active women's disadvantage, for several reasons. What substituted for the high level of ignorance were deeply embedded social and cultural prejudices against women exerting themselves and appearing scantily clad in public, and a general belief that sports and exercise were a man's province, not suitable for "ladies."

Many exercise scientists still practicing today can clearly remember the stifling climate of a generation ago. "Back in the 1950s I started wondering why the sports medicine books all said that women were incapable of running more than eight hundred meters. I discovered that it was because no woman had ever run further than that in a race. They were not allowed, and the reason was because the sports medicine books said so. It all turned back on itself," reminisces Barbara Drinkwater, Ph.D., who is now a professor of exercise science at the University of Washington in Seattle. Drinkwater pioneered research into women's physical capabilities. Her efforts were rewarded when she became the first female president of the American College of Sports Medicine in 1988.

Thanks to the work of Drinkwater and many other female—and some male—scientists, research on active women and girls has moved forward dramatically in recent years. Of course, much progress has still to be made, claim those who have paved the way. The late Dorothy Harris, Ph.D., a pioneering researcher in the area of female sports psychology, pointed out before her death in January

1991 that the ACSM is still only about 20 percent female, and that there are very few females in distinguished and leadership positions in academia (full professors of sports science, chairs of university departments and so forth). "The barriers are down, now women have to take advantage of the opportunities that are out there waiting for them," Harris said.

Of course, what we have learned about active women and how that knowledge affects cross-training could fill a book of its own—one I would love to write someday. I want to focus for a moment here on a few of the most important recent findings and to point out how they might affect the planning and execution of a cross-training program designed for women.

1. *Exercise may help reduce a woman's risk of osteoporosis.* Osteoporosis is a disease in which the natural loss of bone mineral (which takes place in all people starting at about age thirty to thirty-five and accelerates markedly in women after menopause) progresses to the point where the bones are easily damaged or broken under little or no stress. The condition is far more common in women than men, particularly those women who have passed menopause, at which point the body's production of the female hormone estrogen drops precipitously. In women, estrogen production is instrumental in helping the body lay down bone mineral, and one of the reasons some postmenopausal women take estrogen-replacement drugs is to ward off the threat of osteoporosis in old age. Osteoporosis is one of the leading causes of death in women over the age of sixty-five. (In most cases death is the result of infections that set in during the prolonged bed rest that is necessary after a hip fracture.)

Many studies conducted on women (and some on men) have shown that regular, moderate exercise reduces the risk of osteoporosis. The research has been conducted on women both before and after menopause, on those who have no significant bone mineral loss, those with some and those well on their way to developing osteoporosis. Most (but not all) of the studies show that women who exercise regularly at a moderate level have stronger, denser bones than those who are sedentary. Of course, the studies control for factors such as age, race, weight, smoking status, menstrual history, diet and family history of osteoporosis, all of which can also affect the disease's risk.

The research also points out that the *type* of exercise performed makes a difference. Those activities that seem to be of the greatest benefit are "weight-bearing" ones, that is, those in which muscles, joints and bones support the body in an upright position. These would include brisk walking, jogging, aerobic dance, rope jumping, cross-country skiing and any competitive sport in which the participants stand up, such as tennis, soccer and field hockey. The positive bone-strengthening effects seem still to be there for non–weight-bearing sports such as swimming, rowing and cycling, but to a lesser degree.

The effect that this information could have on a woman's choice of activities for a cross-training program is clear: It might give her good reason for including some weight-bearing exercise in her training, especially if osteoporosis runs in her family or if she already knows she has thinning bone mineral. (Sports science labs and hospital facilities can test the density of bones in various parts of the body with a process called dual-photon absorptiometry.) No studies so far have suggested that exercise can *reverse* bone thinning, but many projects suggest that it does seem to be able to slow the process.

2. *If properly trained, conditioned and fueled, women can handle the same physical challenges as men*—factoring in, of course, their differences in body composition, muscle mass and cardiovascular endurance. This truth should be evident: There are hundreds of millions of women all over the world working out and otherwise engaging in strenuous physical activities at levels equal with or superior to those of similarly trained men. Still, there are many women who don't realize their physical capabilities and sell themselves short. (Unfortunately, there are also plenty of men who actively encourage them to sell themselves short, too.) As a result, women may design cross-training programs that don't really challenge their full physical potential. While everyone should start an exercise program modestly and progress gradually, the idea generally is to work at a level that provides a challenge in order to maximize fitness gains and avoid boredom, burnout and injury.

Of course, every active person is different, and generalizations about men and women don't apply to every individual. However, in my years of coaching men and women through the New York Road Runners Club and watching men and women of all ages and ability levels compete in road races, I've found that in general, men tend to push themselves harder physically.

I do not think that this is because men are "naturally" tougher or better able to handle pain than women are. Rather, I believe that women are still not socialized to press themselves to excel, to get the most out of themselves, in the sports and fitness realm. Indeed, I found myself that it was only after I had been competing on a running team for more than a year that I was really able to push myself in workouts and races.

Some men, on the other hand, may push themselves *too* hard in workouts and competitive situations. For example, they may consistently train at too high a level for their ability, frequently breaking down from overtraining, illness or injury. They will play a game or compete in a race when injured in order not to "lose face." Of course, among those who remain at the top over time, common sense and proper training practices will usually prevail over the "macho" urge to push oneself through pain, but that urge is still there nonetheless.

In designing a cross-training program, men (and some women) who have the tendency to do too much have to learn to keep their energies in check, to parcel them out carefully and sensibly, in order to stick with their commitment to sports and exercise over the long haul.

3. *Women can safely, comfortably and effectively exercise during their menstrual periods.* Historically, women have (to use a well-worn but appropriate phrase) truly come a long way in the freedoms they've gained to live normal lives during the time of month known for centuries as "the curse." Today women do everything from windsurfing to running ultra-marathon races during their "time of the month." Indeed, more than one female runner has told me that this is actually when she feels strongest and most comfortable in training and racing!

While some women, particularly those in their teens and twenties, are bothered by cramps, bloating and other symptoms, they tend to find that some moderate physical activity actually helps improve the situation. "Taking a walk, going for a swim, or just stretching and doing some light calisthenics makes me feel 100 percent better," one woman work colleague once told me, echoing sentiments I'd heard many times before. "I usually don't feel like doing anything, especially on my first day. But once I get started I feel invigorated, and my cramps bother me less. I'm always *really* glad I made the effort."

What this all means to the woman who cross-trains is that she probably doesn't need to drastically change her program during the time she is menstruating. While some women are more comfortable making minor adjustments and avoiding super-strenuous efforts such as racing for a couple of days, most find that fitness is business as usual, all month long.

4. *A healthy woman can remain physically active during a normal pregnancy.* Like the old myths about exercise during menstruation, beliefs concerning exercise during pregnancy have undergone a radical transformation over the past generation. Whereas "civilized" women were once kept out of public view, and certainly not allowed to do anything remotely strenuous while "in the family way," they now work out safely, healthfully and happily throughout pregnancy. Most medical experts urge women to "listen to their bodies" in terms of how hard, long and often they should exercise at various stages of pregnancy, although raising pulse rate over 140 beats per minute, exercising while lying on the back after the fourth month, and other cautionary advice is given by some doctors and other professionals. The consensus, though, within these guidelines, is: Don't

Long gone are the myths that once prevented healthy women from exercising during a normal pregnancy. Credit: Cliff Grassmick.

be afraid to experiment to see what works best for you, because every woman is different.

I have known women who have continued to walk, jog, swim, cycle, take aerobics classes and more up until the day they gave birth. Other women—even committed athletes—have chosen to drastically cut back their programs, though no one I know who was active before pregnancy has become completely sedentary. The point is, every woman, and every pregnancy, is unique.

Women who have engaged in a cross-training program before becoming pregnant have an advantage over those who have pursued just one sport because of the restrictions pregnancy may put on some forms of physical activity. Runners, high-impact aerobic enthusiasts and contact-sport participants, for example, may have to modify or even give up their programs. On the other hand, those who are used to doing a variety of sports will have a less restricted selection of activities to choose from.

One runner I know, a member of the elite women's running team Atalanta, in New York City, is also a former dancer and competitive swimmer who still logs laps several times a week even when training for a marathon. When she became pregnant with her third child in 1990, she found running increasingly uncomfortable, so she gave it up completely by the fifth month. Instead she swam for an hour every morning, walked in Central Park during the day while her older two children were in school and did calisthenics and stretching a couple of times a week. On the day she gave birth, she did her customary morning swim, started having contractions in the early afternoon and walked to the hospital with her husband to deliver her daughter just before dinnertime.

Men's and Women's Cross-Training Programs

In general, women and men can cross-train in basically the same fashion, as long as they both keep in mind the natural limitations on their physical capabilities that every active person faces. Despite their general physiological differences, neither men nor women need to give up nor play down any component of fitness—nor should they.

For example, the average man, although he may be less flexible than the average woman, can improve his flexibility and exercise more comfortably by following a regular stretching program—even though he may not be able to stretch as far or as long as his female training partner. Likewise, an elite female marathon runner, although she may hope to complete the 26.2-mile race in the American women's Olympic trials qualifying standard of 2 hours and 45 minutes (compared to her male counterpart's aspirations for a 2:20 Olympic trials qualifying time), will probably set up a training program very similar to his—high mileage, speed work, cross-training for injury prevention and variety—with just slight reductions in the speeds attained (although her *intensity* should be the same as his).

I have trained successfully with several male runners who shared training and racing goals and competed at or near my ability level, much to our mutual benefit. Certainly as newcomers to any sport or physical activity, men and women should never let their gender differences dictate variations in their training programs. As always, their guidelines should be fitness level, previous exposure to the activity, interest, schedule and other activities included in their cross-training program.

Cross-Training's Benefits for Children

If you haven't yet heard all the worrisome facts and figures on the poor physical condition of America's children, you must have been living under a rock for the past several decades. Everyone from United States presidents to actor and former Mr. Universe Arnold Schwarzenegger (now chairman of the President's Council on Physical Fitness and Sports) has put in his or her two cents on the sorry state of affairs. Without rehashing too much of the relevant data, suffice it to say that since the mid-1950s, when the Kraus-Weber report landed on President Eisenhower's desk, informing him that only 42 percent of American children could meet fitness standards that 92 percent of their European counterparts were able to meet, American children's physical condition has been considered sad indeed. Steps taken in the 1960s and 1970s through school and community programs unfortunately were somewhat thwarted by budget cutbacks in the 1980s.

Fortunately, however, things now appear to be changing, although greater efforts are needed. Thanks in part to Schwarzenegger's inspiration and insistence on improving school physical education programs, more kids are being given opportunities to move at school, as well as at home and in their communities. However, the forces of television, our increasingly industrialized society and poor parental example still hold sway. It's a sad but true fact that, despite two decades of the so-called fitness revolution, two-thirds of American adults still get no formal exercise. And the children, sadly but inevitably, emulate their parents.

The situation seems a bit odd, since most children seem naturally to love to "burn off steam." Parents, teachers, child-care workers and others who spend time with kids are always commenting that the youngsters are in constant motion, although the children may constantly flit from one activity to another.

This very inability to stick with one pursuit for more than a few minutes actually can make children ideally suited to cross-training—although the way in which they pursue it may be quite different from a typical adult training program.

How do children become fit? They benefit from attaining and maintaining fitness in the same five areas as do adults: cardiovascular fitness, muscular strength, muscular endurance, body composition and flexibility. Several organizations that concern themselves with children's and youth fitness, including the President's Council on Physical Fitness and Sports; the American Alliance on Health, Physical Education, Recreation and Dance; and the Chrysler Fund/ AAU Physical Fitness Program (see Appendix for information on contacting these and other organizations), set standards for physical fitness performance on tests administered to children between the ages of six and seventeen. The standard levels for average and superior achievement set by the President's Council are reprinted on pages 93–94.

Widespread discussion of the low achievement levels of American youngsters in the area of physical fitness has prompted many fitness-oriented groups and individuals to work to raise these standards through testing and training programs. As you can see, the tests rate children in a variety of areas. This makes clear that it isn't sufficient for a child to be fit in one or two areas; he or she must strive for fitness in *all* components. In order to receive the prestigious President's Award from the President's Council on Physical Fitness and Sports, for example, a child must score above the eighty-fifth percentile in *all five* of the fitness areas included.

Balanced fitness is important for children for basically the same reasons that it is crucial in adults. Being in good cardiovascular shape gives kids greater endurance for their daily activities; muscular strength and muscular endurance can help them perform ordinary tasks more easily (such as getting lids off jars or carrying packages) and protect them from injury; flexibility is another way to prevent injury (in activities ranging from ordinary daily tasks such as toweling off after a bath to strenuous sports activities such as leaping into the air to shoot a basket).

Achieving a healthy body composition (muscle-to-fat ratio) is a special concern for an increasing number of American children. Unfortunately, however, alongside reports of youth unfitness over the past several decades have been a

Components of Children's Physical Fitness Testing and Conditioning Programs

Item	Primary Fitness Component Measured
President's Council on Physical Fitness and Sports (The President's Challenge Test)	
one-mile run/walk	cardiovascular (aerobic) endurance
curl-ups (modified sit-ups)	abdominal strength/endurance
V-sit reach (or sit and reach)	lower-back/hamstring flexibility
shuttle run	leg strength/endurance/power/agility
pull-ups	upper-body strength/endurance
Institute for Aerobics Research (Fitnessgram)	
one-mile walk/run	cardiovascular (aerobic) endurance
sit-ups	abdominal strength/endurance
sit and reach	lower-back/hamstring flexibility
pull-ups/flexed-arm hang	upper-body strength/endurance
skinfold test/body-mass index	body composition
American Alliance for Health, Physical Education, Recreation and Dance (Physical Best Fitness Test)	
mile or half-mile run	cardiovascular (aerobic) endurance
sit-ups	abdominal strength/endurance
sit and reach	flexibility
pull-ups/modified pull-ups	upper-body strength/endurance

All three testing programs are for children ages six to seventeen and are designed to evaluate fitness in the areas most closely related to health. (See Appendix for contact information.)

number of studies showing that children's weight, body-fat content and early risk factors for heart disease have been increasing alarmingly.

The health risks of obesity generally won't affect children while they are still in their youth; the problem, of course, is that they set the stage for trouble later in life. In addition, unfortunately, overweight children are frequently subjected to the ridicule and teasing of their peers. This in turn can discourage them from participating in physical activity and taking advantage of its health and enjoyment benefits. A vicious cycle is set up that becomes hard to break.

All children should be encouraged to take part in a variety of sports and

The Presidential Physical Fitness Award
(Qualifying Standards)

Age	Curl-Ups (Timed one minute)	Shuttle Run (seconds)	V-Sit Reach or Sit and Reach		One-Mile Run (minutes/ seconds)	Pull-Ups
			(inches)	(centimeters)		
Boys						
6	33	12.1	+3.5	31	10:15	2
7	36	11.5	+3.5	30	9:22	4
8	40	11.1	+3.0	31	8:48	5
9	41	10.9	+3.0	31	8:31	5
10	45	10.3	+4.0	30	7:57	6
11	47	10.0	+4.0	31	7:32	6
12	50	9.8	+4.0	31	7:11	7
13	53	9.5	+3.5	33	6:50	7
14	56	9.1	+4.5	36	6:26	10
15	57	9.0	+5.0	37	6:20	11
16	56	8.7	+6.0	38	6:08	11
17	55	8.7	+7.0	41	6:06	13
Girls						
6	32	12.4	+5.5	32	11:20	2
7	34	12.1	+5.0	32	10:36	2
8	38	11.8	+4.5	33	10:02	2
9	39	11.1	+5.5	33	9:30	2
10	40	10.8	+6.0	33	9:19	3
11	42	10.5	+6.5	34	9:02	3
12	45	10.4	+7.0	36	8:23	2
13	46	10.2	+7.0	38	8:13	2
14	47	10.1	+8.0	40	7:59	2
15	48	10.0	+8.0	43	8:08	2
16	45	10.1	+9.0	42	8:23	1
17	44	10.0	+8.0	42	8:15	1

The National Physical Fitness Award
(Qualifying Standards)

Age	Curl-Ups (Timed one minute)	Shuttle Run (seconds)	V-Sit Reach or Sit and Reach		One-Mile Run (minutes/ seconds)	Pull-Ups or Flexed-Arm Hang	(seconds)
			(inches)	(centimeters)			
Boys							
6	22	13.3	+1.0	26	12:36	1	6
7	28	12.8	+1.0	25	11:40	1	8
8	31	12.2	+0.5	25	11:05	1	10
9	32	11.9	+1.0	25	10:30	2	10
10	35	11.5	+1.0	25	9:48	2	12
11	37	11.1	+1.0	25	9:20	2	11
12	40	10.6	+1.0	26	8:40	2	12
13	42	10.2	+0.5	26	8:06	3	14
14	45	9.9	+1.0	28	7:44	5	20
15	45	9.7	+2.0	30	7:30	6	30
16	45	9.4	+3.0	30	7:10	7	28
17	44	9.4	+3.0	34	7:04	8	30
Girls							
6	23	13.8	+2.5	27	13:12	1	5
7	25	13.2	+2.0	27	12:56	1	6
8	29	12.9	+2.0	28	12:30	1	8
9	30	12.5	+2.0	28	11:52	1	8
10	30	12.1	+3.0	28	11:22	1	8
11	32	11.5	+3.0	29	11:17	1	7
12	35	11.3	+3.5	30	11:05	1	7
13	37	11.1	+3.5	31	10:23	1	8
14	37	11.2	+4.5	33	10:06	1	9
15	36	11.0	+5.0	36	9:58	1	7
16	35	10.9	+5.5	34	10:31	1	7
17	34	11.0	+4.5	35	10:22	1	7

fitness activities. The problem—as anyone who has worked with children certainly knows—is that kids don't like to "exercise." Rather, they want to play games and have fun. The challenge to an adult—a parent, teacher, baby-sitter, friend or other supervisor—who is trying to get kids to move more is to stress the fun in such a way that the exercise takes care of itself, without the youngsters even realizing what is happening.

And that can be where cross-training fits in. A child's cross-training program is likely to differ from an adult's in that the variety will be more within each workout than between different sessions. For example, a cross-training adult might play an hour of tennis one day, swim for half an hour two days later, then take a forty-five-minute bike ride or brisk walk for the final workout of the week. Very few eight-year-olds, however, would put up with that type of workout schedule for even one day. It would be too boring, and the sessions too long and not varied enough. The activity might even be harmful to the child. However, that same child might easily include half an hour or more of activity in his or her day three times a week that involved enough heart-rate-raising, calorie-burning, muscle-building, flexibility-enhancing activity to maintain an excellent level of fitness.

The following are sample activities that you might want to consider introducing to children. In all cases, if a child doesn't "take" to an activity, never force the issue. Fitness for children should always be fun, not work. Let your child's wishes and imagination pave the way—not your own rigid expectations of what he or she "should" be doing.

- Walking/hiking
- Swimming/water games
- Jogging
- Bicycling
- Racquet sports
- Soccer
- Frisbee
- Cross-country skiing
- Canoeing
- Rowing
- Kayaking
- Motion/action games
- Jazz dance
- Low-impact aerobics
- Jumping rope

For children, as for adults, any physical activity is better than no activity at all. However, for a child to maintain balanced fitness, he or she must have a varied cross-training program. The following are sample activity schedules for children of various ages. They are based on information provided by the Institute for Aerobics Research's "Fitnessgram" program, the "Physical Best" program of the American Alliance for Health, Physical Education, Recreation and Dance, and the "President's Challenge" conditioning program of the President's Council on Physical Fitness and Sports.

Use the schedules merely as guidelines. They are not intended to be absolute rigid frameworks. Most children and teenagers in this country simply need to move more, and in general, moving in varied ways will offer them more balanced fitness—and more fun.

A Program to Develop Balanced Fitness in Children The President's Council on Physical Fitness and Sports is dedicated to helping the nation's children enjoy balanced fitness—cardiovascular endurance, muscular strength, muscular endurance, flexibility and body composition. The council supports a program that includes a variety of activities designed to keep children interested in physical activities and help them see results.

Of course, as is true for adults, where a child starts with a fitness program depends on what kind of shape he or she is in to begin with. However, any child can develop balanced fitness—and it doesn't take too much time or involve a lot of "boring" exercises and drills.

Aerobic endurance: Pick activities that get the heart beating above its resting rate, such as jogging, swimming, bicycling, dancing or rowing. Start with two minutes of the activity, alternated with one minute of rest (which could be walking between the jogging segments or coasting on the bike between the cycling segments) for a total of fifteen minutes of activity. Do this three times a week (you may pick different activities each time) for two weeks. Don't worry about how much ground is covered (miles jogged, yards swum and so forth).

After two weeks, increase the length of the activity segments from two minutes to four minutes. Continue with the one-minute rest segments. Total activity time should be fifteen to twenty minutes. After two weeks, cut the rest breaks to thirty seconds. Over the next few weeks, build up to thirty minutes total of the activity per session. Remember, you can vary activities.

By the end of ten weeks, you should be able to exercise aerobically for twenty minutes without a break. Then, if you wish, you can gradually increase session length up to sixty minutes.

Muscular strength and endurance: Any activities that develop the muscles' ability to support the body's weight will help build strength and endurance. Sit-ups or curl-ups, push-ups or modified push-ups (on knees rather than toes), gymnastics and calisthenics are among the most effective and enjoyable activities. Weight-lifting exercises are also helpful, but should be performed under adult supervision for younger children, or after thorough instructions for older ones.

It takes two to four exercise sessions per week to effectively build strength and endurance in the muscles. For sit-ups or curl-ups, start with ten repetitions or the number that can be done without a rest, and add two a week. Work up to as many as desired, but there is really no need to do more than about fifty, three times a week.

Upper-body strength can be built with modified pull-ups: Instead of pulling oneself up while hanging from a horizontal bar, place a bar on two secure chairs, lie on the back on the floor, slide under the bar, grab it with both hands and pull the chest up to the bar, keeping the body straight. Work up to doing this ten times, three times a week. Then gradually work up to doing the exercise hanging from a horizontal bar.

Push-ups are best done on hands and knees to start, slowly lowering the body until the chest touches the floor. Once it is possible to do twenty to twenty-five with bent knees, try the straight-knee type, and work up to ten repetitions.

For weight-lifting, pick eight to ten exercises that work various muscle groups, and do one to three sets of eight to twelve repetitions.

Flexibility: It's a good idea to stretch before engaging in any vigorous activity, which means stretching at least three times a week, and up to seven times weekly. Make sure to warm up before stretching with light physical activity—just enough to sweat slightly. Always stretch just to the point of slight discomfort, not pain. Stretches should be held for ten to sixty seconds, so that the total stretching session lasts between three and twenty minutes. Always stretch slowly and steadily, without bouncing, working specific muscle groups. For most activities and for daily living, the quadriceps, hamstrings, calves, abdominal muscles, lower back, shoulders and neck muscles are the most important ones to stretch.

Body composition: The best way to achieve a healthy ratio of fat to lean tissue is through continuous activity that uses the large muscle groups and is vigorous enough to induce sweating but not so difficult that you are out of breath. Walking, jogging, active games, swimming and water activities, bicycling, dancing, calisthenics and gymnastics are all good choices. You should exercise in this way for thirty to sixty minutes at a time, three to five times a week.

Cross-Training for Senior Citizens

Not too long ago, the concept of an older person exercising and being con-cerned with fitness was at least as remote as that of a woman moving vigorously and regularly to stay in shape. Of course, in times long gone by, most people stayed active all their lives because they *had* to in order to survive—raising crops, hunting game, traveling, making clothing, keeping house and other life-sus-taining activities were all incredibly physically taxing, and the vast majority of people did them all under their own steam.

In addition, of course, people's lives were also much shorter than they are now: As recently as 1900 the average American lifespan was only forty-nine years; in the Middle Ages to survive to age thirty was to have lived a remark-ably long life. In the years since, as the average lifespan has lengthened and the concept of retirement has gained ground, the tendency has generally been —and often still is—to show the elderly respect and consideration. We have tried to tax them as little as possible in their "golden years" and let them en-joy the rest their years of hard work and sacrifice had led them to so richly deserve.

A good bit of this attitude and practice has changed dramatically in this century, at least in Western culture. The average American born today can expect to live to be almost seventy-five years old, according to the National Center for Health Statistics. This is one of the longest lifespans in the world.

Women, on the average, live longer than men, an estimated 78.3 years for those born today, compared to 71.5 years for males being born today in this country. While much of this gain is due to reductions in infant and childhood mortality, quite a bit also comes thanks to medical progress against diseases that strike a disproportionate number of people over fifty, such as cancer, heart disease, diabetes and osteoporosis. There were roughly 31,560,000 people age sixty-five and over in the United States in 1990, representing 12.6 percent of the total population; by 2010 the projected figure is 39,362,000, or 13.9 percent of the population, according to the United States Census Bureau.

Thanks to the nationwide passion for health and fitness that began in the 1970s and continues today, millions of these older people are physically active. No doubt many pursue fitness programs based on a lifetime of physical activity. Many others, however, have become regular exercisers only late in life, over-coming years of the conventional wisdom that "you can't teach an old dog new tricks"—meaning in this case that starting regular physical activity late in life was not only impossibly difficult, but also dangerous and probably useless anyway, since the damage of years of sedentary living was already done, and therefore could not be overcome.

These and other beliefs about activity in old age are being proven by scientific studies to be largely myths. It is easy to see how they have given rise to a host of false ideas: Old people are told that they shouldn't exercise because it's too taxing and possibly dangerous, so they sit around and get out of shape; eventually even mild movement becomes difficult and hazardous, reinforcing the belief that it should be avoided as much as possible. A vicious circle is created.

The fact is that *anyone* of *any* age who doesn't exercise will become weaker, less flexible and less cardiovascularly fit, and will settle into a lower metabolism. There are, of course, the "natural effects of aging" that we hear so much about to contend with: Maximal oxygen uptake does indeed fall slightly and gradually starting at about age thirty; the skin becomes less elastic; flexibility decreases slightly; metabolism may drop, especially in women, weight gain is likely to occur unless caloric intake is cut.

However, there is a vast amount of evidence that these and other aging effects can be largely compensated for by regular, moderate activity. And, it turns out, the best type of exercise program is one that includes—you guessed it—a variety of aerobic, strengthening, flexibility-promoting and fat-burning activities. In other words, cross-training.

How should someone sixty-five or older go about designing a cross-training program? If the person has been active in the past, it may be natural to first think of activities that have been enjoyed. However, these are not always practical. For example, someone who played on a high school or college football team will have a tough time finding an appropriate league to join after graduation. In some cases, physical restrictions may rule out a range of activities: For example, an older person with arthritis in the hands may well have trouble with any activity that requires holding, catching, throwing or grabbing an object, such as most ball sports, rowing and cycling.

In general, the following activities are found to be suitable to the greatest number of people over age sixty-five. Those that are aerobic should be done in the training range, starting at the lower end if the person is exercising for the first time or coming back after a layoff:

- Swimming and other moderate water sports (such as water aerobics)
- Walking
- Jogging
- Cycling

* Moderate weight-lifting or other resistance training
* Golf (walking and carrying clubs preferred)
* Low-impact aerobics
* Tennis
* Moderate canoeing or rowing (either outside or indoors on a rowing machine)

Like other adults, people over age sixty-five should follow the American College of Sports Medicine guidelines for cardiovascular activity (three to five fifteen- to sixty-minute aerobic sessions a week) and strength-building exercise (two sessions of one set of ten to twelve repetitions of eight to ten different exercises to stress various muscle groups). Again, as with younger adults, remember that from a health perspective *any* regular physical activity is better than none at all, and the exercise can be part of one's regular daily activities: climbing stairs, walking, gardening, housework and so forth.

Following are two sample cross-training programs for elderly people. The first is for someone who has been moderately active and thus is able to comfortably tolerate a higher level of activity than someone who hasn't worked out at all, at least not in a long time. The second is for someone who has not recently been a regular exerciser but wants to safely, comfortably add more activity to his or her life. Either program can be increased gradually from the levels given, or one can back off if the level is found to be too strenuous. (Note: For both of the programs below, the order of the days can be varied, but you should not exercise more than three days in a row, or take off more than two consecutive days unless you are ill, injured or otherwise incapacitated.)

Moderately Active Program

Monday: Forty-five minute stretching and aerobics session, plus a warmup and a cooldown.

Tuesday: Thirty minutes of stretching and resistance training (calisthenics, weight-lifting or both).

Wednesday: Rest day.

Thursday: Thirty- to sixty-minute brisk walk, jog or walk-jog combination.

Friday: Twenty- to sixty-minute swim at a moderate pace.

Saturday: Thirty minutes stretching and resistance training (calisthenics or weight-lifting).

Sunday: Rest day.

Program for Someone New to Regular Exercise

Monday: Twenty to thirty minutes walking, light aerobics, or stair climbing (at level that raises heart rate but still allows one to talk comfortably); you may want to join an exercise class for instruction and companionship.

Tuesday: Rest day.

Wednesday: Twenty to thirty minutes doing gardening, yardwork or housework.

Thursday: Rest day.

Friday: Twenty to thirty minutes of light stretching and lifting, pushing or resisting objects to stress, but not strain, major muscle groups.

Saturday: Twenty to thirty minutes swimming, rowing, cycling or another nonpounding activity.

Sunday: Rest day.

For both programs, to make sure heart rate stays in the training zone, take your pulse frequently until you get a sense of what moderate exercise should feel like. Many people of all ages push themselves harder than necessary and become injured or burned out.

Cross-Training for the Disabled

It wasn't long ago that people with physical disabilities were referred to as "handicapped" and by and large excluded from vigorous physical activities. All that has changed as physically challenged people in this country and overseas have taken to the streets, sidewalks, exercise paths, gyms and aerobics studios by the hundreds of thousands to enjoy fitness in essentially the same ways as those who exercise without disabilities. People with all sorts of physical and mental disabilities participate and compete in marathons, triathlons and other events, play every type of team sport imaginable, work out with free weights and on weight machines, take aerobics classes or work out to videos and join in a variety of wilderness and adventure sports.

There are organizations, exercise programs and other resources all over the country providing opportunities for people with all kinds of physical and mental disabilities to exercise in every way imaginable, achieving full, balanced fitness. Special Olympics are held around the world for mentally retarded children and adults in a variety of track and field and other pursuits. The Disabled Olympics are held quadrennially, offering competitive opportunities in sports ranging from wheelchair basketball to slalom skiing. Wheelchair racing has become an extremely competitive, high-tech sport alongside the American road-racing (long-distance-running) circuit, with the physically challenged athletes covering the same course as the able-bodied, and given prime-time television coverage and generous prize money along with their able-bodied counterparts. Craig Blanchette, currently considered the top wheelchair racer in the world, trains full-time for races on the track and roads at distances from eight hundred meters to the marathon, is sponsored by Nike, and competes in a custom-designed chair weighing under twenty pounds.

A large worldwide network known as the Achilles Track Club (see Appendix for contact information) gives people in wheelchairs and with other physical challenges opportunities to train and enter races far and wide. To give just one example, the New York City Marathon draws hundreds of Achilles athletes from all over the globe to compete in the 26.2-mile event.

Obviously, an individual cross-training program for someone with a physical disability will depend on the nature of that person's particular challenge, as well as his or her interests, fitness goals, lifestyle and other factors. It should be noted, however, that the emphasis on balanced fitness—aerobic endurance, muscular strength, muscular endurance, flexibility and body composition—is no less important to someone who is in a wheelchair or has some other physical challenge than to someone who does not. In fact, achieving fitness in the five basic areas can enhance the quality of life for a disabled person even more than for someone who is able-bodied. In some cases (such as some types of arthritis), a regular, balanced exercise program may even prevent a physical impediment from being completely disabling.

See the resource list in the Appendix for organizations to contact for information on fitness opportunities both for the disabled and for the general population. Check with local health and fitness clubs, YMCAs, YWCAs and other groups for fitness and sports classes and other opportunities in your area. Don't be limited by the expectations of the past. The world of fitness opportunities for physically challenged people is expanding day by day, and with interest, determination and a sense of adventure you will likely be able to enjoy activities that disabled people of a generation ago never dreamed of.

As is true for anyone beginning an exercise program, it's a good idea to start gradually, particularly if you have been sedentary for a long time. Work with someone who can help you set and achieve realistic goals without injury, so that you can enjoy balanced fitness for the rest of your life.

As you can see, cross-training is an ideal way to work out and get fit for many different kinds of people; in fact, there is virtually no group whose members cannot benefit in some way from a multiactivity fitness schedule. Again, your approach—no matter who you are, how long you have been exercising or what activities you want to pursue—should be to experiment, remaining open to possibilities and not considering *any* activity out of the question until you have tried it.

By this point, I hope that you have become truly committed to cross-training and have started to make it a regular part of your life. If so, you will probably want to learn something about one of my favorite topics: eating well to fuel your body for this activity.

SIX

FOOD AND

NUTRITION

Fueling our many, varied sports and fitness activities with the many, varied foods that we are fortunate enough to enjoy is one of the greatest pleasures of living an active cross-training lifestyle. Eating well, however—no matter what your activity level and choice of exercise—isn't as easy as it may appear. Indeed, many cross-trainers find that eating healthfully can be fraught with more challenges than their sports and fitness activities themselves!

More than one well-meaning, determined cross-trainer has fallen short of fully benefiting from an active lifestyle because of problems with diet. The sources of the troubles are many, ranging from ignorance, to lack of access to the right foods (or, more often in our fast-paced society, lack of the time to properly prepare and enjoy them), to underlying unresolved psychological issues.

As with most things in life, many of us make eating well to fuel sports and exercise a lot harder than it really has to be. The key, however, to keeping fitness-oriented nutrition simple is to learn and adhere to a few basic principles. Don't worry, that doesn't mean that healthy eating is, by definition, a dull, repetitive and joyless prospect. In fact, quite the opposite: The very first of the federal government's "Dietary Guidelines for Americans," which apply to all healthy people age two and over—no matter how much or how little they exercise—is "Eat a variety of foods." In addition, the basic rules of healthy eating can be adapted to myriad tastes, cultures and lifestyles. As is true in your cross-training exercise program, you are limited in your choices for healthy eating only by your imagination.

In order to fully understand and appreciate the principles of eating as they help you exercise your best, you will need to pick up a few bits and pieces of nutrition science along the way. Of course, a full understanding of human nutrition requires a deep knowledge of chemistry, biology and other basic sciences and is beyond the scope of this book. However, I have tried to make the basic information you need as understandable and "user-friendly" as possible. I promise that nothing will be overly complicated; in fact, you should find these mini-lessons no more taxing than the exercise science principles that I slipped into Chapter Two. You have my promise—after all, the principles weren't easy for me to learn, either.

The Basics of Sports Nutrition

More than forty nutrients have been identified as necessary for the health of the human body. Since, for the most part, these nutrients cannot be manufactured within our systems, they must be obtained from the diet. A few nutrients can be made in the body, such as certain fats manufactured in the liver; vitamin D, generated in part from sunlight absorbed through the skin; and vitamin K, made in the lining of the intestines.

The forty basic nutrients—called *essential* because they are not optional; they must be eaten for survival—include carbohydrates; fat; nine of the twenty-two amino acids that make up proteins; thirteen vitamins; fifteen minerals (including the three principal electrolytes) and water. A brief look at each of these categories of nutrients will help you understand why they are so important—no matter what sports and activities you engage in, how frequently or at what level.

Carbohydrates An active person would have to have been living under a rock for the past two decades not to have become somewhat familiar with "carbos." Technically they are organic compounds made up of carbon, oxygen and hydrogen atoms arranged either as single or double sugar molecules (monosaccharides or disaccharides). These arrangements are either short, uncomplicated chains known as *simple* carbohydrates or less simple chains of sugar molecules linked together—consisting of up to thousands of units—called *complex* carbohydrates.

Because of their straightforward chemical structure, carbohydrates are relatively easily broken down by the human digestive system and made available for energy. Every carbohydrate gram contains four calories of energy. They are present in all foods from plant sources (that is, all fruits, vegetables and grains, nuts and legumes and any processed food that contains them) as well as a large variety of foods from animals, such as milk and dairy products, and in small amounts in some meats (as glycogen). For a list of top-choice high-carbohydrate foods for active people, see page 117–18.

In recent years, nutrition and medical experts have been paying more and more attention to the crucial role that carbohydrates play in the diet of all people, not just those who work out. Indeed, the federal government (through its "Dietary Guidelines for Americans," a booklet published by the United States Departments of Agriculture and Health and Human Services) now recommends that carbohydrates make up 55 percent to 60 percent of the diet of healthy Americans over the age of two. Many sports nutritionists urge active people to consume even more—up to 70 percent of total calories, and even more in the days before an important athletic event. Later in this chapter you will see examples of the important role carbohydrates can play in maximizing the sports and fitness efforts of people in all activities and at all levels.

Fats If you are like many active people, you probably think of dietary fat as "the enemy," a substance to be avoided at all costs in the pursuit of health and fitness. Actually, our systems could not get along without fat—both in our diets and on our bodies. We need to get a certain amount of fat in the diet, in the form of linoleic acid, a *free fatty acid,* found in vegetable oils, that the body cannot make on its own. However, it should be noted that we need only about a teaspoon a day of linoleic acid for survival (less than 1 percent of the total calories eaten); all the rest of the fat needed by the body can be made from other nutrients within the body.

Present-day Americans—exercisers and sedentary people alike—are often chastised for consuming far more fat than we need for our optimum health. For example, the 1988 *Surgeon General's Report on Nutrition and Health* reported that the typical American diet derives 37 percent of its calories from fat, and a significant portion of that from saturated fat, the type considered most likely to raise our risk of heart disease. The federal government (in the "Dietary Guidelines" booklet mentioned above), the American Heart Association and many individual medical experts recommend reducing the dietary fat content to 30 percent of total calories—still a hefty portion in the opinion of many experts, but for millions of people a vast improvement.

It should hardly be surprising to health educators that the connection between fat in the diet and heart disease risk is poorly understood by the average person; it's a complex series of links with several confounding factors. The key is understanding that in most people, dietary fat contributes to the production of cholesterol, a waxlike substance in the blood that, over time, can form a plaque on the insides of arteries capable of narrowing and even completely blocking them. (Note: Cholesterol in the diet, which is chemically identical to that circulating in the bloodstream, also has an effect on serum [blood] cholesterol levels, though the relationship is not as clearcut. The impact of dietary cholesterol on blood cholesterol in most people is less than the impact of fat, especially saturated fat.)

If the buildup of plaque happens in the large vessels feeding the heart, a heart attack may occur; if it happens in the brain's blood vessels, the result is likely to be a stroke. The fact that cholesterol is also a component of the diet is confusing, and it's not clearly understood why dietary cholesterol doesn't seem to contribute to the formation of serum cholesterol nearly as much as dietary fat does. This misunderstanding, however, is why people who "cut down on cholesterol" may still be unwittingly putting their health at risk if they are consuming excess fat. For tips on cutting the amount of fat in your diet, see page 114.

Another confounding fact is that people vary enormously in ways in which their body handles excess serum cholesterol. Some people seem to be able to tolerate above-average levels for decades without developing buildups of plaque, while the vessels of others may become dangerously narrowed with much more moderate levels. It is also crucial, from a health standpoint, to remember that *saturated* fats (the term, much bandied about, simply means that the fat's chains of carbon molecules all have hydrogen molecules bound to them, making them relatively stable chemically) contribute more to raising heart-disease risk than do other types, namely *monounsaturated* and *polyunsaturated* fats (which have one and two or more unbound carbon molecules, respectively, in their chemical chains and are therefore less stable). Health experts generally recommend substituting unsaturated for saturated fats in the diet whenever possible.

Fats of all types are in so many of the foods we eat (many of them rich in other nutrients as well and therefore part of a healthy, balanced diet) that it's virtually impossible to ignore them. Most sports nutritionists see no reason for normal, healthy people to consume less than the 30 percent of total fat calories recommended for healthy Americans, particularly if they are active. Some experts, however, do consider the 30 percent maximum too high, especially for people with special medical conditions (such as those who have suffered from a heart attack), who may be advised by their doctors to eat less fat. Indeed, a study in 1990 found that arterial plaque buildup was actually reversed in a group of people put on a special 10 percent fat diet for several months. Obviously, research continues apace in this important area.

A 30 percent fat diet is not overly restrictive for most people. Indeed, it leaves plenty of room for splurges. And as a regular exerciser, keep in mind that you can burn more calories, and thus consume more food daily, than someone of a similar size and build who doesn't work out. While this doesn't give you license to ignore sensible nutrition and eat as much fat as you want (see "Thirteen Sports Nutrition Myths Refuted," page 116), it may give you a little more leeway than you would otherwise have.

Protein The question of whether athletes need more protein than sedentary people (even after adjusting for the active people's overall increased calorie needs) has perhaps generated more inquiry than any other sports nutrition topic of recent years. The vast majority of sports scientists have retreated from their position of decades past that massive meals of steak and eggs are the way to attain superhuman levels of strength and endurance. There is still quite a bit of disagreement, however, over the role protein can and should play in the diet of people who exercise and participate in various sports.

Protein is not a single substance but rather a group of thousands of different chemical structures found in all parts of the body. All human proteins are made of twenty-two different *amino acids*—the so-called "building blocks" of protein—arranged in a seemingly endless variety of ways. The important thing to remember about amino acids in terms of diet is that the body needs to have all twenty-two of them on hand at one time in order to make a single protein.

You have probably heard the terms "complete" and "incomplete" proteins. The former refers to a protein that has all twenty-two amino acids (and therefore can be used by the body), while the latter is a protein that lacks one or more of the amino acids; it is therefore unusable in its current form. Proteins from animal sources—that is, meat, poultry, fish, milk and dairy products—are complete, while those from plant sources are incomplete. This means that plant proteins must be eaten either along with or within several hours of eating complementary plant-protein sources in order to be used. Getting complete proteins is a concern of vegetarians (especially those who eat no milk products or eggs), who must learn the rules of matching complementary proteins in order to make them complete.

Nine amino acids are termed "essential," meaning that they cannot be made in the body and therefore must be obtained from the diet. The other thirteen, known as "nonessential," are every bit as important; however, they are not called essential because they can be made within the body from other nutrients, including fats and carbohydrates as well as proteins. Therefore, it is not necessary to eat them.

There is a mistaken idea that athletes—particularly those engaged in sports that call for intense bursts of muscle power—need significantly more protein in their diets than sedentary people. This concept probably arose because one of the roles of protein in the body is to build muscle. What in the past was poorly understood, however, is that the body actually needs very little dietary protein to build muscle protein. This is true for two reasons: One, as noted earlier, proteins in the body can be made from nonprotein sources in the diet; and two, the creation of muscle protein is a process that can recycle the same amino acids a number of times.

What this means for the average person who cross-trains—regardless of the activities involved—is that there should be little worry about getting enough protein from food, as long as the diet is well-balanced and contains adequate calories to support the level of activity. The federal government's Recommended Dietary Allowance (RDA) for protein, 0.8 grams per kilogram (kg) of lean (non-fat) body weight, applies to sedentary and active people alike. A kilogram is approximately 2.2 pounds. Using this formula, someone weighing 55 kg (about 121 lb) would need to eat 44 grams of protein to meet the RDA; someone tipping the scales at 70 kg (154 lb) would require approximately 56 grams daily; and a person whose weight was 85 kg (187 lb) should get about 68 grams of protein each day. (Lean body weight is used as a measure since fat contains very little protein, but for nonobese people, total weight is close enough to total lean body weight to get an approximate figure.)

The RDA is for all healthy people. Nutrition experts have estimated that the average American gets twice as much dietary protein as he or she needs. You may have heard of a few scattered studies showing that people who exercise very heavily may need more protein. Indeed, there have been studies on long-distance runners and other active people suggesting that they may need up to twice the RDA of protein—1.6 grams per kilogram of lean body weight instead of 0.8 grams. A number of sports scientists have conceded that this may in fact be true. They hasten to add, however, that unless someone is eating an unusual diet (such as no animal foods whatsoever, including eggs and dairy products) and paying no attention to combining nonanimal sources of protein, the active person should be getting plenty of protein simply by eating the additional calories that are naturally consumed to fuel the extra activity. Thus, most people have no need at all to worry.

What this means, however, is that the thick steaks and raw-egg concoctions of the athletes of yesteryear are out—they are unnecessary at best and unhealthy at worst (because of the large amounts of fat and cholesterol they pack along with the protein). Also off the contemporary training table are the protein and amino-acid supplements, powders, drinks and other concentrations still hawked to unsuspecting athletes today. They are expensive and unnecessary, and may even be dangerous. The body is not very good at disposing of extra protein. The nutrient puts a strain on the kidneys and may get in the way of consuming enough nutrients from other important sources, especially carbohydrates.

If you still feel you need more protein than your diet provides, see a doctor or registered dietitian. The chances are good, though, that you are already getting more than enough of what you need.

How Much of Each Nutrient Do You Need? The pie chart on page 112 shows the proportion of fat, carbohydrates and protein in the diet of the average adult American. The chart on the left shows what those proportions *should* be for a person active in a cross-training program (any program, but particularly one that includes large-muscle-using endurance activities—which most programs should include). Notice the increased carbohydrate and decreased fat proportion in the ideal cross-training chart. The percentage of carbohydrates (ideally of the complex variety) can go even higher in the few days before a major endurance-event competition.

Vitamins and Minerals Vitamins are organic (that is, carbon-containing) compounds that exist in foods and in the human body in very small amounts. In fact, all the vitamins we need to eat to meet the RDA each day would fill up only one-eighth of a teaspoon! Since many different scientists working separately discovered vitamins over the past several hundred years, the naming of them may seem a bit haphazard—vitamin A, the eight B-complex vitamins, C, D, E, then a big jump (over F, G, H, I and J) to vitamin K. The missing letters correspond to vitamins that were once thought to exist but were later shown not to, or proved to be identical to other already identified nutrients. The profusion of B's is due to the fact that they are all chemically quite similar and were once thought to be all the same vitamin. While it is possible that other vitamins may be discovered and given other names, these are the only recognized ones at the moment—don't let any hocus-pocus supplement salesperson tell you otherwise.

Each of the vitamins has an RDA (Recommended Dietary Allowance), an amount that nutrition and medical experts convened by the United States government have determined to be both adequate and safe for consumption by healthy people. The important thing to remember about RDAs is that it is *not*

Current and Recommended Proportions of Fat, Protein and Carbohydrate in the American Diet

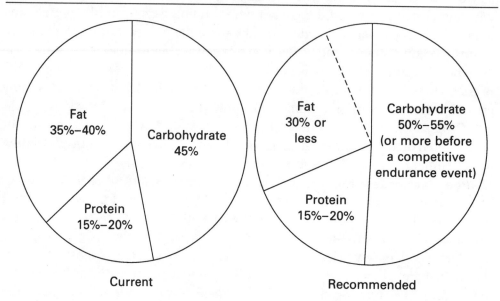

Current

Recommended

absolutely necessary to meet all of them each and every day, because the body is capable of storing vitamins for various lengths of time, and deficiencies may take weeks, months or even years to show any symptoms. If your diet is basically varied and balanced over time (more later on these important principles of variety and balance), then you are very likely getting all the vitamins you need.

It is also important to keep in mind that overdosing on vitamins, either in food or—more often, for most people—as supplements, can be harmful to health. You will read more on this later.

Minerals are another group of elements and chemical compounds needed in minute amounts to sustain life and carry out essential bodily functions. The twelve minerals deemed by nutritionists to be essential (that is, obtainable only through the diet) are the macrominerals, calcium, magnesium and phosphorus, and the nine microminerals (also known as trace elements), chromium, copper, fluoride, iodine, iron, manganese, molybdenum, selenium and zinc. Three other macrominerals (chloride, potassium and sodium), known as electrolytes, perform functions slightly different from those of the other minerals, being involved primarily in the regulation of fluid balance within and outside the cells.

Recommended Dietary Allowances have been set for the three macrominerals, as well as for copper, iron, selenium and zinc. As for the other micro-minerals, nutritionists have thus far agreed upon "safe and adequate levels." These are usually ranges of figures within which consumption of the nutrient will likely meet nutritional needs as far as they are understood without creating excesses or toxicities in the body. However, the experts do not feel that they yet have enough information to give those figures the government's stamp of approval.

Water Although it has neither caloric nor, in any strict sense, nutritional value, water is the one substance we take into our bodies without which we could not survive for more than a couple of days. (Most people can live for several weeks, on the other hand, without food.) Active people in particular depend on life-giving water in order to stave off the potentially fatal effects of dehydration—a state in which the body loses a sufficient percentage of water to raise body temperature, thereby compromising various bodily functions. If not treated, dehydration can result in a sudden sharp rise in body temperature, triggering convulsions, coma and, eventually, death.

As you probably know, exercise raises the body's needs for water by raising body temperature and creating the need to replace water lost through breathing and perspiration. Humans perspire in just about every sport, from skin diving to badminton, not just the obvious land-based large-muscle-group-using ones. In order to meet that deficit, athletes engaging in virtually any sport need to consume more water than sedentary members of the general population.

You may think that, in order to meet your body's water needs, all you have to do is drink fluids when you are thirsty. Unfortunately, the formula isn't always that simple, because the human thirst mechanism, while it is generally a reliable indicator of when you should "wet your whistle," does not always let you know how *much* fluid you should take in to maintain the levels of fluids and chemicals in the body that are so crucial to carrying out vital processes. This is why many experts recommend that *everyone*—sedentary as well as active people engaged in all types of sports and exercises—make an effort to drink at least eight eight-ounce glasses of water a day. Active people, as well as those who are overweight, have had kidney stones, or spend time outdoors in hot, dry climates should drink even more.

Many sports scientists feel that people who don't consume enough fluids may end up going around in a chronic state of semidehydration. Unlike severe dehydration, this condition is far from life threatening. However, it can imperil health in minor ways. If you suffer from unexplained fatigue, sluggishness, muscle or joint soreness, if your face appears drawn and pinched when you look in the mirror or if you urinate fewer than five or six times every twenty-four hours (particularly if your urine is dark-colored or sparse), consider upping your fluid intake. If your performance in any type of exercise suffers, drinking more water should be one of the first remedies you attempt, especially if you have recently increased your training level.

As a runner, I am constantly gauging my intake, especially during the hot summer months, and most of the people I train with do the same. To the classes I coach at the New York Road Runners Club, I repeat the same advice over and over: Drink, drink and drink some more.

And what if water is not your beverage of choice? Fruit and vegetable juices (without added sugar or sodium), noncola carbonated beverages, low-fat milk and high-carbohydrate "sports" drinks can help fill your eight-glass-a-day quota, but they probably should not be the bulk of it, for a number of reasons. They are more expensive, they may not always be accessible, they contain calories (which may or may not be a problem for you) and, in some cases, quite a bit of sodium or sugar or both. In addition, unless the drinks are diluted with water, they may not leave the stomach quickly enough to meet the needs of working muscles. Along with many other sports-active people at all levels, I have always found that water, pure and simple, is the best way to help keep my system functioning at peak capacity.

Now that you know the basics of sensible sports nutrition, here are some words of advice on how to apply them in order to perform your best whenever you work up a sweat.

How to Eat the Low-Fat, High-Carbohydrate Way

Many active people who have their diets analyzed by a registered dietitian or nutritionist are surprised to learn the actual nutritional breakdown of what they eat. Typically, they find they eat more fats and protein and less carbohydrates than they had imagined. They are discouraged and puzzled, wondering where the unwanted fat could be.

Why the discrepancy? Often, these people have the best of intentions, but are simply misinformed in some areas about just where unneeded fats and extra protein in the diet reside and the many ways in which they can get more carbohydrates. Some may even be avoiding certain high-carbohydrate foods in the mistaken belief that they are fattening—although this seems to be less of a problem now than it was in the past.

Subtracting fats and adding carbohydrates will help improve the diets of most people. The suggestions below should help you point your diet toward a low-fat, high-carbohydrate way of eating—and keep it headed permanently in that direction.

First, root out the hidden sources of fat. Many people *think* they eat a low-fat diet, but when they sit down—often with the help of a registered dietitian or a nutrition-savvy physician—they find that there are gobs of fat hidden in places where they would have least expected to find it.

Certainly you know enough to trim all visible fat from your steak and remove the skin (it harbors about half the fat calories) from a piece of chicken, turkey or duck. Many other sources of fat, however, are much tougher to find and to root out. The positive side of that fact is that the best-hidden fats that you locate may be the ones that you end up missing the least. For example, most people can't tell the difference between a three-egg omelette made with all three yolks and one which contains only one or two, but removing just one yolk gets rid of 7 grams of saturated fat, as well as 210 grams of cholesterol. In many baking recipes, you can substitute two egg whites for every yolk with minimal adverse effects. Few people will be able to tell the difference.

Many condiments are fat-filled land mines. Holding (or at least going easy on) not only the mayonnaise, but the mustard, butter, margarine, salad dressing, tartar sauce, sour cream, cheese topping, cream sauce, dessert topping and other common adornments to our foods will go a long way toward saving you fat and calories. Nutritionists like to point out, for example, that while an average-size baked potato contains about 100 to 150 calories (virtually none of them in the form of fat), putting a tablespoon of butter—not an unusual amount—on top adds 120 calories and more than 13 grams of fat. It does give you incentive to pass the butter on down the table.

The methods you use in cooking also have a significant impact on how much fat ends up in your food. For example, anything fried, deep-fried, creamed or sautéed will almost certainly contain more fat and calories than the same item baked, broiled, boiled, steamed, blanched, simmered or grilled. If you do fry foods, you can minimize the damage by at least not breading them as well, and by draining them thoroughly on paper towels before serving. When preparing meat, choose the leanest cuts (or grades of ground beef, turkey and other meats) and remove as much fat as possible both before and after cooking. For example, you can chill meat-containing soups (such as chicken) and skim the layer of fat off the top before heating and serving them.

Then replace fats with complex carbohydrates. Once you get as much excess fat out of your diet as you can, you need to take the next important step—replacing those fats with carbohydrates, preferably of the complex variety (the differences between simple and complex carbohydrates were explained back on page 106). If you are exercising regularly—even if your level of activity doesn't seem like a lot compared to that of other active people—you are still burning significantly more calories each day than a sedentary person. You need to replenish the calories lost, as well as those you have given up as fat, in ways that will fuel your system for action.

The foods listed in the table on pages 117–18 are among the best sources of complex carbohydrates. Rather than just finding a few that you like, why not experiment with all of them to give your diet as much variety, and your meal-planning as much flexibility, as possible? I've just tried to cover the foods most commonly eaten by exercise-loving people. However, you may eat other terrific sources of carbohydrates not included here. But keep this list handy as a reference whenever you want to give your high-carbo diet as much variety as you can.

With much of the fat out and the carbohydrates in, you should be on the road to healthier eating to fuel your cross-training lifestyle. Before you start dealing with the specifics, however, take a look at some of the common sports nutrition myths that thwart the efforts of cross-trainers eager to eat as healthfully as they can. How many have you ever put stock in? Read on for the pitfalls—and the facts to help you avoid them.

Thirteen Sports Nutrition Myths Refuted

When it comes to giving advice on what active people should eat, it sometimes seems that everyone is an expert—or at least they would like to think they are. The result, unfortunately, is that there is a great deal of misinformation floating around out there in the area of what, how, when and why physically active people should get their daily calories. Read on for a review of some of the most common misconceptions in the sports nutrition realm and the correct information to set them right.

Myth 1: If you are physically active and don't have a weight problem, then you can eat whatever you want.

For many people, this is probably a case of wishful thinking. Others are simply ignorant. I counted myself in the latter category for many years. I come from skinny stock and would almost certainly be underweight even if I didn't exercise at all. Since I never had to watch my weight, I always allowed myself whatever high-fat food I wanted. The skin of the chicken, whole milk, buttered

High-Carbohydrate Foods

Food	Grams carbohydrate per 100 grams (3.5 oz)	Calories	Food	Grams carbohydrate per 100 grams (3.5 oz)	Calories
almonds	19.5	598	crackers		
apples (raw)	14.5	58	graham	73.3	384
apples (dried)	71.8	275	whole-wheat	68.2	403
apricots (dried)	66.5	260	dates	72.9	274
bananas	22.2	85	doughnuts	51.4	391
beans (white)	21.2	118	figs (fresh)	20.3	80
beans (red)	21.4	118	figs (dried)	69.1	274
beans (lima)	19.8	111	grapes	17.3	67
biscuits	52.3	325	guavas	15.0	62
blueberries (raw)	15.3	62	kumquats	17.1	65
			lentils (cooked)	19.3	106
bran flakes	80.6	303	macaroni	30.1	148
bread	47.7–56.4	243–276	(enriched,		
bread pudding	28.4	187	cooked)		
bread sticks (Vienna)	58.0	304	mangoes	16.8	66
			miso (soybean)	23.5	171
cake			muffins	41.9–51.9	261–324
angel food	60.2	269	nectarines	17.1	64
sponge	54.1	297	oatmeal	9.7	55
cashew nuts	29.3	561	(cooked)		
cherries (sweet)	17.4	70	pancakes (cooked)	34.1	231
chestnuts (fresh)	42.1	194	parsnips	14.9	66
			peaches	68.3	262
chick-peas	61.0	360	(dried)		
cookies			peanuts	17.6	568
fig bars	75.4	358	peanut butter	17.2	581
lady fingers	64.5	360	pears (fresh)	15.3	61
raisin	80.8	379	pears (dried)	67.3	268
corn (fresh, cooked)	18.8	83	persimmons	33.5	127
			pie	23.4–43.7	198–418
cornbread	29.1	207	pineapple	13.7	52
cornflakes	85.3	386	pizza (cheese topping)	28.3	236
corn puffs	80.8	399			

High-Carbohydrate Foods

Food	Grams carbohydrate per 100 grams (3.5 oz)	Calories	Food	Grams carbohydrate per 100 grams (3.5 oz)	Calories
plantains	31.2	119	rye wafers	76.3	344
plums (Damson)	17.8	66	sesame seeds	21.6	563
potatoes (baked)	21.1	93	squash (winter, baked)	15.4	63
potatoes (boiled)	17.1	76	sunflower seeds	19.9	560
pretzels	75.9	390	sweet potatoes (baked)	32.5	141
prunes	67.4	255			
raisins	77.4	289	tapioca pudding	17.1	134
raspberries (black)	15.7	73	waffles (cooked, from mix)	40.2	305
rice (brown, cooked)	25.5	119			
rice (enriched white, cooked)	24.2	109	water chestnuts	19.0	79
rice flake cereal	87.7	390	wheat and barley cereal (cooked)	13.2	65
rice (puffed) cereal	89.5	399	wheat cereal (shredded)	79.9	354
rice pudding (with raisins)	26.7	146	wheat germ (toasted)	49.5	390
rolls (hard)	59.5	312			

Source: United States Department of Agriculture "Composition of Foods" handbook (Agricultural Handbook No. 8), Agricultural Research Service, Washington, D.C., U.S. Government Printing Office, 1975. Actual food composition may vary depending on brand, season, cooking time and other factors.

rolls, bagels slathered with cream cheese, you name it, and if it was high-fat, I ate it.

Then in 1987 I had my cholesterol level measured for the first time at a press conference. By far the thinnest, most active person in the room, I had one of the highest levels, 219. I took a crash course in low-fat eating and quickly learned all the ways I could replace fats with healthy complex carbohydrates—practices that were already second nature to many of the people I knew through sports, as well as anyone who had successfully dealt with a tendency to put on weight.

The point is, being lean and fit does *not* guarantee that you are healthy. The classic example of this truth, of course, is Jim Fixx, the runner and writer who died of a heart attack while out for a jog. Running didn't kill Fixx directly, but it is possible that the confidence that being fit gave him may have caused him to ignore factors (heredity, former smoking, high cholesterol and so forth) that put him in a high-risk category for serious heart trouble.

Remember, fitness is but one part—albeit an important one—of the formula for good health. No matter how active you are, if you don't eat well, you won't be in peak health.

Myth 2: If you want to lose weight, cut out the carbohydrates—bread, potatoes, pasta and so forth.

It always amazes me how prevalent this erroneous belief still is. You would think that simple mathematics would be enough to set people straight: Carbohydrates have only four calories per gram, compared to nine per gram in fat, so ounce for ounce, they are less than half as fattening.

Other factors work in favor of carbohydrates as well: Because they are so readily available as a fuel source for exercise, it's much easier to work out when eating a high-carbohydrate diet than one rich in protein or fat. The extra activity can be yet another contributor to weight loss. Since carbohydrates also fuel the brain, a diet rich in them also keeps you more alert and generally better-tempered than a high-fat and high-protein diet.

It's hard to know how and when the starches-are-fattening myth got its start. It may linger because the high-fat adornments we tend to put on carbohydrate foods make them counterproductive to weight loss. Baked potatoes (almost pure carbohydrates) get covered in butter or sour cream, pasta is obscured by rich cream sauces, greens drenched in high-fat dressing are called a salad, and rolls aren't considered fit for human consumption unless they are covered with margarine or butter. If you cut back on all these and other high-fat extras, a carbohydrate-rich diet—along with exercise, of course—is a surefire way to control your weight.

Myth 3: Don't exercise if you are trying to lose weight. You'll just get hungry and overeat.

It's easy to see how strict calorie-counters can get caught up in this kind of thinking. What they may be overlooking is that exercise revs up the metabolism—and working out regularly keeps it that way. You won't step on the scale and be lighter after your first workout (or if you are, it will be from water weight lost through perspiration, which is temporary). Over the long term, however, the vast majority of sedentary people who take up exercise do reduce their stores of body fat—even if they don't diet at the same time. (Those who both eat less and work out, of course, tend to lose more weight.)

Appetite tends to be somewhat depressed immediately after heart-rate-raising physical activity. Studies have shown that in the long term the appetites of people who work out moderately tend to stay the same or increase slightly, leading to the loss of weight. But even if an exercise regimen doesn't cause you to shed pounds, it will probably alter your body *composition*, which will make you both look better—if leaner and trimmer means "better" to you—and be healthier if you were significantly overweight to begin with. (For more on weight loss and exercise, see the next chapter.)

Myth 4: People who work out need to take supplements to get all the extra vitamins and minerals they need.

There is no—repeat, no—evidence that active people have any increased vitamin, mineral or other nutritional needs over the sedentary population. However, the supplement industry probably makes billions of dollars a year off of active people who believe otherwise. A healthy diet supplies more than enough proteins, fats and carbohydrates for most of us, exercisers or not. Those who exercise, with their average higher calorie intake compared to the sedentary population, and generally greater interest in and knowledge of good nutrition, probably get even more nutrient value from the diet than the average nonexerciser. Any extra calories in the form of protein, fat and carbohydrates, as you know, are either excreted from the body or stored as fat.

As for vitamins and minerals, remember that they are needed in very small amounts and generally can be reused a number of times. Again, a healthy diet supplies all of them in adequate amounts. That's true even if you aren't active, so if you are, and are presumably consuming more calories to fuel a lifestyle that includes more physical activity, you are probably even further ahead of the game.

It has been suspected, but never proven, that the only two nutrient shortages that seem to occur more than rarely in this country—iron and calcium—bear some sort of relation to one's level of physical activity. A few small studies suggest that some (but not all) runners and other people who engage in activities in which the feet pound the ground or floor might lose iron through bleeding of minute blood vessels in the bottoms of the feet. The possibility of this phenomenon, known as *footstrike hematosis,* should only be investigated in cases of anemia in which all other possible explanations have been ruled out. Other studies of athletes have shown that some seem to lose blood through bleeding (again, small amounts of blood) in the gut, but the prevalence of the problem has never been compared to that in a group of nonathletes.

Finally, it appears that relatively large numbers of people who go from being sedentary to even moderately active develop what is called "sports anemia" or "pseudoanemia." This is a harmless condition in which the blood volume increases in response to increased physical activity before the system has a chance to make enough red blood cells to "keep up." The result, temporarily low red-blood cell and iron counts, is often diagnosed as anemia. Technically it is, but in most cases, the condition rights itself within a few weeks without treatment. So if you are new to cross-training, or returning after a layoff from exercise, and you're feeling tired, be wary of the results of any blood tests that indicate anemia. By all means eat an iron-rich diet. However, you are probably better off refraining from aggressive therapy beyond that (such as high-dose supplementation) until you've had another test in a few weeks. If it shows that the problem has not diminished, consult a medical professional about what action to take next.

As for calcium, used to help keep bones healthy and strong, again there is no suggestion that the average active person needs more than someone who is sedentary. The only exception might be a woman who works out at such a high level that she ceases to menstruate. There is some evidence that the lack of the female hormone estrogen—one of the functions of which is to help build bone—circulating in her body can raise her risk for losing enough bone so that her chance of later developing osteoporosis goes up. Osteoporosis is the "brittle bone" disease that causes bones to become dry, brittle and more likely to fracture. It affects a disproportionate number of women after menopause (when estrogen production plummets) and can cause death from the complications of a fractured hip (see Chapter Five).

Moderate exercise, especially "weight-bearing" types (those done on land in an upright position, such as jogging, walking, aerobic dance, tennis or volleyball), may protect against osteoporosis by strengthening bone. A calcium-rich diet also may help ward off the condition—but again, the effect is there whether you exercise or not, and at all levels.

Myth 5: Muscle turns to fat when you stop exercising.

It may appear that way, but it isn't so. That the two events take place at the same time when you stop exercising does not mean that the one causes the other. Rather, muscle and fat are two completely separate entities, and it is impossible for the one to "turn into" the other. If you are consuming calories and cross-training at a certain level and maintaining your weight, and you stop the physical activity but don't eat fewer calories, chances are very good that you will put on fat. At the same time, if the muscles you have used in your activities are not exercised for a few days, they will begin to *atrophy* (see Chapter Two, page 40). You will notice this as the muscles getting smaller and weaker. So, it may appear that your muscles are directly converting to fat. However, you will not put on fat unless you consume more calories than you expend in activity. Likewise, you can gain fat even while you are engaging in a cross-training (or any exercise) program, as long as your caloric intake exceeds your output.

Some people who stop exercising *lose* weight, although the amount of fat they are carrying may go up. This usually is what happens to me. The reason is that muscle tissue weighs more than fat tissue. As my muscle tissue shrinks, the overall weight of my body decreases, even if I do add pounds in the form of body fat. My clothes will be tighter, my thighs more jiggly—but the number on the scale will be smaller. This is another reason why dieting without exercise isn't such a great idea. (For more on weight loss and exercise, see the next chapter.)

Myth 6: Exercising on a full stomach burns more calories than exercising on an empty stomach.

No study has ever proven it. This myth probably got started because of a physiological reaction that definitely does happen after the body ingests food. Digestion itself is a calorie-burning process—the act of eating food and processing it, no matter what else you may be doing at the same time, will use up some calories. So it's true that more calories are being burned if you exercise after eating than if you do the same exercise on an empty stomach, but since you'd have to eat (and burn the calories) at some point anyway, there really isn't any calorie savings.

It's really up to you when to cross-train in relation to when you eat your meals and snacks. Having a lot of food in the stomach during workouts doesn't seem to work well for most people because of the likelihood of indigestion. But it depends on the activity, the food and the individual. For example, long-distance cyclists eat on the road all the time, while most joggers and runners wouldn't dream of it (except for ultra-long-distance competitors, who usually have to). Many people find eating something light and rich in carbohydrates, such as a banana, just fine before a workout, while a steak would be a disaster. Very sweet, milky, high-fiber and high-fat foods top the list of most people's no-no's for any time within a few hours of vigorous exercise.

Exercising without anything in your stomach at all (not having eaten for, say, six to ten hours) may also produce a suboptimal workout or competitive effort. If you are hungry an hour or so before a scheduled exercise session, experiment with eating something light and rich in carbohydrates, such as a piece of fruit, some crackers, a bagel, a piece of bread or a sports drink. Some people can tolerate such things up to a few minutes before a vigorous session (again, it depends on the individual, the food and the activity). A workout attempted without enough fuel in your system may indeed burn fewer calories— if you end up being too hungry and tired to finish what you set out to do.

Myth 7: A calorie is a calorie is a calorie. Eating too many carrots is just as bad as eating too many potato chips.

Well, yes, and no. In theory, eating thirty-five hundred extra calories of carrots (and believe me, that is a *lot* of carrots!) should cause you to put on a pound of fat just as eating thirty-five hundred calories of potato chips, ice cream or anything else, or so it would seem. However, it turns out that the more fat a food contains, the more easily it puts fat on the body, because fat calories are more easily converted to body fat than are carbohydrate and protein calories. In experiments on both animals and people, those overfed a high-fat diet gained more weight than those overfed on protein and carbohydrates.

On the other hand, there are people who think that the calories in some foods, such as those high in carbohydrates and low in fats, are completely "free," meaning that the foods can be consumed with reckless abandon. Unfortunately, such is not the case either. *Any* food, if enough of it is eaten, will add pounds on the scale and inches to the waistline.

Myth 8: Top athletes get their competitive edge by following special diets that they keep secret from their competitors and the rest of us.

When I speak to groups of active, sports-minded people, both informally and at talks and seminars, I'm pretty much guaranteed to get questions about what I eat—the underlying assumption being that the secret to my running success is a terribly complicated, restrictive, arcane diet.

Sorry to disappoint anyone, but I fuel my body pretty much the same way most of the people I know do—both those who work out and those who don't. I don't make a habit of eating at Burger King, but I'm not a fanatic. I happen to enjoy red meat, ice cream, beer, M&M's, fried eggs and New York hot pretzels, so I make all of them a part of my diet—in moderation, along with other healthier foods and in amounts that allow me to balance food intake with energy outlay.

The very first of the United States government's "Dietary Guidelines for Americans" is "Eat a variety of foods." I really believe that no food, when eaten in moderation as part of a balanced diet, is a so-called "junk" food. The "junk" is overindulging in a food—any food, from french fries to bean sprouts—because doing so may detract from the balance of your diet.

Active people—from world-class athletes to those breaking a sweat for the first time—do not have to give up foods or food categories, or cook meals in special ways, in order to fuel their lifestyle and activities. World records have been set on meals ranging from spinach salads to rib-eye steaks. If you choose to adopt a special diet, based on your moral, religious, philosophical or health beliefs, that is fine. Just make sure that you educate yourself about what you are doing so you can eat responsibly and nutritiously. For example, you shouldn't turn to vegetarianism without understanding what a complete protein is. And you should learn to tune out anyone who tells you that a special diet will make or break your involvement in and commitment to a healthy, active cross-training lifestyle.

Myth 9: Salad is always a healthy choice as part of an active person's diet.

Dangerous thinking. A "salad" can be anything from a few pieces of iceberg lettuce glopped over with high-calorie, high-fat French, Thousand Island, bleu cheese or Russian dressing to a nutritious, mouthwatering collection of greens, grains, fruits and veggies bursting with vitamins, minerals and low-fat, high-carbohydrate goodness.

Like any food, salad involves making healthy choices. Go easy on the dressing, choosing low-fat or reduced-calorie types, or none at all, fresh ingredients, a balance of nutrients and variety from one meal to the next. If you rely on salad bars, make sure the conditions are sanitary and the makings fresh and wholesome. Steer away from heavily creamed and sauced items (such as creamy cole slaw, potato salad, egg salad or creamy pasta salad), bacon bits and oily croutons. Go with dark greens such as spinach and romaine lettuce rather than iceberg. Add fruit when you can. A salad certainly *can* be part of a healthy diet, but it can also be a diet saboteur if you aren't careful.

Myth 10: Don't drink water before or during a workout—it will give you cramps.

Following this advice could get you in a lot of trouble. The opposite is true: You *must* drink to fuel physical activity—before, during and after your workout, and beyond the point of slaking your thirst. This is especially true if you are in a warm, dry climate, the activity raises your heart rate for long periods, you're exposed to sunlight or you have recently consumed anything containing caffeine or alcohol, both of which are diuretics.

Water is almost never the cause of cramps during exercise. Moreover, there is no truth to the belief that cold water is more likely to give you a gut-ache than warm liquids. To prevent dangerous, even life-threatening dehydration, drink plenty of cold, clear water or other noncaffeinated, nonalcoholic fluids without excess sodium or sugar at regular intervals before, during and after your workouts.

Myth 11: If you want to trim the extra fat from a certain part of your body, you must exercise that particular area.

This is known as "spot reducing," and it simply doesn't work. Fat loss is an overall body process that occurs whenever caloric output is greater than intake (when you exercise more than you eat, in other words). The pattern of loss depends on your genetic inheritance, not on which muscles get the workout. Doing sit-ups will strengthen your abdominal muscles, but it will not necessarily remove the fat you carry over those muscles (see Myth 5).

Cross-training takes advantage of the principle of total-body fat loss by making sure that as your exercise program makes you leaner all over, it makes you stronger and more flexible all over as well, by working out muscles and joints in all parts of your body.

Myth 12: Sugar, alcohol and other "empty" calories can never be a part of a healthy, active person's diet.

Sure they can—as long as you keep the principle of moderation at the forefront of your thinking. For example, an ice cream cone for dessert is fine, polishing off an entire half-gallon of ice cream probably is not. By the same token, you can have a glass of wine with dinner, but if you later drink the rest of the bottle, you could be in some trouble.

Every person must find his or her point at which moderation turns to excess— as you know, what's "too much" for you may be "just right" for somebody else. But in general, denying yourself something you enjoy (like ice cream cones) is a surefire way to create an irresistible craving for it. You may temporarily feel as though you have more control over your eating when you give up certain tempting foods. In the end, however, learning to enjoy them in moderation as part of a healthy diet is a lot more liberating—not to mention more fun. (See also the next chapter, on weight control.)

Myth 13: Downing a sports drink will give you a boost of energy when you exercise.

This is true only if the exercise continues for ninety minutes or longer. That's how long it seems to take the carbohydrates in a sports drink to pass from the mouth to the stomach, to the digestive tract and into the bloodstream, and for it to be converted into glucose to fuel the working muscles. This would eliminate the effect for most people running ten-kilometer races; taking hour-long aerobics classes; playing many tennis, racquetball and squash games; going through sessions in the weight room and engaging in quite a few other endeavors.

The drinks might well help, on the other hand, when running longer races (or while training), or on longer hikes, long bike rides, long tennis matches and during many team sports events. But you must drink them early on if you want to get any benefit at all before the end of play.

I know, I know, you say that you feel better *immediately* upon taking a swig of Gatorade or Exceed. I swear I feel the same way. Sorry, say the folks in the sports science labs: All you are feeling is the beverages' *placebo effect:* You feel better because you *think* you're going to feel better. Chances are, if someone told you the drink was a sham, you would report no surge of energy whatsoever. If you do want to try to get a benefit, and your activity lasts less than ninety minutes, your best strategy is to have a sports drink about an hour to an hour and a half before the activity starts.

There are plenty of other sports nutrition myths out there, but this covers the main ones I have heard—and, I hope, sets you straight with the right information.

Now that you know enough to fuel yourself wisely for all the hard work you do as a cross-trainer, you may think that my next step is going to be to tell you how and what to eat. Sorry, but I can't do that. Eating is something you have to learn to do yourself—with the assistance of a doctor or registered dietitian, if necessary. Registered dietitians (R.D.'s) can be enormously helpful in helping you understand nutrition, planning your overall diet, and working on specific problems. In most larger communities you should be able to find one with a sports and fitness orientation—ask around at health and fitness clubs and sports medicine centers. There are also a number of resource organizations and sports nutrition books available, several of which are listed in the Appendix.

Eating well to fuel your cross-training lifestyle is a crucial ingredient to the success of your program. Following the basic rules of good nutrition can enhance a sound training program, while ignoring them can cause unnecessary problems. However, you need not be a fanatic in order to eat well. As in your cross-training plan, the key is finding a plan that incorporates balance, variety and moderation, and with which you can enjoy yourself and have fun. Learn the basics, ask questions, spurn the myths—and happy eating.

SEVEN

CROSS-TRAINING AND

BODY WEIGHT

I have yet to meet many people who can say they are, and have always been, completely happy with what they weigh. Indeed, to hear some people tell it, you would think carrying around five or ten pounds too many to be the bane of any self-respecting person's existence.

You might imagine that those who engage in regular physical activity, with their leaner, better-toned physiques, would be immune to despairing thoughts about the size of their thighs and the jiggle of underarm flab. Alas, not so. In fact, it has been my experience that those who work out regularly—even though they may feel stronger, more in control of their bodies and better disciplined as a result—are, if anything, *more* concerned with their girth and that supposedly tell-all number on the bathroom scale. Indeed, studies and surveys have proven it over and over: From the weekend stroller to the Olympic-caliber champion athlete, all of us can at times fall prey to concerns about our weight and body fat.

The Two Extremes of Thoughts About Fat

Our concern about weight covers a wide range of intensities. On one end of the spectrum, these thoughts can be altogether normal and healthy. Indeed,

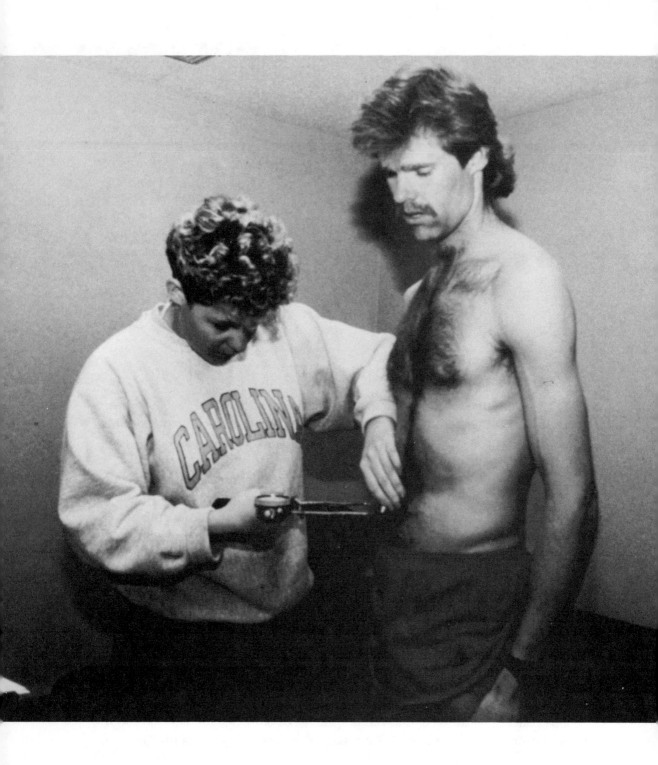

concern about being severely overweight is well-founded. Obesity—defined by most experts as being 20 percent or more over the ideal, or "desirable" weight for one's height and frame size—is considered a health hazard. Many scientific studies have shown that it is a risk factor for heart disease, diabetes, some cancers, gallstones and other disorders. The connections, however, between being overweight and developing the various conditions aren't always completely understood.

Unfortunately, obese people may also be socially isolated and discriminated against culturally and in employment, housing and other areas. In addition, the obese require more energy than normal-weight people to perform daily physical tasks such as walking up and down stairs. Some report that they find it more challenging than normal-weight people do to start an exercise program because of the real or perceived physical, social and psychological hurdles. The federal government, the American Medical Association, the American Heart Association and many other professional groups urge the general public to avoid obesity and to make efforts to lose weight sensibly (under professional supervision if needed) if they are obese.

At the other end of the spectrum of concern over body weight, however, lies an unhealthy, inappropriate and even dangerous obsession. Unfortunately, the society we live in can contribute to this problem. There is no question that we in the West live in a culture that worships thinness. A climate favoring thin bodies—particularly women's—began to gain ground in Europe and North America in the nineteenth century, when the Industrial Revolution moved countless millions of people from lives of hard physical labor, generally subsistence farming, and insecurity about the consistency and stability of the food supply to a more sedentary, often more gustatorily secure lifestyle. More and more people adopted lifestyles in which little physical work was required. At the same time, the worldwide risk of starvation from famine, which had been around since the dawn of history, was gradually pushed back by advances in technology, transportation and communication. Thanks to these developments, by the beginning of the twentieth century, it was no longer either necessary or desirable for many of the world's people to carry extra fat to sustain themselves during periods of heavy labor or little food.

As soon as stores of excess fat were superfluous, thinness became desirable. Thinness came to be seen first as a symbol of wealth, and then—as less-physical work spread to all levels of society—as a sign of self-control, elegance and sophistication. Again, while the thin-is-beautiful standard has been applied to a certain degree to both sexes—fat men generally are not considered particularly

Credit: Courtesy U.S. Olympic Training Center.

sexy or attractive—women usually have been expected to measure up to it to a far greater extent.

Today, in a world where the vast majority of people—everyone from corporate executives, lawyers and financiers down the financial and social ranks to clerks, typists and assembly-line workers—spend their working days in a state of relative inactivity, most of us find that if we don't make some effort to control our caloric intake, we tend to carry more weight than society considers attractive. And in quite a significant number of cases, people who eat whatever they want without exercising regularly can put on enough extra body weight to create a health hazard. It should be noted, however, that the point at which the risk for various conditions starts to noticeably increase appears to range quite widely among individuals, and that a few people can be extremely overweight without raising their risk of serious diseases.

Regardless of the health risks, fat is widely shunned in our society. Numerous surveys show that vast numbers of people are unhappy with their weight. As might be expected, the overwhelming majority would like to *lose* pounds rather than gain. That this concern is often excessive or even completely misplaced is one of the most unfortunate developments of late-twentieth-century Western culture. Surveys by the dozen have revealed that large numbers of women (and some men), athletes and even children want to lose significant amounts of weight. While some are overweight, many are in the normal weight range, and significant numbers are *under*weight.

Obsession with thinness and weight loss, when taken to an extreme, can lead to potentially life-threatening eating disorders, such as anorexia nervosa and bulimia. And, as noted above, active men and women are not immune to such problems; indeed some surveys suggest that they may even be *more* vulnerable than people who don't exercise. In addition, the prevalence of unhealthy food-, eating- and thinness-related thoughts and behavior—short of out-and-out eating disorders—is more widespread than has been believed.

The Road to Healthy Weight Control

As was discussed in the previous chapter, exercising regularly can (and in most cases, probably should) be a crucial part of a successful program to lose weight or maintain weight at a healthy level. To see why this is so, and why weight-loss programs that do *not* include exercise tend not to be successful over the long haul, you must first understand a few important pieces of information about body weight and body fat, how both of them relate to exercise and sports activities of various types and intensities, and how some of the many myths about exercise, weight and fat got started and have been perpetuated.

After you have grasped these things, you will see how one of the best possible ways of losing weight and controlling weight at the healthiest level for you is through a well-planned cross-training program, preferably one that uses as many of the major muscle groups as possible. You'll also see, perhaps to your surprise, that keeping yourself at the right weight (for you) through cross-training need not depend on exercise that is violent, painful or excessively long. In fact, believe it or not, the *best* weight-loss and weight-maintenance activities are gentle, regular and sustained for at most about an hour at a time.

Body Weight versus Body Fat

Have you ever heard anyone complain—or perhaps noticed in yourself— that starting a regular exercise program, rather than leading to weight loss, as hoped for and indeed expected, has led instead to a *gain* in pounds? This seemingly frustrating result, which is not the least bit uncommon, may have the unfortunate result of causing people to abandon sports and fitness activities as a useless and even counterproductive way to reduce that number on the scale.

If you have ever followed such a course of action—and I admit that I have myself, as have a number of people I know—you have a few things to learn about body weight, body fat and the important differences between the two. Read on.

The Not-So-Magic Number When you step on the scale, the number you see (usually in pounds) represents the sum total of your various body organs, tissues and food and fluids that you have ingested and not yet excreted. This is why weight can vary in most people by a few pounds depending on the time of day, month (for women who menstruate) and year (many of us tend to gain in the winter, for reasons that are not completely understood) one happens to weigh oneself. Most people are aware of these differences, and would expect to weigh more than normal after, for example, eating Thanksgiving dinner, or less after running a marathon and before replenishing lost fluids and nutrients.

What is less well-known is how changes in the composition of body tissues can affect weight. Recall that any exercise that uses any of the body's muscles to a significant degree will cause an increase in the size of the muscle fibers used (see Chapter Two). As body tissues go, muscle fibers are relatively heavy. It follows that a gain in muscle fiber, if it is at all significant, will result in a gain in overall body weight.

This gain can be offset, in part, by an exercise-induced loss of body fat—which is the only thing many people say they care about when they first undertake an activity program. Fat, however, is actually a relatively light-weight form of body tissue. If you need any proof of this, simply pour a bit of any type of oil—or drop some margarine or butter—into a glass of water. The oil, which is more or less pure fat, will float because it is less dense than the water.

Now try the same thing with a piece of lean meat, which contains some fat, but proportionately more muscle tissue. The meat (if it is sufficiently lean) will sink to the bottom of the glass. Why? Because it is denser than both the water and the fatty oil. By the way, if you're not interested in such experimentation in the kitchen, you can observe the same effect by taking two people, one fat and one lean, for a swim. I guarantee that the fat person will float more easily in water than the lean one. The reason, again, is that fat floats, while muscle tissue sinks, because one is less dense than the other. And you may be surprised to know that the *weight* of the two individuals relative to each other does not make the least bit of difference.

Since muscle outweighs fat, you would need to lose proportionally more fat than you would gain in muscle to see a net weight loss from an exercise program. Some people do accomplish this, and are thrilled to report they have lost weight through exercise. Others, however, find that their weight stays the same, and some even gain. I find, for example, that a layoff from running generally produces a loss of a couple of pounds after a week or so. Obviously, I'm losing muscle weight, although I may be gaining some fat at the same time.

The logical corollary to this fact, which has been observed by more than a few exercise participants, is that since you can *gain* weight, yet still reduce your girth, through regular exercise, what you weigh if you are active and healthy shouldn't really matter a whole lot—or at least not as much as we have been led to believe. Really, it is not uncommon to hear women say they have dropped two or more dress sizes, or men to find themselves buying pants two to four inches smaller in the waist than they did when they were still sedentary—*while losing few or even no pounds on the scale.*

If you have concluded from the previous discussion that weight loss really isn't a terribly important measure of the "success" of a fat-reducing exercise program, congratulations. This brilliant deduction puts you miles ahead of most of the people attempting to reduce their weight in the gyms and dance studios and on the roads, sidewalks and trails all over the world. And it follows that what *does* matter, in terms of health, fitness and how you look and feel as a result of exercise, is the *fat* you end up losing (and keeping off—but you'll read more on this topic later), *not* the weight.

Fat versus Weight Some of the country's top doctors, scientists and public-health experts realized the greater importance of fat loss compared with loss of weight when they convened in 1990 to update the federal government's "Dietary Guidelines for Americans," a publication put out approximately every five years to advise healthy people on how to eat and control their weight for optimum health. The guidelines consist of seven points, the second of which is "Maintain healthy weight." The wording was altered in 1990 from "Maintain desirable weight." To obtain a free copy of "Dietary Guidelines" write to Consumer Information Center, Pueblo, CO 81009.

The difference, and the thinking that went into it, is significant. In past versions of the guidelines, "desirable" was defined on the basis of the ranges given by the well-known Metropolitan Life Insurance Company's height-weight charts, which represented levels for men and women at which all-cause mortality was lowest. Intuitively, this definition made sense, and the tables were seen as a useful index of health as it related to fat and weight in a time when scientists understood little about the connections among the three.

Where's the Fat? However, understanding has advanced markedly in recent years. There is increasing evidence that it is a high proportion of fat carried on the body, not overall weight, that increases the risk of conditions such as heart disease, diabetes and some cancers. In addition, it has been strongly suggested that the places where fat is stored on the body affect health as well. Specifically, fat stored in the abdominal area seems to pose a greater health risk than fat stored below the waist, such as on the hips and thighs. The reasons for this aren't entirely clear, but seem to be related to chemicals produced by fat cells in the abdominal area.

Unfortunately, it appears that there is a limited amount that people can do to change their tendency to put on extra weight in the abdominal versus the hip-and-thigh area. (See Chapter Six on "spot-reducing" on page 125.) In general, as you may have noticed, men seem more likely to put on extra fat in the abdominal area (you often hear sedentary men complaining of their "spare tire" or "potbelly"), while women are more prone to fat gain in the hips and thighs (delicately referred to as "problem areas" for the typical sedentary female). While this fact doesn't make women immune to heart disease, it may in part explain why they have lower rates, before age sixty-five, than men do.

The important thing to keep in mind, however, is that anyone can bring about an overall loss of fat through a regular, moderate exercise program, especially if it is combined with a sensible low-fat diet. And the loss of fat will include fat (and inches) taken off the abdominal area.

If You Can't Trust the Scale, What Can You Trust?

It may now occur to you to wonder how, if the numbers on the scale generally are not a reliable indicator of your weight-related health and fitness level, you are supposed to know whether you are at a healthy body-fat level. The answer is that it isn't always easy to know exactly—which may in part explain why people tend to go by the number they see on the scale in deciding whether they need to go on a diet or start exercising, or both. There are a number of more-or-less accurate, reliable methods for measuring the percentage of fat that a person is carrying on the body, but unfortunately, most of them are not readily available to the average person, the way a bathroom scale can be.

Fat-Measuring Methods Exercise science and physiology labs employ a range of body-fat—measuring techniques. One of the best known and most widely used is underwater weighing, in which a subject to be measured is first weighed on dry land, then submerged in water wearing a special weighted belt and told to blow as much air as possible out of the lungs. The speed at which the person then sinks to the bottom of the tank provides an index of the body's density. Contrary to what you might expect, the less body fat a person has, the faster he or she will drop to the bottom. This makes sense if you keep in mind that muscle tissue weighs more, proportionately, than fat tissue.

Once the speed is measured (several trials are usually performed) a formula is then applied to calculate the percentage of the body that is fat. The method is imperfect—it assumes a standard bone density, for example, and relies on the subject's ability to blow absolutely every bit of air out of the lungs (something I, for one, have had trouble doing)—but its results are generally considered accurate and can be helpful in tracking trends over time.

What is a healthy range of body-fat percentages, anyway? Unfortunately, the answer to that question is not a simple one. The average American woman seems to log in at somewhere around 25 percent to 30 percent fat, whereas the typical man will measure in the neighborhood of 20 percent. These figures vary widely, however. Male marathon runners and other athletes who have been deemed perfectly healthy have recorded body-fat percentages as low as 2 to 3 percent, and women measured at less than 10 percent are not unheard of among elite gymnasts, ballerinas and runners. At the other end of the scale, measures in excess of 50 percent are not uncommon among the severely obese.

A special note on women, who typically have a greater percentage of fat than men to sustain their menstrual, pregnancy and breastfeeding functions: Women who lose body fat through dieting or exercise may menstruate irregularly or not at all and may find they have trouble getting pregnant. These conditions usually revert to normal when the women stop exercising so intensely and gain some weight.

As for other body-fat–measuring methods and devices, unfortunately, most are even more complicated, expensive and hard to secure access to than underwater-weighing tanks. The one exception that I am aware of is the hand-held caliper. This is a device, common in many exercise physiology and sports science labs, for measuring the thickness of the layer of fat under the skin (known as subcutaneous fat) at various body sites. I have had my fat measured in this way on many occasions; it is, for example, the method employed by the exercise scientists working with elite athletes at the United States Olympic Training Center in Colorado Springs. The skinfold test always reminds me of the old "pinch an inch" test from commercials for Special-K breakfast cereal.

Most calipers can be held in the hands and look something like a large pair of tweezers. The procedure is very straightforward: The tester grabs a fold of fat in the area to be measured and pinches it with the device. The thickness is indicated on a small gauge. Generally, two or three measures are obtained and averaged, although experienced "pinchers" may rely on just one test. The sites on the body most commonly measured include the underside of the upper arm, the area over the shoulder blade, the abdomen, the hip area, the thigh and the calf. Since body-fat measures may vary in the different spots among individuals, the most accurate assessments take all these sites, and sometimes others, into account.

If performed properly by a well-trained person, the caliper test is considered a highly accurate measure of body fat. This has certainly been my experience: The results of tests that I have had performed on several occasions at the United States Olympic Training Center have consistently fallen within no more than a percentage point of one another.

A good set of calipers costs between $50 and $100—an amount that is very small change compared to the thousands of dollars exercise science labs must pay for complicated dual-photon absorptiometers, TOBEC machines and other body-fat measuring devices. However, the suitability of the low-tech, hand-held devices for the general public is limited because of the need for taking very precise, careful measurements. The spots selected on the body, the amount of fat grasped for measuring, and even the calibration of the calipers all should be performed by an experienced professional if accuracy is to count for anything. During one of my stays at the Olympic Training Center I was measured by an intern under the supervision of one of the lab's scientists. Even after a careful review of the procedures, the intern was made to repeat each of the measures at least half a dozen times to meet the standards of accuracy of his supervisor. I was told that this was not the least bit unusual when training people to use the calipers. This insistence on getting it right—essential if the test is to have any value at all—stretched a ten-minute procedure to almost half an hour. Clearly, this makes the procedure not quite the same thing as jumping on the bathroom scale for two seconds first thing in the morning.

Barred from these and other fat-measuring options, what then is the average person to do when it comes to monitoring flab? About the best suggestion I can offer is one that appearance- and health-conscious people have been following for years: Find a quiet place by yourself where you won't be disturbed, take off your clothes and stand in front of a full-length mirror. Stand normally—don't suck in your gut or puff out your chest—and take a good, hard look at your body. Observe and feel the places where you tend to put on fat (you know where they are) and look at yourself from the front, the back and the sides. Are you more or less satisfied with what you see and feel, or would you be happier with some changes?

It is probably not a bad idea to get in the habit of doing this regularly—say, once a month or so. For one thing, it will allow you to become comfortable with the process. Many people feel a bit weird the first time they take a long, hard, critical look at themselves naked, and aren't really able to respond to what they see. This can cause them either to become paralyzed, and do nothing, or to take inappropriate action, such as going on a severe diet when they have little fat to lose.

Second, looking at yourself regularly will help you evaluate your current body-fat situation honestly and realistically. You will be able to say, "Yes, this is me, this is how I look, and no, it's not quite the way I want to be. I am going to do something about that in a sensible, realistic, nonpunishing way." You can then adapt a well-planned cross-training program (combined with a fat-reducing diet if you wish), designed to tone and strengthen the body, promote overall fitness and, if you think it necessary, reduce your stores of fat.

Alternatively (and equally honestly and realistically), you could look at your reflection in the mirror and say, "At the moment, I believe I am happy with the way I look. I may not have the body of a movie star, but then again, I never did. Given what I have to work with, I don't think I need or want to make any changes right now. Therefore, I'll just go on eating and exercising about the same as I have been and be satisfied with this aspect of my life. But I'll take another look at things in a month or so."

Over time, I believe that you will find this to be a healthy approach to monitoring your fat and making decisions about trying to change your girth, shape and tone through cross-training. I haven't owned a scale for years, and I don't miss having one. As a competitive runner, the only significant weight fluctuations I experience are related to my hydration level. After a hard race such as a marathon on a hot day, I probably lose several pounds, even if I have drunk fluids before, during and after the event. I make sure to keep drinking until my urine is clear, a sign of being fully hydrated. I also take a look at myself unclothed in a full-length mirror every so often, to get a sense of whether my fat levels are where they should be. It's a rough estimate, I know, but I have found it's all I need.

When I do weigh myself (a couple of times a year when I'm involved in one sports science test or another, or have to go to the doctor), my weight very rarely deviates by more than a pound or two. So I must be doing something right.

From what you have read up to now, it should be clear that if you look in the mirror and are not particularly happy with what you see, your solution should not be a crash diet or some similar drastic (and, most likely, doomed to fail) method of "weight loss," but rather a program of sensible exercise. This is the point at which cross-training can enter the picture.

How Cross-Training Can Help You Control Fat

Now that you have accepted the fact that weight loss is neither an expected nor even necessarily a desirable result of exercise (although it may indeed take place), I want to say a few words about the proven benefits that a cross-training program can have in helping you control the amount of fat that you carry around on your body.

"I just want to exercise enough and in the right way so that I can eat whatever I want without worrying about getting fat" is a statement I hear again and again from people wanting to start exercising, those new to regular physical activity and those whose fitness programs have lapsed. As you learned in the previous chapter, it's probably not a good idea for most of us—no matter *what* our activity level—to completely throw caution to the wind every time we sit down and pick up our forks. However, if "eating whatever you want" means making healthy food and ingredient choices without having to skimp on calories (and, it is very likely, nutrients as well) and forgo meals, then I can promise that you can combine such a program with a cross-training schedule that is not excessively arduous, complex or time-consuming.

A cross-training regimen can be more beneficial as a fat-regulating endeavor than an exercise regimen involving similar time and intensity that is centered on just one activity. The reasons this is so are related to scientific understanding of how aerobic exercise (that which relies solely on oxygen for fuel, as explained in Chapter Two) burns fat and calories.

You might recall that the increases in heart rate, pumping of blood, muscle-fiber activity and other processes that accompany aerobic exercise call upon carbohydrates (generally those stored in the muscles as glycogen), fats and—if the first two energy sources are not readily available—protein to fuel the activity. It should be obvious that this is one of the reasons people who exercise aerobically regularly find, over time, that they require more calories to maintain their energy level and body processes. As many of these people wish, they can basically eat "whatever they want" (or at least a reasonable approximation thereof) without gaining excessive amounts of fat.

The Afterburner Effect It appears, however, that the calorie- and fat-burning benefits of exercise are not just limited to the changes that take place *during* heart-rate-raising activity. Indeed, many scientific studies have shown that metabolism—the rate at which the body burns calories, which is set by exercise level, genetics, calorie intake and possibly other as-yet-unknown factors—stays higher than its resting-state level for significant periods *after* the exercise is completed. In other words, you can engage in a half-hour jog, brisk walk, bicycle ride, aerobic-dance class or other activity, and your body will still be burning proportionally more calories several hours later than the body of your friend who stayed home for that half-hour and sat around watching television.

This news must be encouraging for any current or potentially active person. (I was certainly thrilled the first time I heard it.) What, however, does it have to say to cross-trainers in particular? The answer lies in understanding *why* metabolism stays up after a sports or fitness session has been completed.

Exercise, by putting stress on the muscles, breaks down muscle fiber in a process known as *catabolism*. The body then has to rebuild the muscle fibers in a process called *anabolism*. Both catabolism and anabolism take energy (calories). In addition, the process of anabolism makes the muscle fibers stronger than they were before exercise, and thus better able to withstand the rigors of further exercise. This is the essence of training the muscles and making them stronger. As you have certainly noticed if you have ever worked out relatively unused muscles for the first time (or after a layoff), the muscles actually get larger over time. The fibers both expand and multiply. It follows naturally that more and larger muscle fibers need more fuel—in the form of calories from food—to sustain them. This is the reason why regularly exercising people can eat more than those who abstain from exercise, and not worry about getting fat.

The superiority of cross-training's effect in this respect lies in the fact that a varied, balanced cross-training program works out a wide variety of muscle groups. More muscles worked, obviously, translates to growth and an increase in muscle fibers involving a larger area. After all, there are limits to how large, powerful and hungry for calories a single muscle or group of muscles can grow. But a wide range of muscles growing bigger and stronger through exercise *all* need more calories to fuel them. In addition, exercise not only raises the number of calories burned *while the activity is being performed*, it also causes the metabolic rate to stay elevated for hours afterward. This lasting metabolism-raising effect of exercise figures prominently into the fat-controlling benefits of exercise, particularly a cross-training program.

One well-known study pointing out the calorie-burning aftereffects of exercise was carried out by Peter Wood, M.D., at Stanford University in California. He compared two groups of middle-aged women; one group played tennis about ten hours a week, while the other group—who on the average were sixteen pounds heavier than the tennis players—were sedentary.

Wood was stunned to find that the active women consumed an average of 2,417 calories a day, while those who didn't work out at all ate 1,490 calories a day, on average. Both groups of women were maintaining their weight at those intakes. Wood's shock was due to his calculations showing that the difference of 1,000 calories between the intakes of the two groups could not be entirely explained by their different activity levels. He found that the tennis players would have to play three hours and twenty minutes of tennis a *day* (that is, about twenty-three hours a week) to burn off the excess 1,000 calories a day in food energy. Since the women were playing well under half that time, there obviously had to be another explanation for the difference in calories burned per day.

There was. The discrepancy was a direct result of the "afterburner" effect of exercise. Clearly, bodies that are lean and toned—in other words, that have a higher proportion of muscle to fat than bodies that have become relatively flabby through inactivity—burn more calories *all the time*, or at least as long as they continue to exercise regularly. And if you wish to maximize this effect, you can hardly come up with a better strategy for doing it than cross-training, which spreads the muscle-building effect to more muscle groups in the body than a single-sport program using a limited range of muscles possibly could.

More Is Not Better There is one final point to keep in mind if you are embarking on a cross-training program (or modifying a current plan) in order to reduce body fat. You may think that your best strategy is to always exercise as intensely as you possibly can. Indeed, I have seen many completely out-of-shape, overly fat men and women, resolved to restore (or capture for the first time) their lean, fit shapes, put themselves through sweaty, gasping, gut-wrenching workouts under brutal conditions—to the point where they were endangering their health, even risking serious mishap. This is done, generally, in the old beliefs of "no pain, no gain" and "if a little is good, a lot is better."

Unfortunately for those tortured souls—and fortunately for those who take a more sensible, less extreme approach to exercising for fat loss—the more-is-better formula does not apply to this situation. In fact, the exact opposite is true. For optimum loss of body fat through exercise, the best strategy is continuous aerobic activity, in the lowest region of the training range (see Chapter Two) that can comfortably be sustained, using as many of the large muscle groups as possible. In other words, success comes through a consistent, reasonably paced cross-training program centered on a variety of aerobic activities.

Aerobic activities, such as running, swimming and cycling, sustained at a faster pace (one that presumably raises the heart rate higher, without taking it into the anaerobic range) provide only a *slightly* increased calorie-burning benefit. Countless tests in exercise-physiology labs have shown this as well: If you want to burn fat through activity, to get the greatest effect you really need only to get your heart beating in the low end of the training range. As long as the activity is aerobic, and the training effect is taking place in the heart, lungs, circulatory system and muscles, moving more quickly in the aerobic range won't really help you.

It may, in fact, actually hurt. Here is why: For most people, the less intense activity in the lower end of the training range has two important benefits. One, it can comfortably be sustained for longer periods of time, thus giving you a better workout. You have probably noticed this yourself: When starting a new exercise program or coming back after a layoff, you are able to complete a forty-five-minute beginner aerobic-dance class with relative ease. On the other hand, you are totally floored, gasping for breath, a mere fifteen minutes into a faster-paced, more intense session geared to people with a higher fitness level. Alternatively, you find that you can easily take a brisk thirty-minute walk, but have to stop after just a few minutes of jogging. In both cases, you are faced with two choices in the more taxing activity: You can either stop completely, or you can slow down and finish out the session.

In terms of fat loss, the second option is the clear favorite. By raising your heart rate and using your large muscles, you are still burning calories. And there is an even greater advantage in terms of losing fat: It turns out that the proportion of fat calories burned, compared to calories used from stores of carbohydrates (glycogen) is actually *higher* for activities that are carried out at lower—but still aerobic—intensities. Ultra-long-distance endurance athletes have known this for years. They realize that to train effectively, they must do long workouts at slow paces. This technique trains their bodies to fuel themselves with fat stores rather than with glycogen.

The result of sustained, relatively slow workouts for the less-serious active person is a diminishment of stored fat greater than that which would be seen in speedier, more intense workouts—sessions that, as noted, might be too taxing for many average people to complete anyway. For this reason, the advice that informed doctors, trainers and other fitness advisers give to overly fat people who consult them about dropping fat through exercise is: Take it slowly. Break a sweat, get your heart rate up, breathe harder than you would at rest and bring a glow to your cheeks. But don't thrash about, pant uncontrollably and push yourself anywhere near the point where you feel as if you are going to pass out or get sick. You won't lose fat any faster—in fact, your efforts will be much more likely to sabotage your goals.

The second reason to keep your exercise intensity within reasonable bounds for fat loss is related to the first. As you will learn in Chapter Eight (if you don't know it already), exercise-related injuries are alarmingly common among those in pursuit of fitness at all levels. And more often than not, an injury is the result of asking the body to do too much (in terms of workout volume or intensity or both) before it is ready. Injury rates are higher in more-intense activities such as high-impact aerobics, running and skipping rope than among gentler pursuits such as walking, nonimpact aerobics and leisurely cycling.

Obviously, an injury at least curtails—if it doesn't completely disallow—your participation in a sports or fitness endeavor. One of the great beauties of a cross-training program is that an injury in one area of the body need not forestall all activity, since so many other exercise options will still be available. In addition, cross-trainers are less likely to get injured in the first place, simply because they spread the burden of activity around to different muscle groups, thereby lessening the total impact on any individual part of the body. However, even cross-trainers, if one of their goals is to trim their bodies of excess fat, would do well to proceed slowly and increase their exercise load gradually to prevent injuries, and thereby to keep themselves moving in as many ways as they possibly can.

How Long Should You Go?

I want to add a final note on the optimal length of time to exercise in order to remove fat. Exercise scientists are far from completely in agreement on this question. The general prescription for aerobic exercise is that sessions should last at least twenty consecutive minutes to obtain a training effect (see Chapter Two for an explanation of this principle), although there is some recent evidence that sessions as short as twelve minutes can be effective. In terms of lowering the percentage of fat on the body, however, experts are continually emphasizing that *any* activity—no matter of what length and at what intensity—contributes to calorie and fat burning. There is some evidence that the greatest gains in loss of body fat through exercise do not begin to take place until the body has been working aerobically for at least thirty minutes, although the differences between shorter and longer workouts may be inconsequential.

Where does this leave the cross-trainer in terms of deciding how long to plan exercise sessions for optimum loss of fat? In the face of all the uncertain and sometimes even conflicting evidence, my advice would be this: In this area, you should set your fitness goals first, not your goals for fat loss. If you achieve your goal of becoming fitter, stronger and healthier through regular, varied aerobic exercise, then I believe that any reasonable goals you have for losing fat through exercise will eventually take care of themselves.

I would recommend following the advice of the American College of Sports Medicine, the renowned Institute for Aerobics Research in Dallas (founded by Dr. Kenneth Cooper, popularly known as "the father of aerobics") and other major health-related organizations to exercise aerobically for at least twenty consecutive minutes, at least three separate days a week. A formula based on these principles has launched countless millions of people on the road to fitness— and along the way, significant numbers have achieved healthy fat loss, as well.

Committing yourself to a sensible cross-training regimen based on reasonable goals of fitness and, if you deem it important, loss of some extra body fat is an essential first step toward maintaining a lasting fitness program. Another crucial part of the formula—as has been hinted throughout this book—is working out in ways that prevent, or at least reduce the risk of, exercise-related injuries. A more detailed look at this at-times-frustrating topic is the subject of the next chapter.

EIGHT

CROSS-TRAINING TO AVOID

AND OVERCOME INJURIES

I have been fortunate enough to have been injured very few times as a result of sports and fitness activities. On the occasions of each of my injuries, however, I have been able to think of extraordinarily few positive things to say on the topic of injuries.

Injuries can be a competitive athlete's worst nightmare: Cropping up at any time, they inevitably disrupt training and competitive events. They may force one to adjust the timing of goals and even to permanently lower sights one has set and worked toward diligently and with perseverance. And if they happen to come at strategically inappropriate moments—such as in an Olympic or World Championship year—injuries can be nothing short of devastating.

Naturally, any elite athlete has only a limited number of years in which to compete at the top levels. Injuries that necessitate significant changes in training and competitive plans shorten the period of time that one can perform at these highest levels. The 1991 experience of professional football and baseball player Bo Jackson, whose career came close to ending, is but one dramatic reminder of the supreme importance top athletes must place on staying as free from injuries as they possibly can.

I have heard the sentiment expressed over and over again by top-level athletes and their coaches and trainers: There is nothing more important to an athlete's

long-term career than avoiding injuries. Along with thousands of other top athletes—many who have learned the truth of this lesson the hard way—I believe it.

However, what I have found is far less well-known and much under-appreciated is the extent to which this fact applies to *all* people who exercise, at every level and for whatever reasons. As noted briefly in the previous chapter, injuries, more often than not, curtail regular physical activity. And in the worst instances, they can even completely prevent it, although these are usually injuries of the traumatic type, such as broken bones, dislocations and serious bumps and bruises. Also as discussed briefly in the previous chapter, curtailing physical activity has the immediate effect of reducing calories burned. This result, of course, can sabotage a cross-training program (or any exercise regime) that has fat loss as one of its goals.

A reduction in an exercise activity also tends in most cases to lead to a loss of various measures of fitness, unless, of course, another activity or activities are taken up to replace the one lost. Later in this chapter I will discuss the many ways in which a cross-training program can lay the groundwork for a safe, sound, sensible way in which to maintain fitness while injured. The problem, of course, is that such a strategy either doesn't occur as an option to most people, or it is difficult or impossible for them because they don't have enough experience doing other activities in place of the one that brought on their injury.

Take, for example, the case of a woman whose entire fitness program for five years has consisted of taking the same aerobic-dance class three times a week. One day she develops a stress fracture in her foot, an injury brought on by the repeated pounding of the activity in a pair of worn-out shoes she has been meaning to replace. Even with new shoes, aerobic dancing is now extremely painful, and the woman's doctor advises her to take four weeks off from dancing and other high-impact activities.

The woman does no regular exercise for the four weeks. Of course, she sorely misses the activity. She feels herself grow flabby, she becomes bored and longs for the social outlet that her classes provided. Worse, when she gets the medical okay to start back in with aerobics, she finds she has gotten so out of shape that she has to drop back to a beginner class. It is another six weeks before she can finally fully participate in the hour-long advanced class that she so loved.

Two things might have been different for this hypothetical woman if she had developed her fitness through a cross-training program. One, she probably would have performed her aerobic-dance activities less often, thereby lowering her chances of bringing on an overuse injury such as a stress fracture (see the

Credit: Cliff Grassmick.

description of this injury on page 153) in the first place. (Actually, after five years of a program based solely on high-impact aerobic dance, it's amazing that she only had this single injury.)

Two, if she still had happened to get injured, the woman would likely have had other activities to turn to. Swimming and other water exercises (such as hydroaerobics and water running), rowing, cycling and nonimpact aerobic dance are all alternatives to high-impact aerobics that still provide an aerobic workout, and yet don't stress the lower legs and feet in the same ways.

The woman could have simply turned to one or more of these activities and used them to maintain her aerobic fitness, muscle tone and desirable body-fat level, ward off boredom and even maintain social contacts (or develop new ones) while her injury healed. The continuation of the other activities would also have allowed her to return gradually and safely to aerobic dance at her previous level without risking a reinjury (which, as you will soon discover, is a frustratingly common occurrence).

How and Why Do Injuries Happen, Anyway?

If you have ever had a sports- or exercise-related injury, you may remember feeling as if the event just happened "out of the blue," when you were least expecting it. At least, that is how I have often felt. Sometimes, of course, the sudden onset of injury is a reality, as in the cases of injuries caused by trauma: A football player is brought crashing to the Astroturf in a tackle and tears a knee ligament; a tennis player steps awkwardly while straining to return a serve and breaks her ankle; an equestrienne's mount stumbles and she is thrown to the ground, sustaining a concussion and bruised ribs.

Yes, such injuries can and do happen when we least expect them. Sometimes, however, poor training, errors in judgment or excessive fatigue contribute to a traumatic injury. For example, the football player might have avoided his opponent's tackle if he had dodged in the opposite direction. A better-conditioned tennis player might not have had to stretch so hard to return a serve that she threw off her foot placement. The equestrienne might have been able to avoid falling off her mount—or at least might have tumbled in such a way as to minimize her injuries—had she not been overly exhausted from hours of practice.

Generally, however, such events are more or less unpredictable. Active people can look back after the fact and assess what they might have done differently, but many times the contributing factor to the injury will be identified as one split-second decision rather than a cumulative pattern of poorly chosen moves.

Quite the opposite is true for the other major type of injury, usually referred to as *chronic* or *overuse* injuries. As I mentioned, this type of problem also may seem to crop up "out of nowhere." I can remember telling coaches on a number of occasions, "My foot (ankle, knee, hamstring, hip, back, whatever) just started hurting while I was running the other day. I wasn't doing anything special."

That I am being honest in these cases does nothing to excuse the fact that overuse injuries generally do not "just start" one day out of nowhere while one is working out in one's sport of choice (or in some cases, during another activity). Rather, more often than not, these problems have been developing gradually over a long period. At a certain point, they manifest themselves, usually as a dull, nonspecific pain.

On several occasions, after recognizing an injury, I have thought back to the days and weeks leading up to it. I have been able to pinpoint other distinct "warning signs" of the oncoming problem, although they were often subtle, almost unnoticeable: an unusual bit of stiffness, a tendency to favor one part of the body over another, a tenderness in a certain area, especially following a hard workout or a race.

Part of being an active person—at any level, not just among the competitive elite—is constantly monitoring these warning signals. Unfortunately, they don't always appear. Or sometimes when they do, they can be too subtle to be noticed before it is too late. When they are recognized, however, they are certainly not to be taken lightly.

An elaborately detailed discussion of the many hundreds of possible sports-related injuries is beyond the scope of this book. However, I have included below a rundown of some of the more common major types of overuse injuries, and noted what sorts of activities are most likely to bring them on. As noted elsewhere in this book, virtually all of the injuries described here are less likely to occur if you follow a cross-training program designed to use all or most of the major muscle groups, thus minimizing the impact to any one particular area of the body.

I have chosen not to include trauma injuries sustained during exercise, which include complete bone breaks (as opposed to stress fractures), bruises, scrapes, cuts, dislocations, concussions and internal bleeding. Often these problems demand medical attention, or at the very least, first aid from someone qualified to administer it. However, as noted above, they are *not* generally the direct result of an inappropriate or poorly executed exercise program, so there is little I can say about preventing them, other than what is obvious: Use good judgment and be careful.

Muscle soreness: This first category is not really technically an injury—or at least it shouldn't be, if you heed it as a warning sign when it first appears. It is normal for muscles to feel sore within forty-eight hours after exercise. This soreness is caused by the breakdown of the muscle fibers, which triggers a flow of blood to the area to bring oxygen and nutrients to begin repairing the damage. This process makes the area slightly swollen and inflamed, but it is both a necessary and healthy process. It is part of the pleasant aftereffect, the "ahhhh" feeling, that most active people are familiar with upon completing a workout and for several days afterward.

Normally, this type of muscle soreness gradually diminishes over a couple of days. Unless the exercise has been particularly lengthy or intense, the soreness is all but gone by the second day after a workout, as the muscles have completed the process of self-repair, and there is no longer the need for extra blood flow to the area. (Note: This tendency of muscle soreness to diminish markedly within forty-eight hours of vigorous activity is one of the main reasons why most exercise experts recommend that all but the most committed active people, and elite competitive athletes, work out the same muscle groups no more frequently than every other day.)

As you gain experience with various sports and exercise activities, you will learn to recognize and even appreciate this "good" muscle soreness. You can use it as a way to gauge the fact that you are getting stronger. As you progress with your training program, you are likely to discover that the same workouts that used to make you tired and sore now no longer do so. This is because your muscles have adjusted to the workload. To become stronger still, you will have to increase the duration or intensity (or both) of your activities.

You should be aware, however, of other types of muscle soreness that can strongly signal an approaching or actual injury. Soreness that continues (as the result of one workout) for more than a couple of days, that gets worse over time, that hurts more at the end of an exercise session than it did when you first started out, that is accompanied by excessive redness or swelling or both, or that develops into sharp pain, is a sure sign that something is wrong. If the soreness has not already developed into an injury, it is well on the way to doing so. You may be able to forestall problems at this point simply by resting the affected area—avoiding any activity that uses the muscles—for a couple of days. But you should act quickly, for you are at an extremely vulnerable point.

Muscle pulls and muscle tears: These two types of injury can be the result of either acute (traumatic) or overuse problems. In both cases, the muscle is extended beyond its ability to stretch to meet the demands placed on it. The result is either tiny breaks in the muscle fibers that, with rest, heal themselves relatively rapidly (although a returning to peak muscle strength and elasticity may be slow), or, less fortunately, a rending of the muscle "fabric" itself. These problems generally require a long layoff followed by gradual, painstakingly careful return to form. In some cases, peak levels are never again achieved following a serious tear.

Pulls or tears caused by overuse generally happen because the muscle has become vulnerable through excess work. For example, a runner may be out on an easy training run one day and suddenly feel the muscle in the back of her thigh (the hamstring) "go out." She stops, wondering what she has done wrong. Quite likely, the problem results from nothing she did at that particular moment. Rather, the days or weeks of cumulative overstressing of that part of her body—which, like all areas, can only take so much—finally leading up to the pull or tear, is the culprit.

The most common sites of muscle pulls are whatever area is particularly stressed by a sport or fitness activity. Runners, for example, frequently suffer from pulled hamstring (back of thigh) muscles. An aerobic dancer may likely pull or (less frequently) tear a muscle in the gastrocnemius (calf). A soccer, hockey or lacrosse player, in lunging to make a play, can pull or tear a muscle of the inner thigh. For swimmers, it is often the shoulder muscles that are most vulnerable.

The most obvious warning sign of a muscle pull or tear is muscle soreness, as described above. That is one of the reasons it is so important to learn to recognize the difference between mild, healthy muscle soreness—the type that generally goes away in a few days—and the sort that signals a more serious oncoming problem. Unlike soreness, a muscle pull or tear, as noted above, almost always requires an extended layoff from (or at least a significant curtailment of) the activity that caused it.

Strains and sprains: These injuries can occur not only in muscles, but also to the connective tissues—tendons, ligaments and fascia—that hold the body together at its joints and encase many of the muscles. Like muscle pulls and tears, these problems can be brought on both by acute trauma and by chronic overuse.

The two terms really describe varying severities of the same problem. With a *strain*, the muscle or connective tissue is overworked and becomes inflamed due to the excessive, repeated stress placed upon it. A *sprain* is worse—an actual rupture (break) in the tissue. There is more likely to be swelling in addition to the inflammation, and the injury usually takes longer than a strain to heal.

Like pulls and tears, many sprains and strains can be avoided through sensible training. When the injuries do occur, the general prescription is resting the affected area, keeping it elevated, applying ice to bring down any swelling or inflammation and keeping the area compressed to control swelling and prevent the pooling of blood, which can lead to the formation of scar tissue in the area. Aspirin and other nonsteroidal anti-inflammatory medications may also be taken, although they should not be relied on for extended periods in order to continue training. How soon you will be able to return to activity using the injured part of the body depends on the severity of the injury, whether the site has ever been injured before and how quickly you respond to treatment.

Tendinitis: One of the most common overuse injuries, tendinitis covers many different types and degrees of swelling and inflammation of the tendons, the strong fibrous material connecting all the body's muscles and bones. Many tendinitis injuries occur around the joints: in the foot, ankle, knee, hip, elbow and shoulder. The cause of tendinitis is simple and straightforward: Excess stress (caused by working the area too long or too hard) causes microscopic tears in the tendon. If repeated stress prevents these tiny tears from healing, they can become inflamed, causing pain, swelling and stiffness. Obviously, this can limit movement in the area. The body may compensate by favoring the area, bringing on an injury elsewhere. If the inflamed tendon is stressed further, it may even develop a major tear. This usually requires an extended layoff period, as described above.

Again, it is excess stress—too much work performed by one particular area, rather than spreading the activity out to other parts of the body—that brings on most tendinitis injuries. In general, cases respond to rest, ice, compression and elevation (which will be described in more detail below).

Bursitis: Surrounding the bones and cartilage of the major joints of the body that are involved in exercise (the ankles, knees, hips, elbows and shoulders), are small fluid-filled sacs called *bursae* (the singular is *bursa*) that function to protect the joints. When a joint is worked excessively hard or long—for example, when a swimmer does too many laps of one stroke, or swims them too intensely without adequate rest periods—these bursae can become inflamed, causing pain and swelling.

Often, the symptoms diminish quickly—within a few days—when the activity is curtailed, only to return just as rapidly as soon as vigorous exercise is resumed. This can make bursitis frustratingly chronic. I had a case once in my right hip that popped up every few weeks (whenever I intensified my mileage to a certain point) for almost a year. While it didn't keep me from running, it did cause me on several occasions to modify my training and forgo important races. Finally, it just went away by itself, which I have been told is not uncommon.

Aspirin and other nonsteroidal anti-inflammatory medications can ease the pain of bursitis, making it possible for many people to continue to work out normally while still suffering from the underlying problem. The better solution—as you might by now surmise—is rest, accompanied by frequent icing of the area and keeping it elevated as much as possible.

Stress fractures: Sometimes overdoing it with exercise in one area can nail active people where they may imagine that they are least vulnerable: in their bones. A stress fracture is a minute break in the bone that can occur anywhere there is excess pressure. Stress fractures are most commonly the result of weight-bearing activities—those performed on land and in an upright position, so that the feet and legs are supporting the weight of the body. Common sites for stress fractures in active people include the bones of the feet, ankles, shins, thighs and pelvis. They can also occur in the arm bones—this usually in the case of racquet sports such as tennis, squash and racquetball, and with sports involving a lot of throwing and catching, such as baseball (especially pitching) and football quarterbacking.

A stress fracture usually first announces itself as a dull ache that, if ignored, may progress to a sharp, excruciating pain. The problem is not always easily diagnosed because many stress fractures do not appear on X-rays. While a more expensive bone scan usually can reveal the problem, some doctors do not bother with the procedure, preferring to save their patients the expense, and simply go ahead and treat the problem whenever there is reasonable cause for suspecting it.

Treatment for a stress fracture generally calls for complete rest of the injured area (crutches are sometimes recommended, at least for a few days, while the fractured bone begins to knit), followed by a gradual strengthening of the muscles surrounding the bone in order to protect it and prevent further problems. When properly treated, the bone may even heal to become stronger than it was before the injury.

Prevention of stress fractures is best attained by not overstressing particular parts of the body, and by keeping the muscles and joints around vulnerable areas strong and supple. It is also important to make sure you get adequate calcium in the diet to help supply the raw material for bone building.

Shin splints: This injury may feel like a stress fracture but, fortunately, is usually much less serious. It affects the muscles and connective tissue of the front of the lower leg, causing tenderness and pain that can become quite severe, especially on impact with a hard surface (as during running and high-impact aerobics). A telltale sign of the problem is feeling excruciating pain when the area around the shin bone is squeezed gently with the fingers.

Shin splints are common among people who are just beginning an exercise program that uses the lower legs or who are intensifying an existing regimen (adding speedwork or more mileage to a running schedule, for example, or taking three aerobics classes a week instead of one or two). The added strain on the shin muscles and connective tissues causes them to become inflamed—hence the tenderness and pain.

The best treatment for most cases of shin splints is to avoid high-impact activity entirely for a couple of days and ice the affected area for ten to twenty minutes, twice a day. Resume activity gradually, backing off if the pain resumes. It also helps to work out on soft surfaces, such as grass, dirt or a padded floor. Finally, make sure you are wearing the right type of shoes for your activity and replace your footwear before it wears out (see Chapter Ten, on equipment).

Most cases of shin splints go away if these precautions are taken and are much less likely to occur as the muscles and connective tissues in the lower legs gradually strengthen as a natural result of the activity. For stubborn cases, of course, it is best to consult a medical professional.

How to Get Maximum Results from Exercise Without Injury

As you can surmise from the preceding descriptions of the various possible exercise-induced injuries, the choice between sensible, injury-preventing exercise and that which puts you at increased risk of injury should not be a tough one to make. As I have noted, the cause of a large number of injuries is simply working out too long or too hard. As anyone who has ever been physically active knows, sports and exercise can become a "positive addiction." It is all too easy to push beyond one's reasonable capabilities without intending to, and to have an injury as the unfortunate result. In other cases, active people push too hard and get injured in an effort to achieve certain performance goals, such as beating a friend in a game or race; covering a certain distance on a hike, bicycle ride, rowing excursion or other adventure; or lifting a certain amount of weight.

Fortunately, cross-training can be useful in both situations—as well as others—as a way to curb the tendency toward injury. I've listed below several specific reasons why a cross-training program is the overall *best* way to keep your risk of overuse injury as low as possible—in most cases *without* compromising your fitness or performance goals.

1. *Cross-training uses different parts of the body, so no one area gets overstressed.* This is probably the single most potent factor in cross-training's capacity to reduce the risk of injury. Studies in a variety of sports show that the incidence of injuries increases substantially whenever the frequency and intensity of the activity rises over a certain modest level. For example, studies at the Institute for Aerobics Research in Dallas, under the direction of Dr. Kenneth Cooper, have shown that running injuries are significantly more common among people logging more than thirty miles a week than among those running less. Cooper himself has noted that anyone who runs more than fifteen miles a week—a level that will maintain basic fitness in most people—is performing the activity for reasons other than fitness.

Almost any athlete who takes one sport or another seriously eventually finds that there is a point of diminishing returns in the fitness benefits one can reap from engaging in just that sport. Guy Reiff, Ph.D., an esteemed exercise physiologist at the University of Michigan, has noted, "Most good athletes don't play their sport to get in shape. Rather, they get in shape to play their sport."

Trying to force the fitness benefits of a single sport beyond their reasonable limits results not in greater fitness, but rather the opposite: an increase in the risk of injury. And as you have seen, if injury results, fitness levels are likely to plummet.

There are two possible alternatives to this scenario. One, of course, is limited fitness—which, considering the number of people who pursue just one sport or activity, many people seem willing to settle for. The other option is enhanced fitness *without increased risk of injury,* through a cross-training program. The choice is yours.

2. *Cross-training balances the strengths of opposing muscle groups against each other.* Many of the large muscles used in sports and exercise work in pairs. These duos are known as *agonists* and *antagonists.* The muscle pairs are connected to each other by tendons and ligaments, so that the activity and condition of one set affects the other.

One of the best-known examples of muscle agonist-antagonist groups is the hamstrings, the large muscles that run up the back of the thigh, and the quadriceps, which are in the front of the thigh. Among the best exercises for building up the strength of the hamstrings are brisk walking and jogging. These two activities, however, do relatively little to strengthen the front-of-thigh quadriceps.

The results, over time, of weak quads and strong hamstrings are well-known to many joggers and walkers. As the hamstrings grow stronger, they gradually become larger and tighter. If the quadriceps are not correspondingly strengthened by another activity, a variety of problems can arise. Most commonly, the pull of the hamstrings will exert tension on the tendons and ligaments around the knee area. As these hard, fibrous bands of tissue are stretched over the delicate bones of the knee, the tendons can become inflamed. Alternatively, the stretched tendons and ligaments may put pressure on the knee bones themselves that can shift them into uncomfortable, even dangerous positions. The third common outcome is that the shortened, tightened hamstrings exert painful pressure on the quadriceps themselves, causing them to become painful, sore, inflamed and even torn.

In this example, the walker or jogger could greatly reduce the risk of all such problems by embarking on a cross-training program that included some sort of exercise to strengthen the quadriceps. There are many possible activities, including weight-lifting, cycling, rowing, calisthenics, water-walking or -running, hydroaerobics, and various dry-land aerobic-dance moves. As in any cross-training program, any new activity should be added gradually and, ideally, should be performed no more often than every other day.

Other common agonist-antagonist muscle pairs are the biceps and triceps of the upper arm, the gastrocnemius (calf muscle) and the anterior tibialis of the lower leg, and the pectoralis muscles of the chest and the dorsal muscles of the back. It is always recommended, for the sake of injury-risk reduction, that any activity that strengthens one set of muscles be accompanied by some type of exercise to keep the opposing group strong and supple as well.

3. *Cross-training can combine pounding exercises with those that are easier on the joints.* The sports and fitness activities that tend to cause the greatest joint stress, particularly to the lower body, are those classified as weight-bearing exercises. These include any activities performed on land (so that the joints feel the full impact of gravity on the body) in an upright position, such as walking, jogging, aerobic dance, racquet sports and land-based team sports (especially those involving running) such as football, soccer, lacrosse, field hockey and ultimate frisbee.

Most people eventually suffer from an overuse injury—commonly to the lower half of the body—if they perform such activities day in and day out. A common scenario is a soccer or tennis player who, on the days she does not engage in her sport, jogs to build and maintain aerobic fitness. Over time, she is likely to develop tendinitis in the knee, bursitis in the hip, a stress fracture in the tibia (the prominent bone in the front of the calf) or a number of other possible problems.

In order to reduce the risk of injury from pounding, anyone who engages regularly in a weight-bearing activity is well-advised to balance the exercise with some activities that are not of a weight-bearing nature. These could include swimming or other water exercises such as water-walking, water-running and hydroaerobics; cycling; rowing and canoeing.

There is something of a trade-off here, between injury-risk reduction and improvement or maintenance of cardiovascular endurance: For performing land-based activities that demand some aerobic endurance but do not necessarily do a great job of building it up themselves, running and jogging are the most efficient ways of keeping aerobic endurance at necessary levels. You may well find that you have to perform the non–weight-bearing exercises for slightly longer periods in order to get the same effect that weight-bearing ones offer. However, as long as your primary goal is fitness, rather than competitive excellence, you are almost certainly better off leaning toward a cross-training program that emphasizes injury prevention over cardiovascular excellence. Your swimming, cycling and other non–weight-bearing activities will still help you maintain decent aerobic fitness. And of course, you *can* run, jog, walk or perform other weight-bearing activities on occasion—just not to the point where they combine with the other pounding sports you do to bring on an injury.

4. *Cross-training can extend the length of a workout without your performing any single activity for too long.* Long workouts (say, more than forty-five minutes or so) can have tremendous physiological, psychological and emotional benefits. There is much to be gained in a variety of activities from working out for an hour, as opposed to completing two half-hour sessions. The problem with longer workouts, however, is that they can contribute to injuries by overstressing groups of muscles for longer periods than they are able to handle.

Long workouts are a necessary training element for anyone who is preparing to participate in long-distance endurance events such as marathon runs, "century" (hundred-mile) bicycle rides and hiking excursions. In running, the sport that I know best, it is simply not correct, in terms of preparing to run long races, to treat two ten-mile runs, even if they are performed on the same day, as the equivalent of one twenty-miler. In order to complete a race such as a marathon, your body must learn to have its heart rate up and its large-muscle groups working for periods of time approaching (some even say exceeding) that of the race. The same goes for long-distance swimming, cycling, walking and other events. You don't have to exercise as intensely (and go as fast) as you will in competition. Rather, the important thing is putting in the same exercise time that you will in the event.

You would think that the best way to prepare for long-distance events would be to "practice" by engaging solely in the activity that the event involves. Indeed, this is the strategy that most people follow—runners run, swimmers swim and so forth. Sometimes the method meets with success. However, it is also well known that training for long-distance events can produce an extraordinarily high rate of injuries. For this reason, adding other aerobic activities, to a certain extent, to long periods of endurance training can be effective.

Just how is this done? There are many ways. As one example, someone training for a marathon might take a twelve- to fifteen-mile run (which would take about two hours) and then immediately jump into the pool for forty minutes of swimming or water running. This would keep the heart elevated for the same period of time that it would be for a longer run, but without the sharply increased injury risk that comes from pushing the body to such extremes.

I know several top-of-the-field marathon runners who have trained in this way with great success, and on occasion I have used the technique myself. For example, substituting thirty minutes of stationary biking during a two-hour-and-forty-five-minute-long run (or at the end) leaves my legs feeling fresher afterward and the next day. I have found that not only does this training technique spare my legs, but it also goes a long way toward relieving the tedium of the final miles of a long-distance run. For these important reasons, I recommend it to active people training for endurance events in all areas and at all levels.

You can benefit from breaking up longer workouts into different activities even if you aren't preparing for endurance aerobic events. Such strategies can relieve boredom and rest certain muscle groups while others are being used, all the while improving aerobic capacity and burning additional fat and calories. A formalized way of doing this sort of workout has become popular at gyms and health clubs over the past few years. It is known as "interval circuit training" and involves going from one exercise station to another to perform a variety of calisthenics, weight-lifting and other exercise activities. Often, these moves are interspersed with aerobic-dance or other exercises, designed to increase variety even more and to keep heart rate elevated for an aerobic training effect.

Interval circuit training is popular because it is lively, it is rarely dull and it provides a terrific balanced workout. Classes I have participated in have been notable for the high-spiritedness of both the clients and the instructors, as well as the wonderful rush of overall energy they can provide. Moreover, if properly orchestrated and supervised, they tend to have a low injury rate—even though they may be billed as "advanced" level and can last for an hour or longer.

You don't have to take a health-club class, however, in order to reap the benefits of interval-training–type workouts. Rather, you can engage in short periods of cycling, rowing, walking, jogging, stair-climbing and other activities at any gym or health club (provided the machines are free when you want them—which is not always a realistic assumption), or you can do the activities outdoors, as your specific situation allows. Just be careful to ease gradually into each activity as you begin it to reduce the risk of injury (especially muscle pulls or tears), and to not get so carried away that you exercise longer than is good for you from an aerobic-endurance standpoint.

5. *Cross-training can allow a temporary layoff from (or a reduction of) one activity that seems about to bring on an injury.* As noted earlier, many people are reluctant to discontinue an exercise activity when they sense an injury coming on (or sometimes, even after it has occurred), because they don't want to give up physical activity. However, this is unlikely to be a serious problem when cross-training: If one activity is causing soreness or pain, most cross-trainers can easily switch to another exercise. For example, imagine that someone who plays squash, cycles, lifts weights and jogs for fitness develops shoulder pain after a particularly vigorous game. That person can simply cancel his squash sessions for a week (or until the injury heals), while continuing with the other three activities—most likely eliminating or at least going easy on any weight-lifting exercises that stress the muscles he hurt playing squash. He needn't give up his fitness, nor the social and emotional outlets the other exercises afford. Another benefit is that when he does return to squash, he is unlikely to feel out of shape, disoriented or slow on his feet, because he has stayed fit in other ways.

What to Do if You Do Get Injured

All right, suppose you carefully follow your cross-training program, back off from abnormally sore muscles and other warning signs when necessary, take days off from exercise as needed, and you *still* get injured. Then what? It can happen to the best of us. After all, in addition to chronic problems brought on by overuse, don't forget that acute (traumatic) injuries really can swoop down and strike us when we least expect them.

The following steps, recommended by sports medicine professionals, outline the responses you should take to immediately deal with an injury and bring yourself safely back from the problem to your peak fitness form.

1. *Administer first aid as needed.* In the case of some traumatic injuries, you may need to stanch bleeding, keep the injured person covered to prevent shock,

and even monitor breathing and vital signs. Obviously, summon medical assistance if it is needed. Elevate and protect the injured area as much as possible.

2. *Rest the injured area*. This applies to both acute and chronic injuries, as well as potentially injured areas (usually signaled by soreness). In many cases of muscle soreness, a day or two of avoiding activity involving the muscles in the affected area—or sometimes, even just lowering the exercise's intensity—will allow the soreness and minor inflammation to heal. In other cases, rest may involve a period of weeks or even months.

As discussed above, resting one group of muscles does not necessarily mean taking a complete layoff from physical activity. In fact, following such a course of action, in addition to making you bored, cranky and out of shape, can actually be detrimental to rapid, complete recovery from injury. You can avoid all of these situations if you are cross-training. As noted above, you should simply adjust your exercise program during the period of recovery from your injury to at first eliminate any activities that stress the affected area. Then you can gradually add those exercises back, in small, measured doses, all the while continuing at normal levels with any activities that don't stress the muscles that are recovering.

I have known many runners who started cross-training for the first time because of injuries that forced them to temporarily give up or cut back on running. Grumpy, discouraged, all but kicking and screaming, they grudgingly slipped into the pool, hopped on an exercise bike, sat down on the rowing machine or learned to maneuver on an indoor cross-country skier. Much to their surprise, many of them found that not only did the activity help them maintain their fitness, but they actually felt *stronger* when they recovered and headed back out onto the roads. Moreover, they even *enjoyed* the variety that the addition of the new activities afforded. Those who decided to stick with their newfound sports said they remained stronger and fresher—and were permanently committed to the concept of multisport training to keep injuries at bay in the future.

3. *Apply ice if there is swelling or inflammation around the affected area*. Many people are unsure about whether to treat their injuries with heat or cold. Initially, cold treatment is almost always the preferred option because cold inhibits blood flow in and around an injured area, which has the immediate effect of reducing any swelling and inflammation. Then, after the injury site is iced for ten to twenty minutes, fresh, new blood flows in. This influx brings oxygen and nutrients and flushes away "old" blood and chemicals generated by the injury.

For most cases involving soreness, strain, sprain, swelling or inflammation, periodic applications of ice to the area for ten to twenty minutes at a time for the first forty-eight hours after an injury will help keep pain at bay and hasten recovery. If, after two days of this treatment, you find that pain, inflammation (signaled by redness), soreness and swelling are not noticeably diminished, you should see a medical professional if you have not already done so. You might well be suffering from a more serious problem, such as a muscle tear or a fractured bone, for which icing is of limited value.

Even if this is not the case, you may at this point benefit more from applications of heat than of cold. Heat draws blood to the injury and helps the muscle and connective tissue relax. These conditions can be helpful in treating tightness, muscle pulls (that are not accompanied by inflammation) and other problems. However, before you start using heat applications to treat any injury, your best bet is to consult a medical professional.

4. *Treat the injury with compression to reduce swelling.* Wrapping an injured area in a bandage restricts the flow of blood to the injury site. This helps keep too much blood from flooding the area of injury—which causes an increase in the swelling and inflammation—and directs blood flow from the injury back toward the heart, where the blood can receive fresh oxygen.

Usually a soft, wide, elastic device such as an Ace bandage is the best way to compress the area surrounding an injury. It is important not to compress the site so tightly that the flow of blood is cut off. This will usually be signaled by pain, restricted movement and discoloration of the area; if any of these symptoms occur, you should loosen the bandage slightly and continue to monitor the area to make sure enough blood is being allowed in.

It's also a good idea to consult a medical professional about the length of time you should continue to apply compression to an injured area. Many experts recommend removing the compression for short periods every now and then, but whether this is the best strategy for you depends on the nature and extent of your injury.

5. *Elevate the injured area as much as possible.* Along with the three previous suggestions, elevating an injury site is an example of a strategy that almost can't go wrong, no matter what sort of injury you are treating. Keeping the injured part of your body above the level of the heart as much as you can allows old, oxygen-poor blood to drain away from the area so that blood supplemented with oxygen from the heart can then flow back in greater amounts.

The conditions of your daily life may make elevating an injury a challenge, especially in cases of injury to the lower body. There are a couple of strategies that can help. If the injury is to your foot or lower leg, try keeping a small stool with you on which you can prop up the leg for extended periods. You will find that this really makes a difference in reducing pain, soreness and swelling. Indeed, I do this as much as I can, especially any time my legs feel tired, heavy or sore from long runs or hard speed workouts. Wherever I am, I try to keep my feet up on a chair, stool, table or desk. If I need to ask permission or give anyone an explanation for what I am doing, people tend to be understanding—especially when I suggest that they do the same thing to give their tired legs and feet a break! After working at my desk for hours with my legs elevated, I'm much better able to lace on my shoes and head out for a run than if I have had to keep my feet neatly and properly on the floor.

You might notice that the first letters of the key words of the four preceding suggestions, when strung together, form the word R-I-C-E (rest, ice, compression, elevation). This acronym is easy to remember and can help you keep in mind the four simple, widely applicable ways of treating injuries without medical intervention. While I must emphasize that if you have any questions or concerns about an injury, you should always seek the advice of a medical professional, I also think it is important to note that a simple strategy of R-I-C-E has perhaps forestalled more complications of sports- and fitness-related injuries than all the advice doctors and other professionals have ever given. I do not mention this to knock the experts, just to point out that some of the simplest, most effective ways of treating injuries can be surprisingly close at hand.

As noted, all of these recovery strategies involve a period of waiting before you are able to fully resume the activity that caused the injury and any others that might aggravate it. If you are cross-training, you undoubtedly will want to continue working out in your other activities. You may, however, be uncertain about which exercises are safe and which may cause problems. The guidelines below—on injury treatment from the ground up—should help answer your questions. The information is culled from various resource books, articles, interviews, advice from professional organizations (such as the American College of Sports Medicine) and personal anecdotes from active people at all levels. Of course, questions on any injury you develop should be answered by a medical professional. Consult an expert as well for injuries and problems not covered here, or if you have any other questions.

Guidelines for Alternative Activities for Various Injuries

1. *Foot problems* (cuts, soreness, swelling, bruises, tendinitis, bursitis, faciitis, strains, minor sprains): First make sure your foot isn't broken or badly sprained; if you have any doubts, seek medical attention. Foot injuries will likely impede your ability to walk, jog, run, dance and play sports that keep you upright and on the move, such as racquet games, football, soccer, field hockey and lacrosse. Taping the injury may allow participation in important competitive events but should not be relied on as a long-term solution.

In most cases, you can continue to engage in water-based activities, especially those in which you are not in contact with the bottom of the pool (such as swimming, deep-water running and hydroaerobics); cycling (if the ankle is not hurt); weight-lifting that doesn't aggravate the foot; and rowing. As you recover, you may be able to start back with nonpounding, upright activities such as walking and nonimpact aerobics before gradually easing back into higher-impact exercise.

2. *Ankle injuries* (twists, strains, sprains, breaks, tendinitis and bursitis): While minor ankle twists and strains may require no layoff whatsoever, most problems are serious enough to benefit from at least a day or two away from the activity that caused the problem and others that may aggravate it. If redness, pain or swelling are intense or last more than a couple of days, you should probably have the injury evaluated by a medical professional and follow his or her advice. Of course, a known or suspected bone break should receive immediate medical attention.

There are many activities that you can safely engage in while waiting for an ankle injury to heal. Be careful, however, since the ankle's muscles, bones and connective tissue are involved in a wide variety of sports and exercise movements—not just the obvious pounding activities. You can keep your upper body in shape with weight-lifting, an upper-body ergometer and activities that don't depend on a lot of movement of your feet, such as table tennis. Many types of injuries will allow you to swim; walk, run or do aerobics in the water; row; bicycle; and cross-country ski.

Be aware, however, that while these activities relieve the pounding that can bring on ankle pain, they all still involve flexing the ankle joint. Proceed cautiously (and avoid these pursuits entirely if a medical adviser recommends it), backing off from any activity that brings on a renewal of pain, swelling or inflammation. Sit down as often as possible, and consider crutches as a way of relieving stress to the ankle during times that you must remain upright.

3. *Injuries to the Achilles tendon and calf:* Remember the ancient Greek myth of Achilles? As a baby, this famous warrior was dipped in the river Styx by his mother so that he would be protected against his enemies. However, by holding her son by the back of his heel, Mom left this part of him vulnerable, and Achilles was finally felled by a poison arrow through his heel.

The Achilles tendon, stretching from the heel up to the large gastrocnemius muscle in the back of the calf, is the strongest tendon in the body. However, Achilles problems can be the downfall of walkers, runners, aerobic dancers, skiers, climbers and others whose activities flex and pound the ankle and stretch the calf. Repeated stress, often combined with lack of flexibility in the lower leg, can bring on tiny tears, which become inflamed. Larger tears can become chronic, and are among the most stubborn sports-related injuries.

Achilles problems often respond to R-I-C-E treatment, as well as wearing lifts in the heel of both sports and street shoes. You can keep fit while the injury is healing with most activities that don't involve pounding to the lower leg. Water-based exercises, weight-lifting, nonupright calisthenics and stretching are all good choices. Some people are able to cycle, row and cross-country ski, although you should check with a medical professional about the suitability of these activities for your injury, and proceed cautiously.

Strains, pulls and tears to the muscles in the back of the calf (the gastrocnemius group) tend to respond to the same sorts of treatment as Achilles problems, and allow for the same type of alternative activities while the injury is healing. Severe pulls and tears should always be evaluated by a medical professional.

4. *Shin mishaps:* Pain in the shin (front of the calf) is frustratingly common among people starting with a program of any high-impact activity. I know of almost no runners who have never had a case of shin splints, either when they first took up the sport or during a time of trying to increase the volume or intensity of their training. The problem frequently is caused by inflammation of the two muscles running down the front of the lower leg, the *anterior tibialis*, on the outside, and the deeper *posterior tibialis*. Injuries can also occur in the *tibia* (the large, prominent shin bone), which is prone to stress fractures; the tendons attached to the tibialis muscles; and the *periosteum*, a thin membrane that covers the tibia. Some people also develop *compartment syndrome*, which is caused by sudden swelling of the tibialis muscles, putting pressure on the tight sheath of fascia around it (called the muscle compartment). This pinching can harm the blood vessels and nerves in the muscles. Symptoms are pain, becoming severe during exercise, and tingling down the leg and into the foot. Medical

attention as soon as possible is important in treating compartment syndrome, and the condition can have permanent consequences if not treated.

Shin problems generally demand at least a short layoff from any pounding activities, and usually respond readily to R-I-C-E treatment. During your rest period, you will probably be able to continue with nonimpact activities such as swimming, walking, rowing, cycling and possibly nonimpact aerobics.

5. *Knee injuries:* There is such variety here that it is hard to summarize the effects of various knee problems and what can and cannot be done while your injury heals. In general, activities that pound the leg are not a good idea during recovery. These include jogging (a notorious knee-injury triggerer) and any sports that involve jogging or running, aerobic dance and vigorous ballet. Contact sports such as football and rugby also have a high traumatic-injury rate. Other problems are aggravated by hiking, climbing, cycling, rowing and skiing. However, these activities can be good alternatives during recovery from some types of knee problems; talk to a medical expert about what is best for you. In addition, swimming and other water activities are almost always a safe bet because of their nonimpact nature.

6. *Quadricep and hamstring problems:* In many cases here, changing the way in which an activity is done can allow healing of minor problems and a reduction in the risk of their cropping up in the future. For example, quadricep pains are often the result of walking or running downhill or performing high-impact aerobics that overstress these front-of-thigh muscles. Often, avoiding downhills on your walks or runs or changing your dance routine for a few days eliminates the soreness. For more serious problems, lay off the offending activity and seek medical attention if necessary (as for muscle pulls or tears). In the meantime, you can usually swim, cross-country ski and possibly engage in moderate sessions of nonimpact aerobic dance. You should avoid cycling, rowing and any calisthenics or team sports that rely heavily on the quadriceps muscles.

Hamstring problems are often caused by walking or running uphill; cycling; straining the muscles in racquet sports, team sports or climbing; and occasionally rowing or cross-country skiing. Activities that don't use the hamstrings at all are hard to find; water running, water aerobics and swimming are generally good choices because they distribute much of the muscle stress to the quadriceps. Cycling and in-line skating (Roller-Blading) may also be good choices while recovering from some injuries.

7. *Hip injuries:* Unfortunately, doing just about any activity too long or too intensely may eventually bring on tendinitis, bursitis or a stress fracture in the hip. The pounding of running causes these problems to flare up for me every so

often, and I find that cross-training on an exercise bicycle, walking or swimming for a week, while continuing to run easily on soft surfaces and avoid racing, keeps the injury from becoming major. If the problem is a stress fracture, *any* impact activity is generally out; this leaves water sports, cycling, rowing, walking and cross-country skiing. These activities are generally good alternatives for inflammation problems as well, although if you continue to feel pain, you may have to curtail them more than you would like for a period.

8. *Back problems:* As with problems in the knees, back injuries cover such a wide range that giving general advice about which activities are appropriate during recovery from injury and which are not is impossible. In many cases, exercises other than those that caused a back problem may also aggravate it. For example, the jolting of running and high-impact aerobic dance may aggravate such problems as a herniated disc or muscle spasm.

In general, when the back is injured non–weight-bearing activities such as swimming are better than those performed upright on land. In addition, weight-lifting and calisthenics may strengthen muscles whose weakness contributed to the back injury. You should, however, consult a medical professional about any problem concerning the back. Self-diagnosis and self-treatment often do more harm than good, and the consequences may be serious.

9. *Shoulder problems:* If injuries to the shoulder are brought on by overuse rather than trauma, sports that emphasize the upper body are usually to blame. These include swimming; weight-lifting; throwing sports such as basketball, football quarterbacking and baseball and softball pitching; and racquet sports.

During recovery from the injury, just about any activity that does not rely heavily on the muscles in the arms and shoulders is usually appropriate. Walking, jogging, cycling, lower-body weight-lifting, hydroaerobics or water-running without arm movements and swimming with a kickboard are all good choices. As the injury heals, the shoulder muscles can gradually be brought back to form with calisthenics, weight-lifting and other strength-building exercises designed to involve the injured area a little at a time.

10. *Injuries to the arm and hand:* Like shoulder injuries, arm and hand problems generally necessitate a layoff from activities that involve primarily the upper body. Unless the injury is severe (such as a bone break), there is rarely a need to stop walking, jogging, cycling and playing all-leg sports such as soccer. Other effective alternative activities include swimming with a kickboard, using a cross-country ski machine without moving the arms, water running, water aerobics without arm movements, and possibly rowing, depending on the nature and extent of the injury.

. . .

So keep moving! The dozens of alternatives offered on the previous pages leave you with no excuse not to.

Tips for Avoiding Injuries in the Future

Once you have been through an injury, you probably have no wish to contend with another. The following tips summarize the best ways I know to stay injury-free throughout your days of sports and exercise activity.

1. Learn to recognize the warning signs that an injury is coming on: Pain, soreness, inflammation (redness) and swelling specific to an area of the body.

2. Back off for a day or two from any activities that aggravate any of the above symptoms.

3. Treat minor problems with rest, ice, compression and elevation of the affected area. This strategy (abbreviated R-I-C-E) can go a long way toward making sure that a small injury is no more than an annoying interruption rather than growing into a devastating curtailment of your activities.

4. Keep muscle imbalances from contributing to injuries by making sure your cross-training program exercises agonist-antagonist muscle groups.

5. Don't stop working out when you are injured. Find alternative activities. This will not only keep your body strong and fit, but also allow you to ease back gradually into the activity that caused the problem in a way that doesn't overstress the injured area yet again.

6. Remember to warm up, stretch and cool down properly when engaging in *any* exercise—whether you are prone to injury from that pursuit or not.

7. Be diligent and committed to the cross-training concept. Don't get "lazy" about keeping your program varied and properly balanced. Cross-training is a proven way of reducing injury risk in a wide variety of activities and at all levels. But you have to stick with it to make it work.

NINE

TRAINING FOR

MULTISPORT EVENTS

The rise in the popularity of cross-training in this country over the past two decades can be tied to the booming interest in multisport events. And one race in particular stands out for the hold it has over the attention of the American public: the Ironman Triathlon.

The Ironman, as it's known, is an appropriately named competition. Its almost superhuman proportions have captured the imagination: Entrants begin with a 2.4-mile swim, then they cycle for 112 miles, and on top of *that* they run a 26.2-mile marathon! The original and best-known Ironman, still held annually in Kailua-Kona, Hawaii (on the volcanic "Big Island"), was put on for the first time in 1978. Only fifteen competitors—all of them men—entered the race, which was referred to by some as a "gruelathlon."

The Ironman's popularity grew quickly, however—perhaps people were simply fascinated by the sheer magnitude of the distances and the toll they could take on the human body and soul. Today, thousands of men and women compete each year in Ironman (or should I perhaps say Ironperson?) events at various locales around the globe. The original Ironman (now called the Gatorade Ironman) has become so prestigious that it must turn away thousands of would-be entrants each year. In 1991, 1,400 triathletes competed, while close to 3,000

were denied entry to limit the size of the field. Those competing hailed from forty-nine states plus fifty foreign countries.

In this chapter, in addition to being introduced to triathlons of various distances, you will learn about a number of other multisport competitions designed to test the skill, fitness, mettle, competitive drive and fun-loving spirit of cross-trainers of every ilk. Of course, nowhere is it written that you ever have to toe the starting line of a race or enter any athletic competition to enjoy and fully benefit from cross-training. In fact, many—if not most—cross-trainers rarely or never test themselves in any formal way against others. However, the opportunities to do so are there in profusion. This chapter provides an overview of the many different ways in which you can cross-train to compete in races and other competitions—at whatever level you choose. Some of the events you will no doubt be familiar with; others will certainly surprise you quite a bit.

The Triathlon: Swim, Bike and Run

No one knows the exact time and place of the very first formal swim-bike-run triathlon, but it wouldn't be surprising if it occurred somewhere in the state of California. Certainly, by the mid-1970s, triathlons and their cousin races, bike-and-run duathlons (see page 177), were being held at least sporadically in the San Diego area. Southern California is considered the triathlon's birthplace and—thanks to its year-round warm climate, its laid-back atmosphere and the migration there of some of the best athletes in the sport—continues to serve as a home base for hundreds of serious triathletes, as well as thousands of not-quite-as-committed and talented folks who enjoy training in the atmosphere there.

After the first Hawaiian Ironman in 1978 (see below), the sport saw a fairly steady growth in popularity. The Triathlon Federation/USA (commonly known as Tri-Fed), the governing and sanctioning body for triathlons and duathlons in the United States, was founded in 1982 (as the United States Triathlon Association; the name was changed in 1983). *Triathlete* magazine was started up a year later (see the Appendix for contact information for this and other cross-training publications).

In 1982, roughly 10,000 people a year were competing in triathlons (although many at shorter distances, not always at the grueling Ironman). By 1985, that number had increased to 120,000, and by last year, it was estimated at a whopping 250,000 to 300,000, according to Tri-Fed.

The vast majority of triathletes entering races today do not train to complete the daunting Ironman distance. The miles in the water and on the roads are simply too great, and the time and energy demands are too heavy to allow most people to live a productive life (hold a job, meet family responsibilities, have a social life and fulfill community obligations) outside of them.

As a result, much more sensible and popular triathlon races have sprung up. "Olympic"-distance and "mini" triathlons field thousands more competitors each year than races at the Ironman distance. The first term refers to a standardized race involving a 1,500-meter (just under a mile) swim, a 40-kilometer (about 25-mile) bike ride, and a 10-kilometer (6.2-mile) run; these distances have been set by Tri-Fed, and were reduced from somewhat longer standards.

Mini triathlons are generally somewhat shorter, although their distances are not set by Tri-Fed and can really be any combination of distances the race organizers feel are best for the athletes they are trying to attract. For example, the Danskin Women's Triathlon Series, organized in 1989 and still one of the few all-women triathlons in the country, consists of an 800-meter (roughly 0.5 mile) swim, a 20-kilometer (12.4-mile) cycling segment, and a 5-kilometer (3.1-mile) running portion.

The swim section of a triathlon can be held in a pool, pond, lake, river or the open ocean. The biking and running can take place on city or town streets, along country roads, dirt trails—anywhere adventurous race directors and athletes can come up with to take their bicycles and their running shoes. The order of the events is perhaps the only thing that almost never varies: swim, then bike, then run.

Suppose you have seen, read or heard about a triathlon and think you might want to train for and enter one. How might you start preparing for the event? Of course, the answer depends on many factors—how fit you are now, what other sports and fitness activities you currently engage in, what distance triathlon you'd be interested in entering, your lifestyle, and where, when and how often you are able to participate in the three sports that make up the event. These variations aside, there are, however, a few pieces of universal advice.

1. *Take it easy the first time.* This is the first pearl of wisdom that most experts hand down to first-timers, and it applies to virtually any amateur sporting competition. Unless you have already competed at a very high level in one or more of the individual sports of the triathlon, or have an extremely high level of aerobic fitness from another activity, do *not* attempt an all-out effort in your first triathlon. Rather, plan to complete the distance at a relaxed pace, or one that is only slightly uncomfortable. Approach the experience in the spirit of enjoyment and adventure. In fact, you might want to consider this strategy even if you are

an elite competitor in running, swimming or biking (or have been in the past) and are entering your first triathlon.

There are several good reasons for taking this relaxed approach. The main one is that the triathlon has several unique aspects that other sports just don't prepare you for. In the first place, you are performing three different activities one right after the other. I have been told that the transition from biking to running in particular evokes sensations in the leg muscles wholly unfamiliar to the just-runner or just-biker. The phrase that people use most often to describe it in polite terms is "rubber legs." However, they immediately go on to explain that the feeling is much worse than that. The sudden shift of the muscles' efforts from primarily the quadriceps (in the front of the thigh) to the back-of-thigh hamstrings makes it virtually *impossible* to run all-out; you simply *must* ease into the new activity. Mark Allen, the 1989 Hawaii Ironman Triathlon champion, told a writer from *City Sports* magazine before the 1990 event that "running off the bike may be an area where there is no plateau." In other words, there is always room for *anyone* to improve.

The earlier swim-to-bike transition is apparently somewhat less excruciating to the muscles. However, the temperature change from cold water to warm air can be a challenge for many competitors. During the running segment things can heat up even more, especially in triathlons that start in the morning, which generally means that by the time the running portion comes along the sun is high in the sky. For this and other reasons, it is absolutely crucial to drink fluids throughout the triathlon, even if you don't feel thirsty, to protect your head, and to take other steps to avoid overheating and dehydration (see Chapter Six, on food and nutrition, and Chapter Eight, on injuries).

Another aspect of triathlons that is unique to the sport, as far as I know (and another reason to take it easy your first time), is the mass swim start. If you think it's hard to dive into a pool at 6:00 A.M. by yourself—or with a few other bleary-eyed diehard fellow lap-swimmers—just wait until you try plunging into a body of water in the early hours of the morning (some triathlons, such as the Ironman, start at dawn) with hundreds of other nervous, overeager, splashing, thrashing competitors at the start of a race. Again, while I cannot speak from the experience of actually having done this, from everything I have heard, this is a mild description of the start of a triathlon.

Again, the advice to beginners and novices I hear and read over and over again is: Take it easy. Don't go for position, or you'll risk being splashed, kicked, and stroked into a near-drowning state by those around you (unintentionally, of course) before you've traveled even one hundred yards. It is much better to take it easy at the start, hanging toward the back of the pack. Once you find your rhythm, you can then pass people and get a second wind after the crush thins out. Or better yet, wait until later when you're on dry land to really "cruise." The point is, don't use every ounce of energy just to keep your head above water in the first five minutes of the race.

2. *Learn how to make transitions.* Another very important distinguishing feature of the triathlon (and other multisport events) is the transition—actually two of them—the switches from swimming to biking, and then from biking to running. You will be urged over and over again by experienced triathletes to practice the actual mechanics of getting out of the water, toweling dry, slipping on your cycling socks, shoes, shorts and helmet and jumping aboard your bike to start pedaling. It is also important, the veterans say, to practice getting *off* the bike, trading cycling for running shoes and shorts (in Chapter Ten, on equipment, you'll learn why all these various pieces of gear are so important to performance in and enjoyment of each individual sport) and hitting the road on foot.

The top competitive triathletes whiz through these transitions in a matter of seconds; most of the rest of the crowd takes at least a couple of minutes at each one. It's a good idea—and perfectly within the rules—to have someone stationed with your gear to lend a hand, and to give you a welcome pep talk.

The same experienced souls who tell you to practice transitions until you feel you can do them in your sleep will also inform you loftily that no matter how prepared you feel, unexpected things can and do happen during the actual race, especially in the transitions. The biggest complicating factor, of course, is that hundreds of other people around you are trying to do the same thing at the same time. You have to be ultraorganized, clear-headed and efficient for everything to go off without a hitch—which everyone will assure you very rarely does. Even the top pros can tell horror stories of losing precious minutes during unforeseen delays.

3. *Don't try the Ironman without doing a shorter race first.* If you have never trained for or competed in a triathlon, it is strongly recommended that you start with one of the mini or Olympic events, rather than at the daunting Ironman distance. The Olympic race is designed to be completed by most moderately fit competitors in roughly two hours; shorter events such as the Danskin women's race take between an hour and an hour and a half for most reasonably fit people. On the other hand, only the top ten or so competitors in the Ironman triathlon are capable of finishing the Hawaii race in under *nine* hours; the majority of entrants take eleven or twelve hours, and some much longer. In addition, some Ironman races may be conducted under extreme weather conditions and in

remote locales. They really are for those "truly committed" to the sport. By starting with more manageable distances, you can get used to the idea of the race without having to exhaust yourself with super-punishing, time-consuming training regimens. Later, if you choose, the Ironman will always be there, inspiring you to move up to a new and exalted level.

4. *Be sensible, but don't be put off by what looks like a huge amount of training.* Preparing for a triathlon, according to those who have made the switch to the event from one of its individual sports, is easier than training to compete in one of those component activities. This may not at first seem obvious when you look at an eight-, twelve- or sixteen-week training schedule for a triathlon, and it is true that training for the event—even at recreational levels—requires a time commitment of at least four or five workouts a week. The volume may be hard to work up to mentally, but the hours and miles are easier on the body than spending the same amount of time training for an individual sport.

The reason for this should be obvious by now: Even though all three of the triathlon's sports are aerobic, each uses very different muscles from the others. Thus, the total training "package" distributes the wear and tear of the activity over the whole body, rather than concentrating it on a few overburdened muscles, bones and joints.

For example, I know several triathletes who have successfully completed a number of events at the international distance, and yet have never been able to make it to the starting line of a marathon, much less finish the 26.2-mile race. Rather, all the hours and miles of just running made them succumb to one injury or another, forcing them to "pull the plug" weeks before race day.

So, all that said, are you ready to get started training for a triathlon? If so, keep reading.

The schedules on the following pages are recommended by the Triathlon Federation/USA (Tri-Fed) for people training for their first triathlon. They are designed to help you train for either a mini triathlon or an international event in either twelve or sixteen weeks. The biggest determinant in setting your current goal should be your current fitness level. If you are starting from being completely sedentary, you should gradually build up to the level of the first week of the program over a period of several months. You should not attempt to train for an Ironman triathlon until you have completed a number of races at shorter distances.

For your swimming training, for example, you can start by swimming one or two lengths of a twenty-five-yard pool at a time, resting for a minute, then swimming another length or two, until you have been in the water, either swimming or resting, for twenty minutes. The amount of time spent swimming should be gradually increased over a period of six to eight weeks, until you can swim at a moderate pace for twenty consecutive minutes.

Bikers should alternate a minute or two of pedaling in their training range with a minute of pedaling more slowly, again for a total of twenty minutes the first few times. Then they should gradually extend the length of the pedaling-in-the-training-range segments until they can bike for twenty to thirty minutes at a time without a break. At this point they can add more strenuous speed sessions if they wish.

For the running regimen, the strategy with the least risk of injury or burnout involves starting out with one minute of jogging, then one minute of brisk walking, again for a total of twenty minutes. Do this three to five times a week, and again increase the length of time of the jogging sections gradually over a period of eight to ten weeks.

As always when starting any new activity, remember to listen to your body, backing off in time, distance or intensity if you feel overly tired or experience any pain beyond moderate muscle soreness, which is normal. By never upping the total distance that you cover with a particular activity more than 10 percent a week (for example, from nine to ten minutes of running), you should keep your risk of injury very low. Always remember to warm up and stretch the muscles to be used before starting your workout, and to cool down and stretch thoroughly to prevent soreness afterward.

Once you've gotten to the week-one level of the schedule you plan to follow, use the chart on page 177 as a guideline for preparing yourself, healthily and sensibly, for race day. You don't need to follow the schedule to the letter; no two people are the same, and you may find yourself more comfortable with a program slightly more or less ambitious than the one outlined. Many people, however, feel most comfortable and confident psychologically if they know they have done everything according to plan. Don't feel hemmed in, though, just heed the warning signs of injury and overtraining (see Chapter Eight for more details) and use your own common sense.

Notice that the schedules in the chart don't assign sports to certain days. This is because your overall aerobic conditioning is what counts most in preparing for your first triathlon. You may also switch the order of the days to suit your schedule; however, try to take at least one day off a week. You should also divide the total number of minutes you spend on the three activities roughly evenly among them. Notice also that one day you do two different activities. This may feel strange at first, but people don't find it hard to get used to.

The Triathlon Federation Training Program for Beginner and Recreational Triathletes

(Times in minutes)

Week	Mon.	Tues.	Wed.	Thurs.	Fri.	Sat.	Sun.	Total
1	Off	40, 35	45	Off	45	65	69	299
2	Off	40, 40	50	Off	45	70	65	310
3	Off	45, 40	55	Off	50	75	70	335
4	Off	45, 45	50	Off	55	75	65	335
5	Off	50, 45	55	Off	65	75	60	350
6	Off	40	30	Off	25	35	25	155
7	Off	30	40	Off	35	45	55	205
8	Off	55, 50	70	Off	65	80	70	390
9	Off	55, 50	60	Off	65	90	75	395
10	Off	65, 60	75	Off	75	90	100*	465
11	Off	45, 45	50	Off	55	45	150*	390
12	Off	45	Off	60	Off	70	45	220
13	Off	20	20	20	20	RACE		

*These two workouts should be combined bike/run or walk, so you can get some experience changing your clothing and doing two sports consecutively.
Source: Triathlon Federation / U.S.A.

As you learned in Chapter Eight (on injuries) one of the secrets of staying healthy while working out physically is alternating times of work with times of rest. You simply cannot "go hard" all the time without eventually breaking down—physically, mentally or both.

The Duathlon: Two for the Road

You may know this event better by its pre-1991 name, biathlon, a term that has been extremely confusing to the sports world over the past couple of decades. This is because the biathlon has long been a winter Olympic cross-country-skiing-and-shooting event that enjoys a small but loyal following in this country and much greater popularity in Canada and Europe, particularly in Scandinavia.

The other event formerly known as a biathlon—and now known as a du-athlon—is a completely aerobic multisport competition in which athletes sand-wich a biking segment between two stints of running. Some people think of it as a triathlon without the water.

At the moment, duathlons have no governing body in the United States; the organization and regulation of the events is under the supervision of the Triathlon Federation/USA (Tri-Fed). To add to the orphaned nature of the event, much of the sports world continues to refer—incorrectly—to the run-bike-run event by its old "biathlon" tag. In fact, misusing the term will probably not embarrass you around most participants in the sport—but just watch what you say if you ever find yourself around a bunch of ski-and-shooters at the winter Olympics.

How did the duathlon—this spinoff, long-misnamed event that hardly existed a dozen years ago—come to be? The key to answering that question lies in appreciating the complaints of many of those who have tried and abandoned the triathlon because they found the swimming segment just too inconvenient to train for and too tough to compete in. After all, running and cycling are events that many people can participate in just by stepping out their front door. Beyond the purchase of a bike (or indoor trainer, or both), exercise clothing and running shoes, not much equipment is needed. Much of the training can be done out-doors, during different seasons, in a variety of types of weather. This is even more true for running than for biking; wet, icy or snow-covered roads and severe cold are often an inconvenience or a hazard for the cyclist, whereas runners can and do head out into just about any sort of precipitation or temperature extreme. And on the worst days, there are always indoor treadmills and stationary cycling machines at health clubs, gyms, Y's or in the home.

Swimming, however, can be another story entirely. In most parts of the country it is a six-month-a-year outdoor sport at best. Indoor pools are of course available in virtually any community nationwide—they are in health clubs, Y's, civic and community centers, schools and even private homes. However, time in the water can be precious, and it may not always be convenient to take the plunge during a facility's hours of operation. There are also the complicating factors of getting to the pool, changing, sharing space with other swimmers, showering and getting back to work or home again.

It should be pointed out that despite these obstacles, swimming is still one of the most popular activities in the country; more than 67 million people participated in the activity in 1990, according to the National Sporting Goods Association (NSGA), putting swimming second behind exercise walking (with 71.4 million participants) among the most popular sports and fitness activities in the country.

Don't forget, however, that the number of swimmers includes *anyone* who took even one dip in a pool, pond, lake, river or ocean. The number of people regularly performing aerobic activities in the water—training in a manner ad-

One of the best-known converts to cross-training is 1972 Olympic marathon gold medalist Frank Shorter (left), now a competitive duathlete based in Boulder, Colorado. Credit: Cliff Grassmick.

equate to prepare themselves to compete in a triathlon—is certainly much smaller, although, unfortunately, no reliable figures exist.

In addition, as mentioned earlier, the swimming section of the race itself can be quite a challenge—particularly for the beginner. The start is a mass event, with lots of splashing and thrashing about, kicking feet and flailing arms. Furthermore, successful swimming—much more so than running or cycling—relies on proper technique and fine-tuned coordination. The top triathletes, while they may devote equal amounts of time to the three components of the sport, say they tend to spend a much greater share of their swimming training time working on technique.

It may be comforting to know that one of the top female duathletes in the world, thirty-three-year-old Liz Downing of Portland, Oregon, has said she switched to the sport from the triathlon because her swimming was just too weak to keep up with the elite. "I swim like a stone," was how she put it.

What kinds of people are attracted to the duathlons? Apparently the ranks are filled with former runners and bikers who have become bored with, injured by or burned-out on a single-sport routine. Tri-Fed estimates that about 75 percent of first-time participants in duathlons are crossovers from running backgrounds. By contrast, only about 5 percent are former cyclists, and a negligible number are defectors from swimming. Of the rest, a small number have no sports or fitness background whatsoever, while perhaps 15 percent have defected—like Downing—from the triathlon.

A Famous Convert

One of the best-known recent converts to the duathlon is Frank Shorter, winner of the 1972 Olympic marathon gold medal—a feat that is credited with helping to inspire the running boom that swept the country in the mid-1970s. Now in his early forties, Shorter has gradually eased out of competitive road running—although he still does enter events and support the sport—and onto the duathlon circuit. Shorter lives and trains in Boulder, Colorado, home to some of the world's best runners, cyclists, triathletes and, most recently, duathletes.

Running and cycling in order to participate in a duathlon can be a complete cross-training program in and of itself (see training chart, page 177). Alternatively, you can come up with a routine that involves other activities as well. For example, many serious duathlon competitors, including Liz Downing, make swimming a part of their weekly workouts. Downing reports that she still swims twelve thousand yards a week, despite having little natural talent at the sport, and does periodic weight-lifting workouts as well. And Ken Souza, the top male duathlete for the past several years, is another avid weight-lifter in addition to his running and cycling regimen.

The general impression among newcomers is that the duathlon, while physically challenging, is neither overwhelming nor intimidating, even when trying it for the very first time. After all, since duathlons are relatively new on the scene, it's hard for anyone to call himself or herself a real "veteran." Show up at any race and you're likely to find large numbers of people who have been participating for less than a year, and many, like you, at their first duathlon ever.

As in the triathlon, one of the biggest challenges of the run-bike-run race is making successful transitions from one section of the race to the other; participants speak of the same "rubber-legs" syndrome afflicting them when they switch from biking to the second running portion of the event. Putting the bike into a low gear to spin quickly for the last few minutes of cycling can help ease the transition into running, where the leg turnover tends to be faster. Beginners may also want to walk briskly for the first hundred yards or so of the second running stint. Of course, practicing doing the events one after the other in training will certainly make the actual race less of a shock. (For training details, see the chart on page 177.)

The truth of the oft-repeated statement "Anyone can do a duathlon" probably holds, as long as one gradually, safely and sensibly gets into decent cardiovascular shape, so that the distances and intensities attempted in the race are not a rude (and painful) awakening. You should be able to run for thirty minutes without a break in your training range (see Chapter Two) and cycle at a comfortable training pace for forty-five before embarking on the race-preparation schedule outlined in the chart on pages 182–83. To extend the schedule beyond the twelve weeks given, simply repeat week one for the first few weeks.

As you should be able to see, a cross-training program like the one just outlined, consisting solely of biking and running, will not really offer you complete fitness. Upper-body endurance training, muscle-strength building of any type, and flexibility improvement all get short shrift and should be added with other activities for the program to truly offer total fitness. As noted earlier, many duathletes do just that.

A good basic guideline for incorporating other activities into a duathlon-training program would be to work up to adding two strength-building workouts a week along the lines of the American College of Sports Medicine guidelines (see Chapter Two) to moderately strengthen the major muscle groups. An exercise that builds the endurance of upper-body muscles, such as swimming or using an upper-body ergometer, once or twice a week, would also be beneficial.

Training for Your First Duathlon

This chart was compiled by Daniel Honig, founder of the Big Apple Triathlon Club in New York City. Under each day is given your mileage followed by R for running, C for cycling. Then you will find the intensity: LSD is long slow distance, which should be two minutes per mile slower than your race pace (ten minutes per mile of running compared to a race pace of eight minutes per mile, for example). INT is interval training, in which you go fast for one- to three-minute intervals, followed by rests of thirty to sixty seconds, repeating until you do the full distance (rest longer if you need to, but try hard to finish the workouts). HIT is high-intensity training, in which you work out at a pace between the previous two, making sure to warm up and cool down before and after the effort.

Week	Sun.	Mon.	Tues.	Wed.	Thurs.	Fri.	Sat.	Total
1	6R/LSD	REST	6R/LSD	15C/LSD	REST	REST	20C/LSD 6R/LSD	35C 18R
2	20C/LSD 6R/LSD	REST	6R/LSD	15C/HIT	8R/LSD	REST	20C/LSD 6R/LSD	55C 26R
3	6R/LSD	6C/INT 8R/LSD	REST	25C/LSD	15C/HIT	REST	6R/HIT	46C 20R
4	20C/LSD 6R/LSD	REST	6R/LSD	6C/INT	4R/HIT	REST	15C/HIT 6R/LSD	41C 22R
5	25C/LSD 6R/HIT	REST	15C/HIT	8C/INT 6R/LSD	3R/INT	REST	8R/LSD	48C 23R
6	20C/HIT 4R/HIT	REST	4R/INT	10C/INT	8R/LSD	REST	25C/LSD 8R/LSD	55C 24R
7	20C/HIT 8R/LSD	REST	6R/HIT	30C/LSD	4R/INT	REST	8R/LSD	50C 26R
8	6R/HIT	REST	20C/HIT 4R/INT	25C/LSD	10C/INT 6R/LSD	REST	10R/LSD	55C 26R
9	10C/INT 8R/LSD	REST	4R/INT	20C/INT	4R/HIT	REST	30C/LSD 10R/LSD	60C 26R

Week	Sun.	Mon.	Tues.	Wed.	Thurs.	Fri.	Sat.	Total
10	10R/LSD	REST	20C/HIT 4R/INT	10C/INT	6R/HIT	REST	30C/LSD 8R/LSD	60C 28R
11	8C/INT 10R/LSD	4R/HIT	REST	30C/LSD	4R/INT	REST	20C/HIT 10R/LSD	58C 28R
12	6R/LSD	20C/LSD 3R/LSD	REST	15C/LSD	3R/LSD	REST		
	Race Day: Run 3 miles			Bike 20 miles			Run 3 miles	

And finally, stretching before each workout (after a five-minute warmup to work up a slight sweat and raise the temperature of the working muscles) and again afterward would take care of the flexibility portion of your program.

Other Multisport Events

The duathlon and triathlon are probably the best-known and most popular multisport competitions available. However, they are not the only ones. The following events tend to attract a small core of loyal and constant followers. Perhaps their limited popularity is caused by lack of exposure—that is, up until now. Note that some are known as triathlons, although they may include few or none of the traditional swim-bike-run components. So be warned: It's a good idea to inquire about exactly what a "triathlon" involves before you show up on the starting line.

1. *The Sugarbush Triathlon, Sugarbush, Vermont.* This fun, family-oriented, generally noncompetitive event is held in late March or early April each year, when northern New England weather is usually at is grayest and slushiest. Despite its name, the race has four components, running, canoeing, cycling and cross-country skiing. The race was formerly known as the Tuckahoe Triathlon and Chamber Challenge and is completed with teams, as a relay.

For the first leg, someone runs five mostly downhill miles from the Sugarbush ski area to the Mad River. There the second team member is waiting with a boat and paddles; he or she jumps in and paddles through six miles of quickwater and whitewater, to a point where the third-leg members are waiting with their bikes to cycle eight miles gradually back uphill to the ski area. Finally, cross-country skiers are waiting to travel three miles over natural or manmade snow to the finish. (For more information contact The Sugarbush Triathlon, c/o Rob Center, Box 858, Waitsfield, Vermont 05673.)

2. *The Craftsbury Center Mud and Ice Quadrathlon, Craftsbury Common, Vermont.* Also held in very early spring, this race is billed in its promotional literature as "not for the faint of heart." The Craftsbury Center, a sports facility specializing in shelling, running, cross-country (Nordic) skiing and other outdoor activities, has been putting on the event since 1987, and usually draws about one hundred competitors. The race starts with a ski segment over snow- and ice-covered streams, then a running section on hilly trails and dirt roads. Next is a mountain-biking portion, through mud that has been known to be hip-deep. Last of all, for those who still haven't had enough, is a canoe and portaging (carrying the craft) segment on the Black River—where as often as not one is challenged by downed trees and huge chunks of ice. Local teams tend to approach the event with a healthy—but strong—competitive spirit. (For more information contact John Broadhead, Mud and Ice Quadrathlon, Craftsbury Nordic Ski Center, Box 31, Craftsbury Common, Vermont 05827.)

3. *The Kaaterskill Spring Rush, Catskill, New York.* Although it has four distinct segments, this race allows single-person (called the Ironman division) or two-person-team participants. It starts at the top of Hunter Mountain Ski Area, which is located about one hundred miles north of New York City.

For the first section, competitors begin by running to their downhill skis, strapping them on, and skiing to the bottom of the mountain. The trail is rated "intermediate" in difficulty, and contains no gates or flags to challenge one's turning ability. The same competitor then changes into running gear and completes the next section, a cross-country sixteen-mile ramble, which can be extremely challenging in parts, especially if the ground is wet and muddy. At the next transition point the second team member can take over, or the same athlete can continue, depending on the division entered. What follows is a hilly, winding sixty-mile bike course. The biker then either continues or tags a canoeist (the original skier and runner, who has been transported to this point), who runs dragging or carrying a canoe to Catskill Creek and puts the boat in the water. Both team members then finally paddle six miles down the river to the finish. (For more information, contact The Kaaterskill Spring Rush, Green County Promotional Department, Box 527 KFK, Route 23B, Catskill, New York 12414.)

4. *The Iditasport Human-Powered Ultra-Marathon, Anchorage, Alaska (triathlon division).* Perhaps you have heard of the Iditarod Championship Dogsled Race,

a grueling multiday event in which competitors cover more than one thousand miles of snow-covered Alaskan tundra with teams of Husky dogs pulling sleds, Eskimo-style. The Iditasport is a somewhat easier, but still daunting, relative of this event that is held in mid-February. It comprises a series of races covering 100 to 200 miles on portions of the same famous Iditarod Trail. The race begins at Big Lake Lodge, near Anchorage. Competitors can choose to either bike or cross-country ski 200 miles, travel on snowshoes for 100 miles or, for the first time in 1991, compete in a triathlon—a 40-mile bike, 60-mile foot race (snowshoes optional), a 60-mile cross-country ski segment, and finally a 40-mile portion in which one chooses any of the three modes of travel.

The race awards prize money (in the true Alaskan tradition, given in the form of solid gold bars) in each division, as well as to the overall winner. With typically horrendous winter weather often a factor, skiing might seem the most logical choice. However, for three of the past four years, biking has proven to be the fastest bet, as well as the venue for the course record of twenty-five hours and fifteen minutes, set in 1989. Although competitors do enjoy themselves, the race is a serious—and potentially dangerous—event. Entrants must sign a disclaimer, which they must have notarized, indicating that they understand the risks involved pertaining to weather, frozen river travel, wildlife confrontations, illness, injury, gear loss or failure, frostbite, hypothermia and the like, and will not hold Iditasport responsible for any mishaps, including death. They must bring with them a sleeping bag with insulated pad, water canisters, a one-day supply of food and a hundred-dollar evacuation bond. Recommended gear includes a map and compass, saw or hatchet, headlamp with extra batteries and a tent or bivy sack. (For more information, contact Dan Bull, 201 Danner Street, Suite 155, Anchorage, Alaska 99518; [907] 344-4505.)

5. *Speight's Coast-to-Coast Triathlon, Christchurch, New Zealand.* Billed as "the ultimate New Zealand adventure," this race combines mountain running, cycling and kayaking across the country's wild, mountainous South Island. It was started in 1983 with seventy-nine entrants, and now accepts six hundred. The competition to enter is so intense that the entry quota for the February event is reached on the day entries are first accepted the previous July.

Covering 238 challenging kilometers through breathtaking terrain, the Coast to Coast is open to individuals aiming to complete it in either two days or one (the latter category open only to those who have previously finished the two-day version), as well as two-person teams. The race starts with a 3-kilometer run, then continues with a 60-kilometer highway bike ride, a river crossing, a

26-kilometer mountain-trail run (this segment is so rugged it takes people up to nine hours), another 18-kilometer cycling portion, a 67-kilometer kayaking stint and finally a 70-kilometer biking finish into Christchurch.

The 1991 entrants came from New Zealand, Australia, Sweden, Japan and the United States. Winner Steve Gurney became the first to finish in under eleven hours—near-delirious, coated with sand and sweat, but exultant. Clearly this is not an event for the faint of heart or unadventurous. (For more information, including a calendar of other multisport events in New Zealand, contact the New Zealand Tourism Office at 501 Santa Monica Boulevard, Suite 300, Santa Monica, California 90401; (800) 388-5494.)

These and literally hundreds of other multisport events keep competitive cross-trainers on their toes year round in all parts of the country. The Triathlon Federation/USA (Tri-Fed) can provide you with information or contacts for triathlons, duathlons and other multisport events nationwide and overseas; see the Appendix for information on contacting this organization. Tourism boards and chambers of commerce can also be extremely helpful. For opportunities in your community, talk to other active people and ask at Y's, health and sports clubs, community centers and local sport-oriented businesses. Or consider starting an event of your own—someone has to plant the seed that grows into a wild and wacky event.

TEN

TOOLS OF THE TRADE:

CROSS-TRAINING

EQUIPMENT

Most of us can remember a simpler era in the history of sports and fitness equipment. There was a time, for example, not so long ago, when the shoes that you exercised and played sports in were the same ones you used to take a stroll, putter in the garden or run errands on Saturday morning. They were called sneakers, and if they weren't Keds or P.F. Flyers or Converse All-Stars, the chances were great that someone visiting you from a foreign country had accidentally left them behind. Also in these bygone times, objects as diverse as skis, baseball bats, lacrosse sticks and even tennis and squash racquets were all made of wood, and were generally kept until they fell apart or were permanently lost in the dim recesses of your closet.

Today, however, so rapid and complete has been the revolution in the technology of sports and exercise equipment that the tools of the trades of the not-so-distant past—say, pre-1980 or so—have ended up looking as if they belong in a museum. Also hopelessly outdated is the notion that equipment isn't really all that important, that one pair of sports or fitness shoes (watch it—even using the term ''sneakers'' now dates you), or one bicycle or wetsuit or rowing machine or pair of cross-country skis is more or less as good as any other.

Running parallel to the new notion that equipment can make or break your participation in sports and exercise—regardless of the activity you pursue or

your intensity, skill or the length of time you have been engaged in it—is the burning need to be continually updating every piece of equipment you own, lest you get left behind, risk injury or, perhaps worst of all, fall behind the latest trend-setting fashion by sporting last season's model.

These factors have combined to make exercise equipment *big business*—to the tune of more than $12.1 billion a year for 1990, according to the National Sporting Goods Association (NSGA), a trade-industry group based in Mount Prospect, Illinois. The figure excludes sports and fitness clothing and footwear, categories that total a whopping $11.4 billion and $6.4 billion, respectively. Another category, recreational transport vehicles (including bicycles and cycling supplies, recreational vehicles, pleasure boats and snowmobiles), adds another $14.3 billion to the annual expenditure, bringing the grand total spent on all sports- and exercise-related equipment and clothing in the United States to $44.1 billion.

Sales figures in almost all categories of clothing, shoes and equipment grew in leaps and bounds through the early 1980s. They leveled off somewhat toward the end of the decade—along with the general flattening of the worldwide economy—and some areas have even shown slight signs of declining in the early 1990s.

In general, however, industry analysts and sports and fitness participants agree: High-tech, state-of-the-art equipment, with a strong emphasis on *performance*, is here to stay. In other words, if you're still out playing tennis in your canvas high-tops, using a wooden racquet and non–neon-colored tennis balls, you are a relic of a bygone era, and will remain one.

As a cross-trainer, you very likely will find the emphasis on state-of-the-art technology in equipment a great blessing, in many ways. Not only are your choices of gear and clothing in most of the major sports and activities seemingly unlimited, but you also stand much less chance than athletes and other active folk in years past of hurting yourself through the use of the tools your activity demands.

The improvements made in the sports equipment of today are often a direct result of the frustrations and agonizing injuries of athletes of the past. Indeed, sporting-goods lore is full of stories of active people who resorted to desperate measures in their quest for goods that would make their pursuits of excellence less arduous. One of my favorite stories, a tale that is a legend in the sporting-goods industry, is of track coach and Nike founder Bill Bowerman coming up with the now-famous "waffle-sole" running shoe by pouring a urethane solution directly onto his wife's waffle iron! I guess he ruined breakfast for that day, but countless millions of runners since have profited immensely as a result of his experiment.

Before I discuss cross-training equipment in particular, a brief overview of the sporting-goods "boom" in modern times should give you more of a sense of how far sporting equipment has come, and where things might be headed.

The Sporting Goods Boom: A Brief History

If any of the athletes who competed in the ancient Greek Olympic Games were to return to Earth and check out the modern-day sporting and fitness scene, they would certainly be in for a few surprises. Naturally, most of the activities that we now engage in would be completely unfamiliar—from football, rugby and tennis to aerobic dance, hang-gliding and in-line skating (Roller-Blading).

Perhaps equally shocking to the ancients, though, would be the preponderance of *equipment* needed to engage in even the simplest sports, such as jogging and swimming. If we are to believe the fragments of illustrated records that have survived the centuries, old-style-Greek athletes competed in everything from wrestling to bull-jumping barefoot and in the nude—or at least very scantily clad. It seems that they definitely adhered to a philosophy of "less is more."

That sports and fitness equipment is big business is clear in this shot of the National Sporting Goods Association Sports Expo, held annually in Chicago.

Credit: Courtesy National Sporting Goods Association.

Today, however, nothing could be further from the truth. But while it has been two millennia since sports and fitness participants decided to give in to modesty and compete wearing more clothes, it has really only been in the twentieth century that such a strong emphasis has been placed on what is worn during exercise, as well as on all the other gear deemed necessary for specific sports.

One classic example of how technological improvement in sporting-goods equipment has affected performance is the modern running shoe. The history of this item shows some more general patterns in sporting-goods equipment development.

How the Modern Running Shoe Came to Be

In the beginning, as I've noted, competitive runners generally did not wear shoes. Records from the first Olympics, in 776 B.C., attest to the fact that they competed barefoot. It is not known whether Phidippides, the first marathon runner (who collapsed and died at the end of his effort after announcing that the Greeks had triumphed in battle), wore shoes or not. However, records indicate that both ancient Greeks and Egyptians wore sandals. In addition, there is evidence that sturdy, hobnailed leather sandals were worn by the Roman soldiers—the ancestors of today's fitness walkers, perhaps?—on their famous marches to the far reaches of the empire.

Leather has been the material of choice for the majority of the footwear of the Western world for most of the modern era, so it is no surprise that shoes for athletic activities were made of the same material. In sixteenth-century Europe, sporting types—presumably runners included—competed in slip-on, lightweight pumps. The first spiked running shoes—still made of leather—were manufactured in England for runners and cricket players in the 1860s. The famous American Indian running sensation known as Deerfoot, who crossed the Atlantic in the early 1860s to take on the top European "pedestrian" runners of the day, created a stir by scorning spikes. He preferred his traditional leather moccasins—and proceeded for several years to blow the competition away.

Toward the end of the century, ultra-long-distance running events—"pedestrian races" of up to five hundred miles and perhaps even longer—caught on in the United States and Europe. Most of the participants wore heavy leather shoes with thick, stiff leather soles. Sprinters were offered lighter-weight, spiked kangaroo-leather shoes, many of which were made by the Spalding company and sold through catalogues for about six dollars.

One American marathon runner experimented with wearing spikes in the 1904 St. Louis Olympics and reported success. It was subsequently discovered,

however, that he had covered part of the course in a car, somewhat detracting from the achievement. Spalding introduced the first rubber-bottomed running shoes in 1909, but unfortunately each one weighed in at about a pound. Lighter-weight models, however, tended to wear out too quickly to be practical.

The next major advance in fledgling running-shoe technology was noted in 1936, when American sprinting sensation Jesse Owens wore a pair of experimental lightweight German-made shoes to win at least one of his four gold medals. The footwear came from the manufacturing plant of Adi Dassler, a German shoemaker. After World War II, Dassler formed the Adidas company and started making even lighter-weight shoes with canvas uppers and soles made from war-surplus rubber.

The complete dearth of comfortable, well-cushioned running shoes was still considered a problem for runners in the 1940s and 1950s, especially over longer distances. When the sensational Czech distance runner Emil Zatopek finished the Olympic marathon in 1952, completing his "triple crown" of three gold medals in long-distance running, the first thing he did—before even approaching the victor's stand to acknowledge the crowds—was to pull off his leather shoes to take a look at his bruised, bloodstained feet. Unfortunately, his experience was the rule, not the exception, as some of his competitors dropped out of the race because of the pain in their feet.

A few companies besides Adidas were also experimenting with lighter, faster, more comfortable shoes for runners, including the Tiger company of Japan and New Balance, an orthopedic-shoe maker in Boston. New Balance's 1962 breakthrough is now considered the first truly modern running shoe. Called the Trackster, it had a single-piece sole (rather than a sole with a separate heel) made of lightweight rippled rubber. The company subsequently added a rubber wedge in the heel to help absorb shock and relieve pressure on the Achilles tendon in the back of the lower leg. This feature soon became standard in the running-shoe "market."

The Trackster's immediate success among runners was limited, mind you, to a sprinkling of serious athletes around the globe—the tiniest fraction of the millions who were to form the "running boom" of people jogging for health, fitness and fun within a decade. However, the race for a technologically superior running shoe was now on in earnest. No real breakthrough was made, however, until the aforementioned University of Oregon track coach Bill Bowerman, working with

---

The running shoe has evolved from a now primitive-looking 1960s model (top) to a high-tech marvel (bottom). Credit: Courtesy NIKE, Inc.

the Tiger company, put out a shoe with a nylon upper. Nylon was much lighter than leather, as well as stronger, better ventilated and quicker-drying.

Bowerman's truly revolutionary contribution, however, came on that morning in 1972 when he heated up some urethane and poured it on the family waffle iron to create a lightweight sole with excellent traction. Following the successful use of the sole by some of his competitive runners, Bowerman and some associates founded the Nike company.

Within a few short years, sales had skyrocketed into the millions. The company rode the crest of the running boom triggered by American Frank Shorter's gold medal in the 1972 Olympic marathon. Yet another Bowerman innovation was the world's first "midsole," a layer of rubber between the shoe's insole and the harder rubber outsole. Midsoles provided the cushioning runners had long been seeking to run over long distances without pain, bruising and worse calamities. The first midsoles were made of rubber. In 1974, however, engineers at New Balance came up with a lighter-weight, more shock-absorbent foam called ethylene vinyl acetate (EVA).

The improvements and refinements in running shoes since the mid-1970s are somewhat less significant, as well as too numerous to cover here even briefly. The advances have concentrated in three areas: cushioning, stability (known in the industry as "motion control") and flexibility. The major manufacturers and even the minor players have whole teams of scientists and engineers whose job it is to develop the best materials, designs and shapes for the latest season's running shoes. The competition in the running-shoe business is so intense that a certain amount of gimmickry is bound to get mixed in with the truly helpful improvements, but the real changes have indeed been impressive. Later in this chapter I will offer some general advice on how you can separate true technological advances from mere hype, not only when investing in a pair of running shoes, but in all your cross-training purchases.

The Running-Shoe Market Today

Today, running shoes are part of a $6 billion annual expenditure for athletic shoes—and that is in the United States alone. It is widely agreed in the industry that companies that "sit still" by merely putting out the same shoes year after year, without state-of-the-art advertising and marketing programs, will get "blown away" by the competition. This has led to such innovations as "energy return systems," "dynamic reaction plates," "gel" protective cushioning, and "nitrogen microballoons." While some of these may give runners at the highest levels something of an advantage over their competition, their value to the average recreational jogger—let alone the person who buys running shoes just to wear while puttering around the house and yard—is questionable in the opinion of many independent research scientists (those not paid by a running-shoe company to promote its products).

Still, runners at all levels today can be thankful for the genius, creativity and dogged perseverance of the runners, coaches, scientists and engineers of the past who stubbornly persisted in their efforts to upgrade running footwear. Were it not for them, runners might still be clunking around in heavy leather sandals or boots. Or perhaps they might have given up in despair, and emulated their ancestors by running barefoot!

The development of equipment in many other sports mirrors that of the running shoe. Generally, the persistence of a few farsighted individuals—who, as often as not, were perceived as eccentrics in their time and place—eventually gave way to the "jumping on the bandwagon" effect of major manufacturers finally jumping in and creating a whole industry around a need that wasn't even there just a few years before.

In a few cases, technology completely changed certain sports. For example, the development of the fiberglass pole-vaulting pole is in no small part responsible for the world record now being over twenty feet, whereas a jump of fifteen feet would have been unheard of when competitors were still depending on wooden poles. The development of materials used to make stronger football helmets occurred parallel to changes in the game making it bigger, rougher and more dependent on brute strength. You may recall that back in the nineteenth century, most players did not even bother with the heavy, usually uncomfortable leather contraptions, despite the rough-and-tumble nature of the game. Hobey Baker, the legendary star quarterback of the Princeton University football squad in the earlier years of the twentieth century, was famous for not wearing a helmet. By the middle of the century leather helmets had given way to stronger, lighter, more comfortable plastic models that could withstand the game's brutal tackling.

It is hard to think of a piece of sports or fitness equipment that hasn't seen huge technological improvement in the past fifty years or so. Downhill and cross-country skis, for example, have gone from cumbersome wooden affairs to sleek models made from metal alloys, kevlar and other materials that are wonders of engineering. In addition, of course, there are whole categories of equipment that didn't even exist a generation ago—or even, in some cases, as recently as a dozen years past. From Frisbees to Windsurfers to cross-country ski machines to weight-lifting equipment, the assortment is seemingly endless. Again, it is all of great benefit to the cross-trainer, seeking to satisfy the person with even the

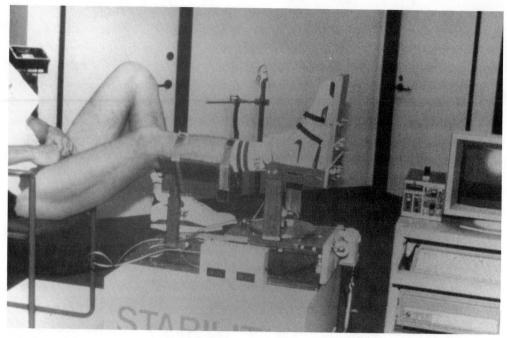

Shoe companies subject athletic footwear to rigorous laboratory testing before putting new products on the market. Credit: Courtesy NIKE, Inc.

most eclectic tastes and demands for material excellence—as long as the purchase fits one's budget.

How to Make Sure You Buy the Best

On the other hand, the blessing of a plethora of high-tech equipment is admittedly a mixed one. The sports-equipment boom leaves you, the intelligent, thoughtful, resourceful, yet admittedly underinformed potential purchaser of sports and fitness goods, in somewhat of a state of turmoil. There is simply *too much* to choose from, and too much information to amass before making your decision. If you are anything like me when it comes to buying sports and fitness equipment, you are almost certainly confused and overwhelmed by your seemingly limitless options. The problem is compounded for cross-trainers, who must buy not for one but several sports.

This book cannot possibly provide you with a guide to buying all the gear and clothing you need to participate in the myriad cross-training sports and fitness activities. There are, however, a number of general tips that I can suggest for purchasing any sports and exercise equipment. You can apply this advice to buying the goods for whatever activities you may choose to engage in.

I speak here from many of my own experiences—both positive and negative ones. Like most active people, I have, over the years, laid out plenty of good money for my share of exercise clothing and equipment that ended up spending far more time sitting in the back of the closet than it did out on the playing fields, courts, roads or trails or in the wilderness. I can bear witness to the many perils and pitfalls on the road to buying a piece of equipment that is right for you and from which you get optimum use. And, while sources of information and advice are many, perhaps even more plentiful are the potential ways in which well-meaning individuals, advertisements, articles and books (with the exception of this one, of course) can steer you wrong. *Caveat emptor*, as the saying goes—no matter what your sport or professed level of "expertise."

1. *Safety always comes first.* If a piece of fitness or sporting equipment or clothing is not going to protect you from the potential dangers and rigors of your sport, *don't buy it or use it*—no matter how flashy, highly touted, bargain-priced or endorsed by superstars or "experts" it may be. There are many ways in which consumers can mistakenly put other concerns in front of safety and later regret it.

For example, many athletic shoe companies make special models for high-impact activities such as running and aerobic dance for big, heavy people, who tend to come down harder on their feet than lighter, leaner types. These well-cushioned shoes are generally among the highest-priced within any given shoe category, simply because they usually have more material to soften the landing blows. The extra expense is invariably worth it, however, when you consider the sharply increased potential for injury that comes with wearing poorly cushioned shoes. If you are a big, heavy person, or you stride heavily, the few dollars you may save on shoes will likely be made up for many times over by what you will have to shell out to doctors and other medical professionals for diagnosing and treating your injury.

On a more dramatic scale, of course, are problems with equipment that can lead to serious accidents such as crashes, falls and strandings. For example, my sister, who works as a salesperson in a bicycle shop, steered me toward a particular brand of bike helmet that comes with a special protective rim made of super-high-impact plastic that reportedly will not weaken or give way under even the hardest of hard knocks. "Just about any bike helmet will protect you the first time you knock your head, but the structure of the helmet can be weakened," she told me. "If the second or third or fourth knock is a hard one, many other helmets will break under the impact. This one won't." Knowing that the difference could literally save my life, I followed her advice—even though the better helmet cost me thirty dollars more than competing models.

Examples such as this show why it is so important to be sure that *any* piece of equipment you buy meets the highest safety standards. Goods should be safety-tested and guaranteed to perform under the conditions in which you will be using them. Don't hesitate or delay in taking or sending back an item about which you have any questions or concern. For example, if your new hiking shoes promise to keep your feet warm and dry when crossing snowfields and fording mountain streams, yet your feet feel damp after a stroll through a dew-spangled meadow, get the problem taken care of *right away*. Waiting until you are out in the wilderness with freezing toes obviously is not a good idea.

Most types of outdoor sporting and adventure-sports equipment must be safety-tested by independent testers (not the manufacturer). Ask a reputable sporting-goods salesperson (or someone you know who knows your activity's equipment well) what the testing organization is for your equipment. For bike helmets and many other pieces of equipment, for example, it is the American Society of Testing Manufacturers (ASTM). Then, before you hand over your money, check carefully for the necessary seal of approval. If it isn't there, *don't buy* the item in question—no ifs, ands or buts!

2. *Consider long-term value over short-term savings in terms of price.* I just can't emphasize this enough—although believe me, as someone who appreciates a "bargain" when I find one, I have often found it tough advice to follow! My husband, Bradley—a more sensible value-finder than I—tells a funny story about how he was converted to the value-over-price philosophy when he was shopping for a backpack in preparation for a summer's trip to Europe. He was an impoverished college student at the time, and he entered the sporting-goods store determined to get the best "deal" he could find. However, after several hours of trying on packs, loading them up with pounds of books, bricks and other paraphernalia and trooping up and down the block outside the shop, he finally became convinced that he had been taking the wrong approach. An extraordinarily knowledgeable, patient and persistent salesperson worked with Bradley to eventually separate him from about one hundred dollars more than he had originally planned to spend. Far from being a con artist, this man simply presented Bradley—who is an eminently logical person—with an eminently logical piece of information: "When you spend a lot for a top-quality piece of equipment, it may hurt, but it really only hurts once. But if you spend less for something of lower quality, it may hurt a lot longer—in this case, every time you sling the

pack on your back!'' Ten years later, Bradley proudly considers the top-of-the-line pack one of the most intelligent purchases he ever made, and will tell the story to anyone who cares to listen.

On the other hand, I have a friend who refuses to buy a pair of running shoes unless they are on sale. If this policy happens to limit her choices to brands with which she is unfamiliar—or worse, those with which she has had bad luck—so be it, she says. At least she saved ten or twenty dollars, and she can therefore feel good about getting a ''bargain.'' Unfortunately, however, that knowledge has done nothing to quell the miles of painful running she has endured, and the days she has been forced to take off, because of her insistence on not paying full price.

I can certainly sympathize with her stance. It is one I have always taken when buying fashion, nonsports and fitness wear. And certainly, if a piece of sporting or fitness equipment you want is on sale, and if it fits, feels comfortable and otherwise meets your wants and needs, then by all means go ahead and buy it. But don't be like my friend, and let a low price stand in the way of your getting the long-term value you deserve. I can guarantee that you will pay for your folly in the end, whether you like it or not.

3. *Buy from merchants whom you trust.* While this makes sense when shopping for just about anything, it can be especially important in the sports-equipment department, where, as mentioned, the technology is constantly and rapidly changing, and last year's state-of-the-art goods are this year's throwaways.

The challenge of finding the best equipment is compounded even more for cross-trainers, who must master the ins and outs of the equipment for not one, but several sports. Rather than try to become the world's expert on the best gear for all of them, it can pay to develop rapport with people who make a business of acquiring such expertise—namely sporting-goods salespeople and store owners.

There are two main types of exercise and sports retail outlets: general and specialty stores. The former may sell equipment for dozens of different types of pursuits, from adventure trekking to billiards. If they are department stores, they may also sell hundreds, even thousands of other unrelated items as well. Nationwide chains such as Sears, for example, have been selling sporting goods for years.

Traditionally, most fair-sized towns and cities across the country have supported at least one sporting-goods outlet, and larger locales have often had dozens. In addition, colleges and universities have also traditionally been home to sporting goods retailers, who have found a ready market among students and townspeople for the basic goods of the most popular American sports, such as football, baseball, basketball, soccer, tennis, volleyball, along with their selections of school sweatshirts and the like. For example, until I left home for college, just about every sporting goods purchase I made—from hockey sticks to running shoes—came from the Princeton University Store in Princeton, New Jersey.

More recently, sole-proprietor shops have been somewhat supplanted by the rise of large franchises; in contrast to department stores, these outlets sell sporting goods and nothing else. The rise of these stores mirrors the national trend toward larger, more centralized companies in the place of traditional "Mom and Pop" operations. Duck into any shopping mall across the country and you will doubtless come upon at least one. Like the single-owner and school-affiliated outlets, they are generally a decent source for general merchandise and offer quite a bit of variety. Imagine being able to buy everything from in-line skates to Ping-Pong balls under one roof.

Specialty sports and fitness equipment outlets, on the other hand, are a relatively new phenomenon. I still remember the first time I happened upon a running shoe store back in the late 1970s. I was dumbfounded. Now, of course, I have been a customer hundreds of times at such outlets across the nation. In addition, I have visited stores specializing in items such as high-end bicycles, aerobics gear, downhill and cross-country skis, wilderness-camping equipment, tennis goods, gymnastics equipment and other esoterica.

Specialty shops are the biggest growth area in the sports and fitness equipment industry, according to data from the Sporting Goods Manufacturers Association (SGMA) of North Palm Beach, Florida. The industry group reports that between 1982 and 1987, specialty sporting-goods retail outlets had an annual growth rate of 10.1 percent. General sporting-goods stores, on the other hand, had only a 2.2 percent yearly growth rate, and the total number of stores declined from 9,252 to 7,959.

These figures make sense to me, because I purchase exercise and sports equipment at specialty sporting-goods stores rather than general outlets whenever I can. The reason is simply that I tend to trust the people who own and work in them to know their merchandise and what they are doing. This is not to say that people who own or work in general sporting-goods stores are know-nothings, but think about it: Wouldn't you find it easier to learn about the equipment needed for one activity than for twenty or thirty? And if you already had an interest in and knowledge of a particular sport or fitness pursuit, wouldn't you rather work somewhere that catered just to that activity, rather than a place where the goods competed with those used in dozens of other sports?

In general, specialty shops are slightly more expensive than general sports-equipment stores, but I have not found the differences to be dramatic. The bigger difference, I have found, is in the level of expertise of the people who wait on you—the specialty-goods personnel generally being leaps and bounds ahead of their general-interest counterparts.

Of course, this finding on my part is not absolute. Every profession has its dolts, and specialty sporting-goods sales is no exception. If you are new to a sport, or have recently moved to a new area, and are about to purchase equipment locally, I'd suggest visiting a number of outlets and talking informally to various salespeople before settling down to make a purchase. In addition, you might ask other people you know who engage in your sport where they have found salespeople they trust. A good working relationship with an intelligent, knowledgeable, patient salesperson can be one of the best long-term shopping "bargains" you will ever find.

4. *Comparison-shop till you drop.* Remember that the booming of the sporting-goods market means that you probably have many more options than you think among brands and models of the item you are purchasing. For this reason, you should not be too tempted to pick up the first choice you see that strikes your fancy.

As for what your criteria should be in making your selection, as I have already noted, price should probably be among your *least* important determinants. It definitely ranks behind safety, durability, a good warranty and the credibility of the company that makes the product. Keep in mind that many stores will let you try out products—running shoes, exercise machines and bikes, for instance—right in the store, or even at home for a specified period of time, with the option to return the item if you aren't fully satisfied. Mail-order companies—the more reputable ones, anyway—often have similar return policies.

Take your time—and don't feel pressured by the time constraints you may imagine are on the salesperson helping you or anyone accompanying you on your shopping expedition. I have a friend who, when buying a backpacking tent, devoted no fewer than three weeks to the project and visited more than ten shops, with her boyfriend in tow to offer advice. As a result of her patience and perseverance, she remains completely satisfied with her $400 purchase to this day—many cross-country treks and one around-the-world jaunt later.

I have found that sporting-goods salespeople are generally accommodating to comparison shoppers, especially in specialty outlets. My sister, the bike-shop salesperson, typically spends a total of three or four hours—sometimes over a period of several days—with a customer who is buying a new racing or mountain bike. This should not come as a surprise when you consider that such a purchase can constitute an outlay of up to $2,000. If you ever feel that you are being rushed or pressured into buying something before you are ready, you probably would do well to take your business elsewhere.

5. *If you find a brand you like, stick with it.* "Which running shoe company makes the best shoes?" is a question that I am often asked by runners whom I coach or meet at talks, clinics or races. My response is always another question: "What are you wearing now?" If the brand that they mention cannot be directly linked to an injury or significant falling off in their running performance, then I tell the person to buy another pair of the same shoes the next time he or she needs them. This advice, which I abide by myself, conforms to a time-honored rule: If it ain't broke, don't fix it. For that reason, I have been wearing Nike running shoes for ten years—not because I think they are "the best," but because I have never had a major injury while training and racing in them. This cannot be said for other brands I have experimented with over the years.

Finding the brand of sporting-goods equipment that works best for you— no matter what the item or activity in question is—can be a frustrating, time-consuming process of trial and error. No wonder the runners I meet wish that I could reveal to them the magical "best" shoe, and no wonder the garages, closets, basements and attics of active people across the country are littered with clothing and equipment that is no longer used because it wasn't quite right.

On a positive note, I can tell you that in general, if one brand doesn't work for you, there are usually scores more to choose from. So the corollary to my initial advice under this point is this: If a brand is giving you trouble, don't stubbornly stick with it. Instead, try another one. Remember, you have a lot of choices out there.

6. *Avoid making impulse purchases, no matter how tempting they may appear.* For the reasons mentioned above, and many others, fitness and sports equipment generally is not an area in which you want to buy too many things on impulse. There are exceptions, of course—a can of tennis balls you remember you need on the way to a match, that on-sale Day-Glo pink pair of biking shorts you just couldn't resist—but most purchases should be a bit more carefully considered. At the very least, by giving in to impulse, you may well do damage to your sports-equipment budget that will later prevent you from spending what you should for top-quality, necessary equipment later. In the worst case, you might end up with a piece of gear that doesn't meet safety standards for your activity, thus putting yourself in a hazardous situation. Protect both your body and your budget by purchasing only equipment that you've planned and comparison-shopped for with time and care.

7. *Don't forget the secondhand option.* This point may seem to go against some of the advice I have already given, but I bring it up for two main reasons. The first, obviously, is that fitness and sports equipment can be expensive, and I have seen many people kept from participating in one activity or another simply because they didn't have the money for the initial investment in the sport.

The second, related point is that I simply cannot stand the thought of perfectly adequate pieces of sporting equipment across the country going to waste in the backs of closets because no one is using them. If there is a piece of equipment you feel you simply *must* have, the chances are good that others before you have had the same impulse and acted on it. Then, of course, for various reasons their purchase has fallen into disuse. You may be able to take advantage of this situation.

There are a number of ways in which you can purchase sports and fitness goods secondhand. The one I would recommend first is going through a reputable sporting-goods outlet. This is the way in which you are most likely to get the same expert sales service, advice and warranty that you would in buying the equipment new. Big-ticket items such as bicycles, exercise machines, Wind-surfers, hang-gliders and skis (water, downhill and cross-country) are available used from stores that sell or rent them. If you are considering the purchase of such a major item, I would suggest calling retailers in your area to ask about used merchandise. Make sure to inquire about their policies for returns and warranties. Make every effort to find and work with a salesperson you feel is knowledgeable and whom you trust, just as you would if you were buying the item new.

Secondhand equipment can also be found through advertisements (in news-papers and magazines, on posted notes in stores and so forth) or word of mouth through friends or acquaintances. However, I tend to be wary of these options, for several reasons. One, you generally will not get a warranty; two, you may have no basis for trusting the person who is making the sale, unless he or she is a close friend (and sometimes, unfortunately, not even then); and three, your options will be limited by what is currently on the secondhand market. If you do consider buying something through one of these sources, I would recommend having someone advise you on the deal who is knowledgeable about the equip-ment in question and unbiased on the outcome of the deal (this would exclude, for example, someone to whom the seller may owe money or a favor).

And as always, take your time. Sometimes these arrangements work out just fine for everyone concerned. Just beware of the pitfalls before you make a decision.

8. *Work on developing a glitz-o-meter to weed out overhyped offers.* Unfortunately,

the sporting-goods market is so overhyped these days that this is easier said than done. The best way I know to avoid being taken for a ride is to become as knowledgeable as I can going into a purchase by talking to people who know more than I do, visiting various stores and reading up on the equipment in catalogues, books and newspaper and magazine articles that cover your sport.

The tricky, frustrating part is that sometimes the hype obscures advances and innovations that are truly worthwhile. For example, Nike's development of the Air sole in 1979 is now considered a true breakthrough in improving the wear and cushioning properties of running shoes (and later other types of athletic footwear). However, coming as it did as part of a virtual tidal wave of "bells and whistles"–type so-called "advances" in shoe technology, it was hard at the time for the casual observer to see the advance's worth. For this reason, I would say that separating the hype from the "real" improvements in the offerings of any piece of athletic equipment involves a considerable amount of patient, persistent research—and a certain amount of luck as well.

9. *Don't be shy about asking others who participate in your sport for advice.* While I think it can be a big mistake to trust every "expert" out there, I want to point out that you almost never need to make purchasing decisions in a vacuum. People involved with any amount of passion in a sport generally fall all over themselves to share information on equipment. Ask friends, acquaintances, salespeople, fellow-shoppers, people you meet at sporting events and those who write about the equipment for a living about anything that you think they may know more about than you do. The very least they can say is that they have no idea how to answer your question—and if they do, they are likely to try to direct you toward someone who might know more than they do.

10. *Always take the endorsement of a sports superstar or an "expert" with a grain of salt.* This is just another aspect of the "hype factor" in sporting-goods marketing—and perhaps it is one of the most powerful. Consider, for example, that the Air Jordan basketball shoe, made by Nike, accounts for well over $100 million in annual sales. Without denying that the Air Jordan is a quality shoe, and its namesake is certainly a top-of-the-line basketball player, you have to wonder for how many people out there the primary reason for plunking down $125 for a pair of Air Jordans was that they are the same pair worn by the glittering superstar.

The fact is, however, that sporting-goods companies have known for years that having products endorsed by stars helps the goods fly off the shelves—no matter that the average person who pays for a pair of running shoes endorsed by a world-class marathon runner will lace up the things in order to do nothing more strenuous than stroll around the mall. In our celebrity-conscious culture, people just cannot help wanting to be somehow associated with fame and dazzle. My advice in this area is no-nonsense: Ignore superstar endorsements. I believe they do nothing to influence the quality of any sports or fitness product, either for better or for worse. As far as I am concerned they are just another form of "bells and whistles."

11. *Make sure any product you buy has a warranty.* This last piece of advice is a fairly obvious one. Whether you are buying table-tennis racquets or a hand-crafted canoe, defects in workmanship, damage in shipping and other defects are *always* possible. If you cannot return an item—no matter how insignificant—for defects or damages, then take your business elsewhere. If you have trouble returning or exchanging a defective or damaged piece of equipment, consult your local Better Business Bureau.

Maintaining and Replacing Your Equipment

With some careful planning—and a bit of luck—the purchase of almost any piece of sports or fitness equipment to be used in cross-training is just the beginning of a lengthy and satisfying relationship. However, in order to ensure that your equipment serves you long and well, it makes sense for you to take the best possible care of it, and to replace it when necessary. Keeping your sports and fitness goods in working order is important for a number of reasons—foremost among them are your safety, comfort, performance and enjoyment in engaging in your activities of choice.

In this area, as with the advice I offered for buying the goods you need for your sport, I can really only suggest some general guidelines—based on research as well as my own experience—about the best ways to maintain your equipment so that it continues to perform at its optimum level. I also include here advice on how to keep your gear clean, as well as guidelines on storing your things safely over both the short and long term.

I must emphasize, however, the importance of finding out the specific information you need to know about each particular piece of equipment you own to keep it in tip-top working order. This is especially crucial where safety is a factor. With that caveat in mind, I offer the following advice.

1. *Find out how long your equipment is supposed to last.* This sounds rather obvious, doesn't it? I am always surprised, however, by the number of people who do not know how to tell when a piece of gear they use for sports and fitness is considered worn out. For example, the roads, sidewalks, jogging trails, aerobics

studios and gyms of the country are filled with people who have been wearing the same pair of athletic shoes for five years—and then wonder why they develop a foot, leg or back injury.

It may help to consult the list below, which summarizes the average lifespan of the principal types of sports and fitness shoes. While you should keep in mind that these are ballpark figures, and may change over the years as technology improves, they may nonetheless help some of you now who persist in working out in shoes that should have been tossed in the trash decades ago.

Shoe type	How long they last
running	500–600 miles
walking	1,000 miles
aerobics	6 months to 1 year of regular use
cross-training	9 months to 1 year of regular use
cycling	1 to 2 years of regular use
basketball	no more than 1 competitive season or 1 year of regular use

(Note: "regular use" means using the equipment roughly three times a week, on average, although figures vary depending on intensity of play, a person's size and weight, the quality of the shoes and other factors.)

For information on other types of equipment, consult the salesperson when you buy the gear, someone else in the shop who can give you an informed answer, a friend or acquaintance who knows your sport well or a recent issue of a reputable magazine pertaining to your activity. Sometimes there are tests that you can perform to give you a rough sense of when it is time to replace a certain piece of equipment. For example, to return to athletic shoes, some podiatrists suggest buying two pairs at the same time, and wearing one regularly, the other only once every couple of weeks or so. Then, when you can feel a discernible difference in the cushioning and support offered by the two pairs, you know it is time to get rid of the frequently worn ones (or at least retire them to lawn-mowing status), start wearing the less-worn shoes regularly, and buy a new pair to become those you only wear on occasion. I follow this practice with running shoes and find it works quite well.

In gauging when to replace equipment, you should keep a record of when you bought something and how often and under what conditions you have been using it. Don't guess or estimate—keep accurate, written records. For example, when I am running one hundred miles a week in preparation to race in a marathon, I will need to replace my shoes a lot more frequently than during my recovery training phase, when I may log only twenty miles a week. Write this important information down. Don't rely on your memory, or you may be the victim of needlessly sore muscles or injuries.

2. *Return defective merchandise.* This point bears repeating. Sometimes a piece of equipment will not reveal its defective nature right away, or perhaps you will keep the gear stored away for a while before using it. Even so, you should be able to return the goods if they are not in good working order—especially, of course, if any problems may be compromising your safety.

If you find that a problematic product's warranty has expired, or if for any other reason the company that makes it or the outlet where you purchased it will not take it back or replace it, then don't stubbornly use the product in its defective state just to make a point or spare your pride or pocketbook. If the gear cannot be replaced—or if you do not feel the expense is justified—then chalk the experience up to bum luck. And of course, be wary of the product, the company and the store where you purchased it in the future.

3. *Replace your goods before they wear out.* This point is really a corollary to the first one made here, and again it depends on keeping careful records of when you purchased a product and started using it in your sport or activity, and under what conditions and how extensively you used it. The advice applies to just about any piece of equipment you might use in your cross-training activities— from cycling socks to the sail of your Windsurfer. Waiting for some unfortunate event—from, say, a blister on your foot during a triathlon in the case of the socks, to capsizing hundreds of yards from shore with a useless sail in the case of the Windsurfer—to signal to you that it's time to invest in some new equipment is a very poorly thought-out strategy. You will save yourself time, trouble and probably even money in the end by replacing your exercise goods regularly.

4. *Keep your clothes and equipment clean.* Yuck! Who would wear smelly, dirty socks to an aerobics class at their health club? However, if you are exercising at home, in the sole company of your VCR and a workout video, you might be tempted to slip into yesterday's pair of still-sweaty socks before you get the heart rate pumping. After all, who will notice besides you?

Unfortunately, aesthetic and olfactory concerns are not the only reason that it pays to use only equipment that's as clean as you can get it. Indeed, your safety, comfort and the prevention of injuries may also be at stake. In the case of working out in sweaty socks, for example, you are sharply increasing your risk of developing a blister, either from the sock bunching or wrinkling if it is still damp, or from the rough surface of a sock encrusted with dried sweat rubbing repeatedly on your foot's tender skin. Wearing sweaty singlets, shorts, tights and other clothing for any type of exercise in which you will be moving vigorously can invite similar problems.

In addition, in many cases keeping your equipment clean can prolong its life by preventing mold, mildew, rust and other forms of decay. Make it a practice to rinse, dry or wipe down your gear after every workout. For example, when I come back from a run of any type or duration, I take off my shoes before I even step in the door. Once inside, I carry them to the windowsill in the bedroom to let them air out.

By the way, I think it is a good idea (and sports podiatrists have suggested this to me as well), if you can, to have two pairs of shoes for any sports or fitness activity you engage in more than once every couple of days. Generally, it takes shoes worn for any sweat-producing activity about forty-eight hours to thoroughly dry, and as noted above, wearing still-damp clothing of any type for a workout is not a good idea. Of course, as a cross-trainer you likely will not be engaging in any single activity for two days in a row. If you do, however—or if you use the same pair of shoes to work out in more than once in a two-day period—my advice is to follow the forty-eight-hour airing-out rule.

5. *Store your gear properly.* Doing so can greatly extend its useful lifespan, no matter how often or seldom the equipment is used. For example, when I visit my parents' home in the wintertime, I can still go ice skating in the same pair of skates I used in junior high school almost two decades ago, thanks to my mother's insistence back then that I rub the blades clean and dry with a soft, dry cloth and then let the skates air out overnight after every use before putting them away, and her keeping them tucked neatly away in boxes and protected from dampness and light during the intervening years.

Most big pieces of sporting-goods equipment are best stored during long periods of disuse indoors (or at least out of the open air), off the floor and away from bright light. This applies, for example, to bicycles, boats, exercise machines, surfboards, Windsurfers and camping equipment. This protects the gear from extreme temperature and humidity changes, the possibility of being scuffed or kicked around, and the potentially harmful effects of bright light. It can also markedly reduce the possibility of an item being stolen. (For this last reason, most people I know who own high-end bicycles keep them indoors all the time if at all possible.)

Always clean your equipment thoroughly and make sure it is completely dry before putting it away for long periods, and wrap or box it (or somehow protect it) to the greatest extent you can. Deflating the tires on your bicycle when it isn't in use for long periods (such as during the winter) prolongs their life. Check up on your stored sports equipment periodically to make sure mildew, mold, rust or other forms of corrosion are not bringing on any problems.

6. *Be careful about using other people's equipment.* You never know whether they have purchased it as thoughtfully and cared for it as lovingly as you have yours. In addition, there are the obvious potential problems of overall size, fit in specific areas (you and your friend may both wear size seven walking shoes, for example, but hers may be much too wide for your narrow feet) and sensitivity to wear.

For example, I once ran for a few days borrowing the running shoes of a friend whom I was visiting. The shoes felt flat and worn-out to me, although she assured me they "still worked fine" for her. Sure enough, though, I developed a pain in my hip, which fortunately quickly cleared up when I returned home and started wearing my own shoes again. Even though my friend and I both wore the same brand of shoes, she must have been less sensitive than I to the shoes' loss of cushioning. I have been careful ever since then to stick with my own running shoes—and, in general, other fitness and sports equipment as well—as much as possible.

A Few Words on Cross-Training Shoes

Hey, Bo knows, doesn't he? You would have to have been vacationing on another planet for the past half-dozen years or so in order not to have seen, heard or at least read about those attention-grabbing Nike advertisements in which the baseball-and-football superstar dazzles with his multisport energy and expertise. The point being, by the way, that he engages in every activity wearing the same pair of shoes, a contemporary creation known as cross-trainers.

Is it really possible, as these and other advertising and promotional plugs so convincingly tell us, to use the same footwear for virtually all of our sports and fitness endeavors? And if it can be done, are there any reasons why this is preferable to lacing up shoes that are made specifically for individual sports and fitness pursuits?

The answers to these questions depend, not surprisingly, on whom you ask. Certainly the athletic-wear companies that make and market cross-training shoes will tell you to go out and buy yourself a pair, and that you can safely, comfortably wear them for all your land-based activities. In the next breath, however, representatives of the same manufacturers may be telling you that for optimum single-sport performance, you are really best off investing in shoes designed specifically for each individual sport in question.

Cross-training shoes come in brands, sizes and styles to fit just about everyone, but whether you need a pair depends on your activities and how hard, long and often you work out. Credit: Courtesy NIKE, Inc.

That advice may be fine for those with an unlimited sports-equipment budget—not to mention endless time to spend shopping around for what to slip on the feet before every workout. Unfortunately, that state of affairs isn't of much help to the rest of us—a group I think of as the perplexed majority.

What I find most interesting about cross-training shoes is that they are not really "new" at all. After all, how many people who are over age thirty today can remember putting on a different pair of shoes as children every time they engaged in a new recreational activity? Not many, I would assume. For my part, I used the same pair of sneakers to participate in running games; play softball, football, soccer, tennis and Frisbee; take hikes; ride my bike and pursue any other activity the day might suggest—and no kid I knew was any different. I remember my younger sister begging my parents to buy her a pair of cleated shoes for soccer one season when I was in high school—and the things being relegated to the back of the closet and finally hauled off to the rummage sale within a year.

Other than that episode, sneakers were *de rigeur* throughout my childhood. Until the past fifteen years or so, multipurpose sneakers were cheap and comfortable, and they lasted seemingly forever (although children's growing feet entailed replacing the shoes far more often than our parents would have liked).

Indeed, after several decades of increased specialization in the athletic-footwear arena, cross-training shoes appear—at least to me—something of an anachronism. Yet at the same time, they hold a certain attraction, at least from a budgetary and space-saving standpoint. After all, what cross-trainer hasn't winced at the prospect of having to shell out several hundred dollars every year for running shoes *and* walking shoes *and* tennis shoes *and* aerobics shoes *and* who knows what else? An all-activities-in-one model does have a certain appeal.

The consensus among athletic-shoe experts—both those who are part of the athletic-footwear industry and those who observe and study it—is that while cross-training shoes may be appropriate for some active people, their suitability is limited to those who don't specialize in any one particular activity. On the other hand, anyone who engages in one special sport or another with any degree of seriousness is usually advised to invest in shoes designed for that particular sport. The reason for this is that the differences in the activities, if they are engaged in regularly more than a couple of times a week, are simply too great to be accommodated by just one type of shoe; the risk of pain and possible injury is too likely to increase.

In order to better illustrate this point, I include here brief descriptions of the shoes used in some of the major sports and fitness activities.

Walking. Until relatively recently, the idea of a shoe designed just for walking seemed ludicrous; after all, hadn't people been using shoes of every variety to walk in since the dawn of recorded history? Yes, and at times they had been powerfully uncomfortable, if historical records are any indication. Hence, the need for a walking shoe arose.

The modern walking shoe is, at least to my mind, a miracle of ambulatory comfort. Slipping on a pair gives me that "ahhh" feeling from the very first footfall. A good walking shoe is well-cushioned throughout the midsole, yet compared to the running shoe has a less-built-up heel and more flexibility in the forefoot area to allow the toes to push off with each stride. It fits snugly but does not bind in the ankle or heel, most models being low-cut rather than the more restrictive high-top types. It does not need to be overly concerned with lateral (side-to-side) motion.

Running. The principal concern with most running shoes (with the exception of the super-lightweight racing flats or spikes worn by competitors in races) is offering adequate cushioning in the midsole. This is especially crucial in the heel area, which bears the brunt of the footstrike for most people. However, a shoe that is *too* highly cushioned will not only weigh too much—thus inhibiting optimal running and raising the risk of injury—but it may also fail to offer adequate support throughout the foot.

Running shoes must also deal with the problem of feet that roll inward (this is known as pronating) or outward (that is called supinating) too much; various models of different brands of shoes are designed to correct these challenges to comfortable, injury-free running. Unlike shoes for activities with side-to-side motion, running shoes needn't be concerned with lateral control, so the uppers are usually made from a lightweight material such as nylon, mesh or some combination, sometimes with small amounts of leather or synthetic leather (although this may be used primarily for embellishment).

Tennis. In the tennis shoe, lateral motion control is much more important than in a walking or running shoe because the sport involves so much side-to-side activity. In addition, a built-up heel can be awkward, or even a potential cause of injury. It is not as important that tennis shoes be super-light in weight, so leather or synthetic leatherlike materials—which are often more durable and longer-lasting than mesh or nylon—can be used in the upper. Tennis shoes also must have a very stable, flat sole, and not an excessive amount of traction, so they can slide a bit, particularly on clay or grass courts. (By the way, I learned the need for this sliding property in tennis shoes the hard way, when I kept falling all over myself when I once tried to play tennis on a clay court wearing running shoes.)

Aerobics. Perhaps more than any other activity, aerobic dance demands support and protection in the foot and heel area. This is especially true if the activity is high-impact. Again, however, the heavily cushioned, raised heel of a running shoe can be a detriment, as it may throw the body too far forward. In addition, the wideness of the running-shoe heel can interfere with side-to-side movement.

Most models come up the ankle at least a little bit, in a high-top or three-quarter-top style. The aerobic-shoe midsole should be well-cushioned, yet there should also be some flexibility, especially in the forefoot, to allow the foot to bend. The uppers are generally made of leather or a synthetic leatherlike material, since super-light weight is not a particularly crucial factor.

Basketball. The ankles are probably more vulnerable here than in any other sport or activity, which is why most players wear high-top shoes. Lateral motion control is another crucial factor, as well as protection in the toe area, because of all the starting and stopping in a typical game or practice session. For all these reasons, most basketball shoes today are made of leather or synthetic leather, which provides durability and control of vigorous movement in all directions. The soles of basketball shoes generally can be made of a slightly firmer type of rubber than that used in other athletic footwear, which helps support the foot. However, a material that is *too* hard will not provide adequate cushioning from the impact of running and jumping on the wooden surface of the court.

Field sports. In the not-so-distant past, most serious soccer, field hockey, football, baseball, softball and other players whose sports took place on grassy surfaces and in which traction was important wore cleated shoes. Now, however, with the widespread use of Astroturf, cleats are less frequently seen, especially among the professional players who compete on the surface often. Noncleated field-sport shoes still rely on durable rubber or rubber-composite soles for optimum traction on Astroturf, which can be slippery, especially when it gets wet.

Both cleated and noncleated shoes rely on the durability and support of leather or a synthetic version of leather in the upper, good lateral motion control, and protection in the ankle area, although some players prefer not to wear high-top shoes because they may somewhat restrict ankle movements in some people.

How do cross-training shoes fit into this scenario? Can you safely, comfortably use them when participating in any of these sports? The theory behind cross-training shoes is that they offer the traits common to the most widely used types of athletic footwear. They are said to provide sufficient stability, cushioning and flexibility for a variety of activities. Therefore they can offer substantial savings in terms of money and closet space, not to mention time spent changing shoes between activities.

So, do cross-trainers deliver? Unfortunately, that is an unanswered question, or rather, a question with a different response for each individual. If cross-training shoes are described in terms of the other types of athletic footwear noted above, they can best be thought of as a combination of tennis and aerobics shoes, with minor elements of walking and basketball shoes thrown in, and almost no specific characteristics of running and field-sports footwear. Their soles are generally well-cushioned, but without a walking shoe's emphasis on flexibility and lacking the raised, widened heel of a running shoe. High-top or three-quarter-top models offer ankle protection, and support across the top of the foot may be offered with a special adjustable strap on some models (a feature you also may see on some aerobics, basketball and tennis shoe models).

Cross-training shoes seem to work best for the following activities: easy, nondaily running and walking; aerobic dance; court sports; field sports such as touch football, baseball and softball performed recreationally; Frisbee; and recreational basketball. People I know who walk occasionally for transportation report satisfaction with cross-trainers, while those for whom walking is a regular fitness activity say they have found greater comfort by investing in a pair of walking shoes. I do not know any regular (three or more workouts a week) joggers or runners who do their training in cross-training shoes, although people I know who run less say they are satisfied with them.

For my part, while I have been comfortable on short, easy runs wearing cross-training shoes, I would be reluctant to wear them during long runs, speed sessions or races. I can feel that the cushioning in the heel is just not there for the long distance, and that the shoes are too heavy for the fast running of interval sessions and races. But suppose I were strictly a recreational runner, someone who jogged, say, three miles, twice a week? And say that in addition I did aerobic dance twice a week for forty-five minutes at a time, and played tennis on Saturday morning? Would cross-trainers fit my needs then?

According to unbiased experts, they might well fit the bill. Opinions vary, of course, but the consensus is that cross-training shoes are adequate for any activity that one engages in at a moderate level no more than three times a week, on average.

If your cross-training regimen fits that description, you may want to give a pair of cross-training shoes a try. When shopping for cross-trainers, you will likely discover that there is no shortage of models to choose from, as virtually all the major athletic shoe manufacturers make cross-trainers for both men and women (and sometimes children), usually in a variety of styles. And you certainly will not be alone in making your purchase: Nike, for example, projected last year that it would sell 10.5 million pairs of cross-training shoes in 1991, compared to 9.9 million pairs of basketball shoes.

There is no guarantee, of course, that cross-training shoes will work for you. The verdict depends on your size and shape, your activity level, the duration and intensity of your workouts, the type of shoes you buy and other factors. As you would when trying out any new product, you ought to carefully monitor your response to working out with cross-trainers, noting any soreness, pain or developing injuries. Serious problems (anything that brings more than the level of discomfort you are used to in your workouts) should prompt you to take a layoff from activity and seek professional attention if the situation does not noticeably improve in a couple of days. You should inform the professional you consult that you work out in cross-training shoes, and carefully consider his or her advice about whether to keep wearing the shoes for your current workout regimen.

It should be noted that many people—myself included, I will admit—also wear their cross-trainers as their "goof-around" shoes. They slip them on to do yardwork, stroll around town or the mall, go out for a casual evening with friends and so forth. Hey, remember when people used to wear their *sneakers* to do exactly those things? Of course, that was back before anyone ever heard of cross-training. In fact, considering that an estimated 80 percent of the sports and fitness shoes sold in this country are not used for the activity for which they are intended, I would not be surprised if most of the cross-training shoes being worn today are on the feet of people who would be shocked and amused to hear themselves described as cross-trainers.

APPENDIX.

RESOURCES AND **R**EFERENCES

There is an abundance of information from a wide variety of sources on the many sports and fitness activities that can be part of a cross-training program. In addition, detailed information abounds on sports and exercise science, nutrition, injury prevention, competitions, coaching, sports psychology and related topics.

The following lists of sports-exercise and health-related organizations and publications will help direct you toward more information in your various areas of interest.

Organizations

> AAU Youth Sports Department
> Box 68207
> Indianapolis, IN 46268
> 317-872-2900

The forty-three-year-old American Athletic Union encourages sports and fitness participation for 250,000 children age eight to eighteen in fourteen different activities. There are fifty-eight local associations around the country.

Achilles Track Club
c/o Personnelmetrics
356 West 34th St.
New York, NY 10001
212-967-9300

Based in New York City, Achilles is affiliated with the New York Road Runners Club and has chapters around the world offering disabled people opportunities to participate in road races. Contact for information on finding or starting a club in your area.

Aerobics and Fitness Association of America
15250 Ventura Blvd.
Suite 310
Sherman Oaks, CA 91403
800-445-5950

Founded in 1983, AFAA is a professional association that certifies aerobics and fitness instructors. It's a good idea to take exercise instruction only from someone who has been certified by AFAA, IDEA, the American College of Sports Medicine or The Institute for Aerobics Research (see below).

American Alliance for Health, Physical Education, Recreation and Dance
1900 Association Dr.
Reston, VA 22091
703-476-3400

AAHPERD promotes fitness for children and youths through its Physical Best program of testing and conditioning for kindergarten through twelfth grade. The emphasis is on achieving balanced fitness, which includes aerobic endurance, muscular strength, muscular endurance, flexibility and body composition.

American Boardsailing Industries Association
99 E. Blithedale Ave.
Mill Valley, CA 94941
800-383-ABIA
415-383-9378

The national trade organization for Windsurfing (boardsailing), with more than fifty chapters across the country.

American College of Sports Medicine
P.O. Box 1440
Indianapolis, IN 46206-1440
317-637-9200
FAX: 317-634-7817

The largest national organization for sports and exercise scientists, ACSM provides a forum for presenting research, holds annual meetings and publishes brochures on sports and exercise topics. For a list of brochures, send a self-addressed stamped envelope.

American Dietetic Association
216 W. Jackson Blvd., #800
Chicago, IL 60606-6995
800-877-1600

A professional organization for registered dietitians (R.D.'s), the ADA provides educational information, including lists of R.D.'s in particular areas, and holds national and regional meetings.

American Heart Association
7320 Greenville Ave.
Dallas, TX 75231
214-750-5300

The AHA publishes dozens of brochures on a wide variety of health- and fitness-related topics. Contact the national office or your local affiliate.

American Massage Therapy Association
1130 W. North Shore
Chicago, IL 60626
312-761-AMTA

A professional association for massage therapists, the AMTA provides information on licensing and certification for massage therapists in your area.

American Physical Therapy Association
1111 N. Fairfax St.
Alexandria, VA 22314
703-684-APTA

The APTA is a professional organization for physical therapists, assistants and students, providing educational information to the public.

American Running and Fitness Association
9310 Old Georgetown Rd.
Bethesda, MD 20814
301-897-0197

Open to anyone with an interest in health and fitness, ARFA publishes a monthly newsletter, *FitNews,* summarizing recent research findings related to running and other activities.

Aquatic Exercise Association
P.O. Box 497
Port Washington, WI 53074
414-284-3416

An organization for instructors and participants in water-based exercise (hydroaerobics).

The Athletics Congress
P.O. Box 120
Indianapolis, IN 46206
317-261-0500

TAC is the governing body for United States track and field, sanctioning track, cross-country and road-racing events, enacting rules for fair competition, funding athlete support programs and overseeing the selection of Olympic and other teams for international competitions.

Center for Science in the Public Interest
1501 16th St., NW
Washington, DC 20036
202-332-9110

A nonprofit educational organization promoting safe, healthy eating. It provides educational materials to the public at a nominal cost and publishes *Nutrition Action* newsletter monthly.

Chrysler Fund-AAU Physical Fitness Program
Poplars Bldg.
Bloomington, IN 47405
812-855-2227

A comprehensive exercise program for children ages six to seventeen, available through schools and community groups. It stresses reduction of risk factors for disease, improved fitness and enhanced self-esteem.

> Fitness for Youth
> 401 Washtenaw Ave. CCRB
> The University of Michigan
> Ann Arbor, MI 48109
> 313-936-3084

A fitness program for children sponsored by Blue Cross/Blue Shield of Michigan and available to children nationwide through school and community programs.

> Hershey's Track and Field Youth Program
> Box 814
> Hershey, PA 17033
> 717-534-7636

This fifteen-year-old program has helped 350,000 children ages nine to fourteen learn about "friendship, sportsmanship and physical fitness." Track and field activities are stressed. A national meet is held each summer.

> IDEA: The Association for Fitness Professionals
> 6190 Cornerstone Court E.
> Suite 204
> San Diego, CA 92121-3773
> 619-535-8979
> FAX: 619-535-8234

Originally founded as the International Dance Exercise Association, IDEA now certifies aerobics and fitness instructors and personal trainers, holds regular meetings, provides educational materials to the public and publishes a monthly magazine, *IDEA Today*.

> The Institute for Aerobics Research
> 12330 Preston Rd.
> Dallas, TX 75230
> 214-701-8001

Founded by Kenneth H. Cooper, the "father of aerobics," the institute conducts research in various health and fitness areas and operates state-of-the-art fitness and sports-medicine facilities.

International Center for Sports Nutrition
502 South 44 St.
Suite 3012
Omaha, NE 68105
402-559-5505

A major research center for nutrition as it relates to sports and exercise activities.

IRSA: The Association of Quality Clubs
253 Summer St. 4th fl.
Boston, MA 02215
800-228-4772
617-951-0055
FAX: 617-951-0056

Formerly the International Racquet Sports Association, IRSA is now a nonprofit trade association for owners and managers of racquet and fitness clubs in the United States, Canada and overseas, with more than fourteen hundred member clubs. You can get a list of clubs in your area by sending a self-addressed stamped envelope.

Melpomene Institute for Women's Health Research
2125 E. Hennepin
Minneapolis, MN 55413
612-378-0545

Founded by a group of active women to provide practical information to fit females, Melpomene conducts research and puts out information packets, available for nominal fees. It also published a book, *The Bodywise Woman,* in 1990.

National Cholesterol Education Program
National Heart, Lung and Blood Institute
C-200
Bethesda, MD 20892
301-496-4000

The NCEP sets guidelines for safe, healthy cholesterol levels for the public and provides educational material for achieving them.

National Dairy Council
6300 N. River Rd.

Rosemont, IL 60018
312-696-1020

This organization provides general nutritional information to the public, focusing especially on milk and dairy products.

National Exercise for Life Institute
Box 2000
Excelsior, MN 55331-9967
612-448-3094

Affiliated with the company that makes the NordicTrack ski machines, this organization provides information to the public on the benefits of regular exercise.

National Strength and Conditioning Association
P.O. Box 81410
Lincoln, NE 68501
402-472-3000

A professional organization for fitness and strength trainers, NSCA holds regular meetings and provides educational material to the public.

New York Road Runners Club
9 East 89th St.
New York, NY 10128
212-860-2280

With 29,000 members, the NYRRC is the largest running club in the United States. It sponsors dozens of races a year, including the New York City Marathon and the Advil Mini Marathon for women, conducts clinics, classes, seminars and other activities, and publishes a bimonthly magazine, *New York Running News.*

Outward Bound National Office
384 Field Point Rd.
Greenwich, CT 06830
800-243-8520
203-661-0797

Outward Bound offers various outdoor and wilderness experiences to people of all ages and in special situations. Contact for a free catalogue.

President's Council on Physical Fitness and Sports
450 5th St., NW

Suite 7103
Washington, DC 20001
202-272-3421

Founded in the 1950s, the council provides fitness testing and conditioning programs to children ages six to seventeen through the schools, with the goal of raising kids' fitness standards.

Rainbo Ironkids Bread Triathlon Series
Traksports
Box 69095
St. Louis, MO 63169
314-241-8100

A national triathlon series for kids ages seven to fourteen, Rainbo Ironkids has introduced more than thirteen thousand children to triathlons since 1985. Events are organized over two days to orient youngsters to the concepts of fitness, nutrition, cross-training, exercise safety and competition. Top performers win trips to the national championships. Ironkids Club members receive the *ProudTalk* newsletter and a jacket patch.

Road Runners Club of America
629 S. Washington St.
Alexandria, VA 22314
703-836-0558
FAX: 703-836-4430

An umbrella organization for running clubs nationwide, RRCA helps govern and sanction American road races and publishes *Footnotes,* a quarterly newsletter covering road running.

The Rockport Walking Institute
P.O. Box 480
Marlboro, MA 01752
617-485-2090

A nonprofit organization that works to educate adults on the health and fitness benefits of walking. You can request free brochures on the Rockport Fitness Treadmill Test and the Rockport Fitness Walking Test.

Triathlon Federation/USA
P.O. Box 15820

Colorado Springs, CO 80935
719-597-9090
FAX: 719-597-2121

Tri-Fed, as it is commonly known, is the governing body of United States triathlons and duathlons. It is responsible for sanctioning events and setting standards and publishes a monthly magazine, *Triathlon Times*. It can provide contact information on multisport events of all types both in this country and overseas.

United States Badminton Association
501 W. 6th St.
Papillion, NE 68046
402-592-7309

The USBA governs the sport of badminton in this country, and provides information to the public on instruction, including USBA-sanctioned camps.

United States Olympic Committee
1750 East Boulder
Colorado Springs, CO 80909
719-578-4500

The USOC oversees the American Olympic movement from its offices in Colorado Springs, although most Olympic sports are also handled individually by their national governing bodies (NGBs). Information is available to the public on topics of general interest, such as the history of the Olympic movement and athlete drug testing.

United States Orienteering Federation
P.O. Box 1444
Forest Park, GA 30015

Orienteering is an outdoor sport that involves finding your way over rugged terrain—walking, running and crossing bodies of water. The USOF can provide information on events (many of which have beginner clinics) and clubs in your area.

United States Rowing Association
201 S. Capitol Ave.
Indianapolis, IN 46225

The national governing body for rowing and sculling in the United States, it can provide information on clubs and organizations in your area.

United States Ski Association
Box 100
Winter Park, UT 84060

The national governing body for both Nordic (cross-country) and alpine (downhill) skiing.

Women's Sports Foundation
342 Madison Ave.
Suite 728
New York, NY 10173
212-972-9170

A nonprofit, educational organization serving girls and women in sports and fitness activities. The WSF promotes equal opportunities for females in sports and sports-related professions, provides grants to aspiring athletes, offers information services to the public and publishes a quarterly newsletter, *Headway*.

YMCA of the USA
101 N. Wacker Dr.
Chicago, IL 60606
312-977-0031

YMCAs exist in virtually every community nationwide, providing multiple sports and fitness opportunities for people of all ages and ability levels. Check your local phone book for the facility nearest you.

Publications

The following magazines and newsletters cover various aspects of health, fitness and sports. Some are available on newsstands, others in libraries, or you can contact the individual publications for subscription information.

American Health
28 West 23rd St.
New York, NY 10010

*American Journal of Clinical
    Nutrition*
428 E. Preston St.
Baltimore, MD 21202

Bicycling
33 E. Minor St.
Emmaus, PA 18098

FitNews
American Running and Fitness
    Association
9310 Old Georgetown Rd.
Bethesda, MD 20814

Health Watch
Stark Bldg.
455 S. 4th Ave.
Suite 1515
Louisville, KY 40202-2511

High School Sports
1230 Avenue of the Americas
New York, NY 10020

IDEA Today
6190 Cornerstone Court E.
Suite 204
San Diego, CA 92121

In Health
475 Gate Five Rd.
Suite 225
Sausalito, CA 94965

*Journal of the American Dietetic
  Association*
216 W. Jackson
Chicago, IL 60606

Longevity
1965 Broadway
New York, NY 10023

*Medicine and Science in Sports and Ex-
  ercise*
401 W. Michigan St.
Indianapolis, IN 46202

NIKE Sport Research Review
One Bowerman Dr.
Beaverton, OR 97005

Outside
1165 N. Clark St.
Chicago, IL 60610

The Physician and Sportsmedicine
4530 W. 77th St.
Minneapolis, MN 55435
612-835-3222

Prevention
33 E. Minor St.
Emmaus, PA 18098

Runner's World
33 E. Minor St.
Emmaus, PA 18098

Running Stats
1085 14th St.
Suite 1260
Boulder, CO 80302

Running Times
Subscription Dept.
P.O. Box 16927
North Hollywood, CA 91615

Self
350 Madison Ave.
New York, NY 10017

Shape
21100 Erwin St.
Woodland Hills, CA 91367

Sports Illustrated
1251 Avenue of the Americas
New York, NY 10020

Sportstyle
7 E. 12th St.
New York, NY 10003

Track & Field News
Box 296
Los Altos, CA 94022

Triathlete
1415 Third St., #303
Santa Monica, CA 90401

Triathlon Times
Tri-Fed/USA National Office
P.O. Box 15820
Colorado Springs, CO 80935

Tufts University Diet and Nutrition Letter
80 Boylston St.
Boston, MA 02116

University of California, Berkeley Wellness Letter
Subscription Dept.
P.O. Box 420148
Palm Coast, FL 32142

Women's Sports and Fitness
1919 14th St.
Suite 421
Boulder, CO 80302

INDEX

Page numbers in *italics* refer to charts.

About the Author

Gordon Bakoulis Bloch was born in 1961 in Princeton, New Jersey, and grew up in an active family. Currently living in New York City with her husband, Bradley, she is a freelance writer and editor and competitive long-distance runner. She competed in the 1988 and 1992 United States Olympic marathon trials and has represented the United States in the World Cup and World Championships marathons.